UNDERSTANDING
AFRICAN
PHILOSOPHY

UNDERSTANDING
AFRICAN
PHILOSOPHY

A CROSS-CULTURAL APPROACH TO
Classical and Contemporary Issues

RICHARD H. BELL

ROUTLEDGE
NEW YORK AND LONDON

Published in 2002 by
Routledge
29 West 35th Street
New York, NY 10001

Published in Great Britain by
Routledge
11 New Fetter Lane
London EC4P 4EE

Routledge is an imprint of Taylor & Francis Group.

Printed on acid-free, 250-year-life paper.
Manufactured in the United States of America.
Design and typography: Jack Donner
10 9 8 7 6 5 4 3 2 1

Library of Congress Cataloging-in-Publication Data is available from the Library of
    Congress.
  Understanding African Philosophy / Richard H. Bell
  ISBN 0-415-93936-4 — ISBN 0-415-93937-2 (pbk.)

To my
wife and children,
Barbara, Jonathan, & Rebecca:
you have given me
great joy in life

contents

Seriously to study another way of life
is necessarily to extend our own.

—Peter Winch

preface

This book reflects many years of engagement with the philosophical and anthropological discussions about understanding another culture—in this case the "other culture" is Africa. This is combined with over twenty-five years of teaching and research on aesthetics and African philosophies. What is at issue is how one who is not an African can go about understanding what is now called *African philosophy*, and furthermore to communicate that understanding to largely non-African readers. Africa, of course, does not have a single culture that is to be understood. It is a large and diverse and sometimes enigmatic continent with a diversity of cultures. There is not what could be called a "philosophical tradition" that can be traced back very far historically in most of the continent. So the issues in "understanding"—cultures and philosophies—are complex.

Parts of Africa—like Egypt and ancient Abyssinia (present-day Ethiopia and Eritrea)—have long traditions of written history and civilizations older than Greek civilization; they also have a philosophical and religious literature of considerable interest. But what are now known as the sub-Saharan nation states, those largely carved out by a few European countries in 1884 for the convenience of their colonizing interests, reflect larger regional cultures and traditions than their boundaries suggest. These regional cultures were broken up and destroyed (or at least radically altered) primarily by the European and Islamic incursions going back some 500 years. The slave trade, introduction of new diseases, forced colonization, foreign language and religious impositions, and alien administration threw most of the continent into social, religious, political, and cultural confusion. Some of these regional cultures once had great civilizations and Kingdoms but a minimum of texts survived to record their ideas and achievements.[1] What remains of them are fragmentary pictures: icons from ritual life, histories of smaller communities passed on orally, some forms of governance preserved in village life, a few written records, judicial judgments, clerical texts, and a rich and a diverse artistic heritage. Most important, however, is a reflective memory carried forward for generations of a people whose dignity and way of life simply would not die. In these pictures many common elements of the cultures do emerge and from these a larger mosaic of Africa's past has been reconstructed. A true recovery, however, of these regional cultures and traditional forms of life, of a precolonial Africa, is extremely problematic—and this is made even more problematic by the nature of developments in the postcolonial experience.

With respect to approaching issues in African philosophy all of this points to the fact that such an enterprise is a fairly recent phenomenon—largely a product of Western and indigenous study and reflections during the twentieth century. It is not that the peoples of Africa have not had the kinds of reflections about the meaning of life or how they came into being. Nor have they given less consideration to the ordering of their life in communities, to fairness and justice, or to the meaning of suffering and love than have other cultures. These are all concerns and interests in human life that are the very "stuff" of philosophical reflection. In most of the subcontinent of Africa, however, what attention was given to such reflections in the first half of the twentieth century must be credited largely to Western social anthropologists. During the second half of the twentieth century, Africans and their philosophical reflections have been brought into dialogue with others who have longer histories of philosophy.[2] This cross-cultural dialogue is itself central to understanding African philosophy. The cross-cultural nature for understanding its philosophy is of particular importance because of the radical—one might say even traumatic—interface that Africa has had with European culture and with Western modernity.

Ludwig Wittgenstein remarked in the *Philosophical Investigations*: "the work of the philosopher consists in assembling reminders for a particular purpose." The following reminders are here assembled for the purpose of understanding African philosophy:

- that as a non-African approaching African philosophy we must begin with those issues central to cross-cultural understanding itself. Central to our thesis here is that philosophy is a product of an *aesthetic consciousness* and that those issues that are genuinely philosophical arise from the very process of our seeing and experiencing the world in which we live; that is, philosophy itself arises from and must be understood within an aesthetic point of view. Both the notions of aesthetic consciousness and an aesthetic point of view will be discussed at length in chapters 1 and 6.

- that African philosophy is currently in the process of formation by an active group of academic philosophers, critical theorists, and writers (almost all of whom are themselves Africans) who are refining its methods of reflections, the range of its concerns, and the particularity of its problems at this moment in time. Their discussions are of inherent and universal philosophical interest.

- that current African philosophers understand their particular task, because of the recent history of their continent, to be necessarily one of dialogue—philosophy itself is understood in the time-honored way as a conversation—ever clarifying and critically refining its reflections of the issues at hand.

- furthermore, that as a conversation, the understanding desired of "African" philosophy must be a two-way conversation, that is, those discoveries made listening to their internal conversation must not just be *heard* but also *seen* as being of value to non-Africans engaged in the conversation with African philosophy.

- because African philosophy is in the process of formation involving a larger intellectual community than just "professional" philosophers, attention must be given to such factors that are expressive of African's ordinary forms of life, i.e., through their orature, their traditional forms of governance, their fictional literature, and their arts. These are all forms of the *narrative* self-expression of Africans, and much that is within them are of critical significance to understanding African philosophy. The specific concept of narrative in African philosophy and its value for cross-cultural understanding will surface often and be developed in several ways throughout the book.

What is here called *cross-cultural understanding* is itself a kind of comparative or interdisciplinary philosophy—a philosophy that draws on different disciplines in order to position the reader "to see" and thus be in a position "to understand" the other's world. In this seeing, however, my hope is that the concept of "other" dissolves, or at least recedes in significance, in the understanding. To engage the African reality requires that we see multiple aspects of that reality through the eyes of Africans themselves—through the eyes of its philosophers, historians, writers, and artists—those who provide us with a critical perspective on the lived experiences of Africans. Some have called this kind of philosophy, which bears the imprint of the African reality engaging the non-African understanding of it, *postcolonial philosophy*.

For Wittgenstein, as with many postcolonial thinkers, linear thinking gives way to disruptions in our ordinary patterns of thought—hesitations, new beginnings, imaginative reconstruals are always the order of the day. Most important, however, is his recommendation that we stop "thinking" and start "looking." By this we shift the emphasis of our critical approach from a "rationalistic," or "meta-theoretical" one to an "aesthetic" one; we extend our vision to overcome "aspect blindness"—an inability to see what is in front of our noses or hear what is clearly auditory. It is such seeing and hearing that bring Africa's reality closer to us and allow it to penetrate how, in turn, we see and understand our own world.

Armed with the above reminders we approach our task with the confidence of listening to and hearing the particulars in the current discussion of African philosophy. The structure for our reading of African philosophy and entering into this conversation is first to discuss those issues related to the philosophical debates about "understanding another culture" and establishing a clear method as to our approach to the problems in these debates (chapter 1). It is in this first chapter that many of the concepts found in Wittgenstein related to meaning and understanding *as an aesthetic enterprise* are developed and we see how they apply specifically to understanding African philosophy as this is given expression by Africans themselves. We also take up what is problematic in the issue of "translation" from culture to culture, from indigenous language to metropolitan language, and from oral to written discourse.

Second, we look at a selection of recent critical developments in the history of African philosophy that has led to a more dialectical or conversational form of philosophical thinking in Africa—there is an active dialogue going on among African thinkers. By recent this means mostly the post–World War II period, though some of the background to these critical developments extend further back in the twentieth century, e.g., the "negritude" movement has its roots in the 1920s and 1930s black consciousness movements in New York City and Paris. Also among critical developments are the refinements of what is called "critical, scientific" philosophy and "sage" philosophy, or philosophy within the oral tradition of African thought. These two developments coexist with some tension within the internal philosophical debate, but by virtue of that dialectical tension African philosophy itself begins to take on a particular shape. Among other recent themes are African socialism, the idea of the "postcolonial" and the more politically charged issues surrounding "race." These issues engage and challenge Western assumptions and enhance the comparative and cross-cultural aspect of our study. These issues and movements discussed in chapters 2 and 3 are part of the inherited background to the current discussion of an *African* philosophy.

Third, specific to African contexts are a number of moral or ethical issues surrounding concepts of justice, community, and civic responsibility. Here the moral debates on the reshaping of African civic society in the postcolonial and post-apartheid context converge and contrast with Western conceptions of justice and communitarian thinking. The contemporary African context also gives us some unique perspectives on understanding the concepts of poverty and suffering and their relationship to the recent debates in international development ethics. Finally, in the second chapter on moral issues (chapter 5) the focus is turned to the grammar of justice as that is being discussed through the recent rise of "truth commissions," especially regarding the South African "Truth and Reconciliation Commission" and the critical debates that surround its process. African philosophy's contribution to the larger conversation on these issues is extremely important and should be carefully listened to and engaged.

Finally, we will examine the role of "narrative" in African philosophy, that is, the philosophical significance of oral narratives, the village palaver as a model for democratic governance, the reflexive value of "fictitious narratives," and the place of art and iconic forms in the formation of African philosophy. The idea of narrative in African philosophy points to the cross-cultural and interdisciplinary nature of the project itself as we have noted above. We further develop the idea of *the aesthetic conscious-ness* and show how it provides us with the fundamental mode for under-standing African philosophy as well as all philosophical reflections that are rooted in human experience and action. Exploring the range of what is meant by narrative and its critical applications to understanding African philosophy through literature, the visual arts, and more complex iconic forms such as music is at the heart of the last chapter.

Overall this study serves as an introduction to and critical engagement with some of the most significant philosophical conversations taking place on the African subcontinent: conversations about the relative value of African oral and written texts for philosophy and issues connected with the concepts of "negritude," "African socialism," and "racism." With respect to international development ethics, issues are explored related to poverty and suffering, community and civic responsibility. These latter issues are linked to the discussions of reconciliation, reparations, and justice swirling around the death of apartheid and the new South African democracy. Finally, there are conversations across the continent on the relative use and value of African literature and iconic forms for philosophical reflection. All these issues are in lively debate in Africa and are of importance for non-African philosophers to consider and embrace in larger cross-cultural and post-colonial contexts.

Uses of This Book as a Course Text

This book stands alone as an introduction to a wide range of classical and contemporary issues in African philosophy and it reflects mostly African writers presenting their own thoughts on the important issues. It also engages non-African readers by placing the African writers and their ideas in conversation with Western philosophical discussions. However, to take the reader a step further in the history and literature of African philosophy and to pursue Africa's self-reflections more deeply, nothing can replace reading the African source materials themselves. Thus, ideally, each set of issues taken up in the chapters in this book should be supplemented by reading more complete texts of African writers.

As a course text in Contemporary African Philosophy or in courses related to "Cross-Cultural Studies," or "Postcolonial Studies" it is suggested that one of several *African philosophy readers* be used and that some critical works of recent African philosophers and works of fiction be used. I would suggest one of the following three recently published readers be selected to complement the chapters of this book:

- *The African Philosophy Reader*, edited by P. H. Coetzee and A. P. J. Roux, Routledge, 1998. This reader offers excellent critical introductory essays opening each thematic chapter. There are nine thematic chapters with twenty-five individual readings, plus the introductory essays. Its essays are current and selected from among Africa's most important philosophers. It is particularly strong in contemporary moral and political philosophy (chapters 6 and 7), which match strengths in my book, but it also selects from among more classical issues reflecting African culture, epistemology, and metaphysics (chapters 3, 4 and 5). Of the three readers, this has the most critically useful selection on aesthetics and African art (chapter 8). This reader best complements my book for course use. As with any of the readers, it would have to be tailored to one's own use and supplemented with a few selected individual essays.

• *African Philosophy: An Anthology*, edited by E. C. Eze, Blackwell Publishers, 1998. This is the most comprehensive collection. It covers African American and Africana issues and recent discussions in post-colonial African philosophy as well as the more traditional issues discussed by African philosophers. It covers these issues in eleven parts and fifty-six essays—from African slavery, race and gender, to politics, ethics, religion and art. It includes some important classical writers such as Du Bois, Fanon, Césaire, Cabral, Nkrumah, and Malcolm X who are missing or only minimally represented in the other two collections. Because of its broad range, however, it is not an easy text to make coherent selections from for a single course. In using this text one has to decide the focus of the course and select only a portion of this large and valuable collection.

• *African Philosophy: Selected Readings*, edited by A. G. Mosley, Prentice Hall, 1995. This is the most modest collection but is the most historically useful. It reaches back to nineteenth-century foundations of African philosophy with readings from Blyden and Du Bois, and does not overlook the important (though sometimes discredited) work of Levy-Bruhl, Tempels, and Mbiti in shaping the mid-twentieth-century ethno-philosophical discussion. There are four sections with twenty-three essays. One should not overlook the inclusion of the very important essays by Abiola Irele on "Contemporary Thought in French Speaking Africa," Paulin Hountondji's "The Particular and the Universal," and a selection from Hallen and Sodipo's work, *Knowledge, Belief and Witchcraft*, not included in the other two readers. However, Mosley is weak in the area of recent discussions in African moral and political philosophy. It would be possible to combine this reader with a new collection of African political thought, such as Teodros Kiros, ed., *Exploration in African Political Thought* (New York and London: Routledge, 2001).

These readers may be accompanied by one or more of a number of important works by African writers that make important contributions to African philosophy. The following works are recommended: K. A. Appiah, *In My Father's House: Africa in the Philosophy of Culture* (1992); V. Y. Mudimbe, *The Invention of Africa* (1988); Paulin Hountondji, *African Philosophy: Myth and Reality*, 2nd edition (1996); K. Gyekye, *Tradition and Modernity: Philosophical Reflections on the African Experience* (1997); K. Wiredu, *Cultural Universals and Particulars: An African Perspective*

(1996); H. Odera Oruka, *Sage Philosophy: Indigenous Thinkers and Modern Debate on African Philosophy* (1990); Wole Soyinka, *Art, Dialogue and Outrage* (1993) and *Myth, Literature and the African World* (1976); Mahmood Mamdani, *Citizen and Subject: Contemporary Africa and the Legacy of Late Colonialism* (1996); and Antjie Krog, *Country of My Skull* (1998).

Other more specific works (books and articles), including some philosophically interesting works of African fiction, are brought to the readers' attention in the endnotes. Also, for easier use of the three "readers," as well as citing essays from their original sources, I have indicated in the notes those essays by African philosophers *that are collected in one or another of the readers*. None of the readers has caught up with the ethical discussions taking place around justice and truth commissions in Africa or with the cross-cultural debates over ethical issues in international development. Nor do any readers that I am aware of adequately treat the theme of "narrative in African philosophy" as I have developed that in this book. Supplementary essays would have to be assigned in those areas. A large Bibliography covering all of my topic headings follows the notes.

acknowledgments

When dealing with such a broad range of issues and a topic as diverse and large as to comprehend the very notion of *African* philosophy, one's debts are considerable. The path that led me into the critical conversations discussed here was first cleared by Malcolm Ruel of the Cambridge University Social Anthropology Faculty and a Fellow of Clare College. In 1979–1980 Malcolm guided me through the ethnographic and cultural anthropological thickets of a wide range of Africanists' debates that lay at the foundations of chapter 1. Malcolm's interest and friendship have helped sustained my interest in African Studies and several valuable conversations with him in the autumn of 1999 helped me clarify the directions of this study. In research in Africa in 1980, I benefited from conversation in Kenya at the Institute for African Studies in Nairobi with Professors Joseph Donders and Henry Odera Oruka, and in 1985 at the University of Dar es Salaam, Tanzania, with Dr. Ernest Wamba-dia-Wamba of the History and Social Studies faculty. This research and these conversations led to the publication of my essay "Narrative in African Philosophy," *Philosophy* (1989).

In 1994, during six months of research in southern Africa based in Namibia and surrounded by the spirit of liberation in both Namibia and South Africa, I wrote the essay "Understanding African Philosophy from a Non-African Point of View: An Exercise in Cross-cultural Philosophy." This was subsequently published in Eze, ed. *Postcolonial African Philosophy: A Critical Reader* (1997).

A research leave from The College of Wooster in 1999–2000 provided time to draft this project. During that period I was affiliated with the African Studies Centre, University of Cambridge, Cambridge, England, the Philosophy and English Literature Departments at the University of Stellenbosch, Stellenbosch, South Africa, and the Department of Philosophy at Rhodes University in Grahamstown, South Africa. These provided me with excellent environments to complete this study. Special thanks go to Ato Quayson, Director of the African Studies Centre at Cambridge, for critical comments on chapter 6, and to Shafiur Rahman, Research Associate at the Centre, for his many valuable recommendations of sources in development ethics and African political philosophy.

Professor Willie Van der Merwe of the Stellenbosch Philosophy Department was a welcoming host and provided general support, friendship, and helpful conversation on chapter 1 and more. Annie Gagiano of the Stellenbosch English Literature faculty was open to endless critical conversation on literature and philosophy and was generally encouraging on the "narrative" aspect of my project. I benefited greatly from reading her newly published book *Achebe, Head, Marechero: On Power and Change in Africa* (2000). I am particularly indebted to Wilhelm Verwoerd of the Stellenbosch philosophy faculty for inviting me to sit in on his "honors seminar" on Justice and the South African Truth and Reconciliation Commission, and for immensely helpful criticism in the preparation of chapters 4 and 5. Wilhelm Verwoerd was a researcher for the "Truth and Reconciliation Commission" (TRC) for two and one-half years and is a treasure house of information on the TRC process and related issues in development ethics and political philosophy.

At Rhodes University, Grahamstown, Professor Marius Vermaak and his colleagues provided a stimulating environment to complete this study. The opportunity to present several parts of this work to faculty and research seminars at Rhodes helped in refining the arguments. Andrew Gleason, doing postdoctoral research at Rhodes, provided valuable criticisms. This project was unexpectedly enriched by the discovery at Rhodes University of the "International Library of African Music" (ILAM). Its Director, Andrew Tracey, underscored for me the importance of African music to the formation and expression of African values, and how African music may serve as a critical tool for understanding African life and its culture. Scores of incidental conversations with Africans and actively listening and learning from living and traveling in a number of southern African cultures have contributed to some finer nuances in this work.

The ideas in this book have been tested under fire. During the fall term of 2000, upon returning to the classroom from South Africa, I used an earlier draft of this book as the basis for my upper division course in African Philosophy. Students read essays from *The African Philosophy Reader* and several pieces of African fiction as illustrative of the issues found in each chapter. Their interest, tough questions, and lively discussion helped refine and clarify many parts of this book. I am indebted to the class—a multicultural group of some 20 young scholars. I am grateful to Greta Dishong from this class for her care in helping prepare the index.

The College of Wooster Research and Study Leave Program and support from President R. Stanton Hales and the Henry Luce III Fund generously supported this leave and research. My wife, Barbara, with her companionship and parallel research interests in Southern African National Libraries and National Bibliographies and her many global contacts, helps keep my energy and interest level high for pushing through on projects. My daughter, Rebecca, who in 1999 and 2000 worked in an international education, women's development, and human rights program in Namibia and South Africa, continues to be an inspiration to me.

Richard H. Bell
Grahamstown and Stellenbosch,
August 2000, and Wooster, July 2001

1.

Understanding Another Culture

We might say "every view has its charm," but this would be wrong. What is true is that every view is significant for him who sees it so (but that does not mean "sees it as something other than it is"). And in this sense every view is equally significant.

Ludwig Wittgenstein[1]

Understanding Others and Ourselves

A central aim of philosophy is to "see something as it is." If this is achieved, we have a reasonable benchmark for approaching another "thing as it is." This simple remark of Wittgenstein's embraces a most fundamental question within philosophy. "A whole cloud of philosophy condensed into a drop of grammar," he once said (PI II, xi, p. 222). The effort to see another's world "as it is," a particular aspect of African culture for example, when one is alien to that culture, poses several difficulties. His remark, however, deflects us from thinking that philosophy is just a matter of one's own perspective, opinion, or point of view. The philosopher cannot say "every view has its charm." It is not that there are not different points of view. Rather the views we have are significant and meaningful in the manner we come to engage and express what *is*—the very being of the world and our being in it. If I come to a significant, that is, considered view of the world I inhabit, then I have a starting point for venturing to understand another's world. In this way there is the possibility of moving toward mutual understanding.

When someone from North America, for example, wants to approach what something is in its significance in an African culture there are obstacles of language, different customs, and perhaps some <u>epistemological</u> differences. Thus in approaching Africa, if we wish to understand the ways in which its people inhabit the world, we must work hard to determine what is significant from the point of view of its people. Understanding anything is always tied to its surroundings, which include language, customs, geography, iconic traditions, and especially the ordinary practices of its people. This applies to understanding features of both my own culture

[handwritten margin note: → studies function of knowledge; its foundations, scope & validity.]

and another's culture. Cross-cultural understanding is to be discussed not only in terms of large Cultures (with a capital C). In fact most larger units referred to as "cultures," such as European or Western or African or Chinese, are in fact a multiplicity of local cultures or multicultural in themselves. What may apply to understanding between, say, Africans and non-Africans, may apply equally between local African cultures. This will become clear as we proceed. *What is important is awareness of differences between cultures large or small and how understanding may pass between them.* Whether understanding is between cultures or within a given culture the difficulties are many, but there are fewer mysteries in this process than philosophers often assume.

Picking up his clues from a lifetime of reading Wittgenstein, Peter Winch understood better than most the difficulties in what became one of the major philosophical debates of the last three to four decades of the twentieth century—the debate called "understanding another culture." Winch is primarily responsible for setting off this debate with his philosophical colleagues and with social anthropologists in his essay "Understanding a Primitive Society" (1964).[2] In this essay, discussing E. E. Evans-Pritchard's description of the Zande poison oracle, Winch raised the specter that however well one might describe the practices of the Zande in their particular surroundings, one may still go away without understanding them. The following concerns followed from Winch's essay: the degree of access that "Western" thinkers have to the ideas and forms of life in cultures radically different from their own; whether there are common logical, epistemological, and cultural features between cultures that point to a common rationality between cultures, or whether each culture has a particular rationality unique to its thought and life. For a decade this essay drew many into the debate, but it remained largely an "intramural" debate *about* understanding other cultures from a Western "rational" point of view, although many attracted to the debate were anthropologists who had studied and lived in other cultures.[3] By the mid–1970s this specific debate was picked up by African philosophers from West and East Africa who responded to these issues from their own point of view and raised the further question "Is there a distinctively African philosophy?"[4] There were, of course, predecessors to this question in African philosophical literature that had their own background and history (which we shall explore in chapter 2). But the question about a distinctive "African" philosophy was now being asked against the background of the "Western" debate in its cross-cultural perspective.

Winch was thought to be a "relativist" on the issue of "understanding other cultures," but this misunderstands his concerns. He clearly stressed the difficulties of cross-cultural comparisons and the indeterminate nature of understanding itself. There are disparate ways in which people express themselves. In this early essay, and thirty-three years later, Winch was to remind us that such cross-cultural understanding was no more difficult than understanding ourselves. "Understanding" is, itself, the primary philosophical difficulty here and not the radical differences between different world views. "It is . . . misleading," he writes, "to distinguish in a wholesale way between 'our own' and 'alien' cultures; parts of 'our' culture may be quite alien to one of 'us'; indeed some parts of it may be *more* alien than cultural manifestations which are geographically or historically remote."[5] Winch is consistent with Wittgenstein in saying:

> We shall hope for a description of the alien practices that creates some pattern that we can recognize; we shall also perhaps hope *to find some analogies with practices characteristic of our own culture which will give us some landmarks with reference to which we can take our bearings.*[6]

In the end, at the center of understanding other human beings, Winch says, is a "practical 'being in tune' with others,"[7] or simply trying to see one another as the human beings we both are, surrounded by the similarities and differences that mark off our respective communities. This is a long way from relativism.

Winch said in beginning his article "Can We Understand Ourselves"— his last before his untimely death—

> I was invited to speak on the possibility or otherwise of our understanding *foreign* cultures. I did not willfully turn my back on the topic, but want to suggest that some at least of the difficulties we see here spring from an inadequate attention to difficulties about how we should speak of "understanding" in relation to our *own* culture.[8]

So where does Winch leave us? And what can be made of claims to relativism in understanding another culture? What are some "landmarks" from which "we can take our bearings?" Social anthropologist Clifford Geertz wrote succinctly:

> The truth of the doctrine of cultural relativism is that we can never apprehend another people's or another period's imagination neatly, as though it were our own. The falsity of it is that we can therefore never genuinely apprehend it at all. We can apprehend it well enough, at least as well as we apprehend anything else not properly ours; but we do so not by looking *behind* the interfering glosses which connect us to it but *through* them.[9]

As human beings we can and do understand another culture's life and practices "well enough," more or less "as [they are]." We can describe many aspects of another culture's world and how it is inhabited just as they can describe ours; we can go on to understand them to a degree hindered only by particular limitations in how we understand our own point of view. *It is primarily by virtue of the limits we have in "seeing something as it is" in ourselves and our own culture that we are inhibited in understanding another's world "as it is."*

There is also this simple fact: I am a philosopher approaching and wanting to understand both philosophers in Africa and what is being explicitly called "African" philosophy. I seem to do this "well enough," as Geertz says, and its overall accessibility seems limited only by my diligence and my imagination (or lack of both). I read philosophers from Africa, and other non-Western philosophers, in English and French, and understand and interpret them well enough to colleagues and students. I do not claim to be an African philosopher, but I do claim to understand what they are talking and writing about. I can accept the prohibition placed by some philosophers in Africa that African philosophy *must be* written by Africans.[10] I would not, however, accept a claim that implied that non-Africans could not *understand* "philosophical texts (whether oral or written) by Africans." *Philosophy may arise from human language situations anywhere. It will be found wherever there are human beings expressing their deepest concerns, interests, and aspirations and where there is sufficient critical reflection on how best to give expression to those concerns, interests, and aspirations.*

The requirement I must adhere to in *understanding* others' philosophy is to be attentive to their modes of expression and sort out both how their concerns and interests are expressed—what concepts and categories are used—and then translate those within myself to sufficiently see and understand such concerns in my own human language situation. Winch has said this very well.

> Since it is we who want to understand the Zande category [of magic], it appears that the onus is on us to extend our understanding so as to make room for the Zande category, rather than to insist on seeing it in terms of our own ready-made distinction between science and non-science.[11]

The key lies with my ability *to see* and "make room for" the others' categories and concepts that give expression to their life. I must be prepared to have the concepts as expressed in African life open new imaginative avenues in me and not expect their expressive forms to conform to how I see the world or to such *Western categories* as I may have. To understand African philosophy I must be prepared to see the world in new ways and appreciate the manner of that seeing. Anthony Giddens noted that "through becoming aware of the dazzling variety of human societies, we can learn better to understand ourselves."[12] More recently philosopher W. L. van der Merwe said:

> [T]here is no neutral ground, no "view from nowhere" in philosophy with regard to cultural differences. . . . This realisation impels one to enter into dialogue with the traditions of wisdom and thinking of other cultures—not so much in the hope that one will reach a trans-cultural, metaphilosophical consensus, but as a way of acknowledging the particularity of one's own viewpoint and discovering the cultural contingency of one's own philosophical presuppositions and allegiancies.[13]

The process of cross-cultural understanding is a reciprocal act whereby I must enter into a real dialogue with the other, and recognize myself as "other" to them. As Geertz said we must "look through the glosses" of the other—through their distinctive concepts, literature, art, and other practices—and hope also to find something of ourselves in them.

Understanding African philosophy—the significant ways in which Africans give expression to the world they inhabit and critically reflect upon that expression—from the point of view of a non-African requires us to establish a specific philosophical procedure that will explore first what it means to "understand" something in our approach to it. This will require that (1) we engage the discussion among African intellectuals about conceptual and critical features of their own self-understanding and its relationship to our own self-understanding. In Winch's words, we "hope to find some analogies with practices characteristic of our own culture which will give us some landmarks with reference to which we can take our bearings; it is here where cross-cultural understanding becomes a genuine dialogue."[14] (2) We must listen to Africa's many voices—the oral narratives and lived-texts of African peoples. And finally, (3) we must attend to the iconic traditions of Africa: its visual art, literature, music, ritual drama, and religious practices and learn to make them somehow our own.[15]

A Procedure from an Aesthetic Point of View

"What's ragged should be left ragged," Wittgenstein once remarked.[16] This is characteristic of how he thought about the origins of philosophy, that is, the well-springs from which philosophical reflections arise, our ordinary language and life. Stanley Cavell images Wittgenstein's approach to philosophy as follows:

> The *Philosophical Investigations* is a work that begins with a scene of inheritance, the child's inheritance of language;.... The figure of the child is present in this portrait of civilization more prominently and decisively than in any other work of philosophy I think of (with the exception, if you grant that it is philosophy, of *Emile*). It discovers or rediscovers childhood for philosophy (The child in us)....[17]

In his *Philosophical Investigations*, having challenged some conventional pictures of how language is said to have meaning, Wittgenstein then provides us with numerous examples of how he sees language to have meaning in the ordinary contexts of life—in its paradigms of use he "rediscovers childhood for philosophy." Among the central features of meaning is that the words and grammar of a natural language are shared within a culture or form of life of a people; the meaning of concepts depends upon their being shared perceptions and customs among a community of language users.

Winch comments on what he regards as "one of the most remarkable . . . examples of one of Wittgenstein's most characteristic argumentative moves [from Sections 286–287 of the *Investigations*]: a shift of attention away from the object to which a problematic concept is applied toward the person applying the concept."[18] He goes on to say that

> This practice of Wittgenstein's is not a meaningless tic, but is meant to emphasize that the sense of the concepts we deploy lies not just in the circumstances surrounding what we apply them to but also in the circumstances surrounding us, who so apply them.[19]

To make this point even stronger, over halfway through the *Investigations* Wittgenstein gives us a new, striking metaphor for thinking about the meaning of language. He writes:

> We want to say: "When we mean something, it's like going up to someone, it's not having a dead picture (of any kind)." We go up to the thing we mean. . . .
>   Yes: meaning something is like going up to someone. (PI, 455 and 457)

The mutual understanding we would like to achieve in "going up to" another human being may be easily thwarted. If the other person is a stranger we may naturally turn away or talk or dwell only reticently in their company; we may fail to spend enough time or give enough attention to meet "face to face" or "eye to eye." "Going up to the thing we mean," involves *me* in the circumstances related to my approach to it. Lack of attention or interest in the "thing"—another person—Wittgenstein sees as a more important drawback in understanding a stranger than believing they have a different way of thinking or a different "rationality" from our own.

What Wittgenstein wants us to do is probe how *we could contemplate* the differences—"riddles," he calls them—we encounter in practices that seem alien to us so we would *connect up* these differences with something familiar or that we did understand. The metaphor of "going up to someone" shifts the meaning paradigm from an epistemic mode to an aesthetic mode—a move from "a dead picture" to "a living one." Meaning is linked more with our human perception and experience (including recognition, interests, and expectation) than with intellectual cognition and empirical fact. I will say more about this aesthetic mode shortly.

Before giving us this very personal metaphor, Wittgenstein had discussions with his friend M. O'C. Drury about their mutual reading of Sir James Frazer's *The Golden Bough*. These remarks go directly to issues in cross-cultural understanding. Among many things, Frazer offered explanations of why children in European Beltane Festivals or elders in an African community's reenactment of ancient regicide rites might burn a straw effigy or kill an aging king. Wittgenstein found an uneasiness in Frazer's too-ready-to-hand causal and theoretical explanations. Frazer's emphasis on explanation seemed misplaced. He failed to note the gravity of the events, even if they were only reenactments or masquerades; he did not see the "darkness" or the complexity in such events. Frazer's "eye" was not cast on the people's activity—on how they went up toward one another. Rather, Frazer sought some explanatory hypothesis that might appeal to the "intellectual eye"—to some bit of Western "scientific" rationality.[20] His explanations were one sided with little apparent attention given to the voice of the other.

A major difficulty in accounts such as Frazer's, and others formed under our "modern" epistemological paradigms, is that they function to make thinking easier; they shift the burden of the investigation *onto* an abstracted level and *away from* the level where the ordinary human activity, with its language, stories or ceremonial acts, are doing something, i.e., their job. The burden of understanding is shifted from ourselves onto a theory.

There is little doubt that "the burning of a man" or the killing of a king is a serious matter and strikes deep roots in us. Matters of life and death beckon to us and demand some understanding. Wittgenstein insists that what gives these matters depth is not to be found in an explanation of their origin, but in how we connect them with our own thoughts and feelings.

> We also say of some people that they are transparent to us. It is, however, important as regards this observation that one human being can be a complete enigma to another. We learn this when we come into a strange country with entirely strange traditions; and, what is more, even given a mastery of the country's language. We do not *understand* the people. (And not because of not knowing what they are saying to themselves.) We cannot find our feet with them. (PI, II, 223e).[21]

It is difficult to "find our feet" or "find ourselves" with those who engage in certain ceremonial acts. With the fire-festivals or regicide we have "come into a strange country." With some attention we can find out what they are saying and how their actions have meaning within their life. Yet, we still may not *understand* clearly. Wittgenstein sees this as the really crucial issue; one that cannot simply be left at an impasse with a culturally relativistic response to fix it in place. We cannot say "every view has its charm" and leave it at that! We must "find our feet" or "find ourselves in them" on the matter and thus move toward a more comfortable (or disturbed) understanding. This is what Winch meant when he said we must "hope to find some analogies with practices of our own culture."

This point was not lost on the Nigerian playwright Wole Soyinka.[22] In his play *Death and the King's Horseman* (1975), the dramatic tension is built around a ritual suicide based on actual events in December 1944 and January 1945 when the Alafin ("King") of Oyo in Western Nigeria died. By custom his leading minister (the Elesin, the "Master of the Horse") would be expected to follow him to the world of the ancestors by ending his life in a prescribed ceremonial way. When Simon Pilkings, the British District Officer, intervened to stop the ritual suicide the world of the Oyo is thrown into chaos—the peace of the Yoruba world has been shattered: "the world is set adrift and its inhabitants are lost."[23] Pilkings, of course, cannot see it this way. He says to the captured Elesin, "It is still a good bargain if the world should lose one night's sleep as the price of saving a man's life."[24] The dilemma in the play, however, is not one of "old values and new ways" as Soyinka puts it, but more like a total lack of respect and understanding of Yoruba ways. Pilkings fails to understand the people he is charged to govern. He believes that only what is Western "makes sense." One is left to ponder what is more sinister, or which is "the better bargain," the "ritual suicide" of the Elesin to save the metaphysical order of the world, or the "mass suicides" which took place over political power struggles during the West's Great Wars.[25] There is no capacity to listen or to see the other in Pilkings' eyes.

Among a number of things, Wittgenstein focuses on understanding "the character" of the people who performed the ceremony and on discerning "the spirit" of peoples' acts. We understand these, he says, by "describing the sort of people that take part, their way of behavior at other times, i.e. their character and the kinds of games that they play. And we should then see that what [may be] sinister [in the Elesin's ritual suicide, for example] lies in the character of these people themselves" (RF, 38). It is not a big step now, with some imagination, to think about what might also be "sinister behavior" in one's own life and thus "find one's self in them"—for example, those "killing games" we played with our childhood wooden weapons—not to mention the "killing fields" left behind in France, Germany, and Russia in the Great Wars or more recently in Kosovo or Serbia. He concludes by asking "What makes human sacrifice something deep and sinister anyway?" and answers, "this deep and sinister aspect is not obvious just from learning the history of the external action, but *we* impute [or ascribe] it from an experience in ourselves" (RF, 40). Think of one's own experiences, find some analogies or some reference point from which to take one's bearings!

On the matter of discerning "the spirit" of the peoples' acts, Wittgenstein zeros in on those things we find common between different people. He writes in notes elsewhere:

> It goes without saying that a man's shadow, which looks like him, or his mirror-image, the rain, thunderstorms, the phases of the moon, the changing of the seasons, the way in which animals are similar to and different from one another and in relation to man, the phenomena of death, birth, and sexual life, in short, *everything we observe around us year in and year out, interconnected in so many different ways, will play a part in his thinking (his philosophy) and in his practices*, or is precisely what we really know and find interesting. (PO, 127–128, my emphasis)

What is *spiritual* in all human beings lies in the connectedness of such phenomena as death, birth, and sexual life, and in our way of acting that expresses the depth of joys, sufferings, hopes, and desires associated with these phenomena. These are what "we really know;" they "play a part in" our philosophies and in what we come to find interesting. Both character and spirit are interconnected with and shaped by community, by its ceremonies, and in individual moral lives. Note that the connection here is made in *an aesthetic mode*, in how we see our world and how we "go up to" one another. "Everything we observe around us, year in and year out, interconnected in so many different ways," is the point of departure for all people. This forms the criterion for how we come to know our world and what we take as true, whatever the particular cultural point of departure might be. It is also what, as Wittgenstein says, allows us to identify the similarities (and differences) in meaning—the thinking, the philosophy, the practices—between one people's conception of life and our own.[26] He is, in all this, preparing us for understanding; creating the possibility of a two-way conversation.

In approaching another's practice(s) we in turn find the room in ourselves to see connections, new aspects of the other's life with our own, and possible appropriations of the practice in our life. The understanding passes both ways in the seeing. Wittgenstein calls this an *"übersichtliche" Darstellung* (cf. RF, 34, 35, PI, 122). For him such a "perspicuous representation" (as it is translated into English) is a way of seeing things and writing things (RF, 35)—a way of setting out the whole field together by making easy the passage from one part of it to another (RF, 35). Connections between parts suddenly become transparent. His idea has an *aesthetic tone* of looking, of seeing things as a whole.

Malcolm Ruel provides this example of an *"übersichtliche Darstellung"* kind of seeing by looking at the meaning of two East African rites. He shows that what people do in their lives, ceremonially, expresses their deepest values. Their rites, he says, are "metaphorical actions" that "carry meaning across different situations," and in turn may be carried across to us. The rites he examines are of a young Nyakyusa chief's "coming out" and the Kuria act of "opening" a slaughtered cow's stomach, a beer pot, or a room. Both rites, when represented fully, link us with important mutually understandable notions of how ceremonial acts are tied to larger social processes, and how they are related to one's natural environment and biological life processes. The Kuria rite also provides a "perspicuous" ["*übersichtliche*"] example of how hospitality and family prosperity are common human sentiments, cutting across cultural boundaries. These rites, and other ceremonial acts, contain in them and commemorate the whole of a community's life. There is not something outside their acts that the people and their stories "wrongly" or "superstitiously" or only "partly" are said to "assert" or "represent." To *understand* their rites and ceremonies is where we must begin to understand the people; it is where the dialogue of mutual understanding begins.[27]

Wittgenstein believes that there is *a way of seeing* how those who engage in creating and transmitting stories actually stand in relation to their stories and practices. With such descriptions, however, the question remains: *is all this sufficient for our understanding?* How are we, for example, to become "convinced" that the gods of other people "have the same meaning" as our own gods? (cf. RF, 34). Not an easy question.

On this point—and *it is the more important one*—Wittgenstein provides us genuinely new insights. He poses a new question that links *us* with the people's life being described: How is it that "we impute" [or ascribe] "from an experience in ourselves" what is deep and sinister, what is fundamentally disquieting, or what is hopeful or uplifting about another's action? It is "in ourselves" that we must see how we stand to the burning of a man or the welcoming of a stranger; we must deal with our own feelings of guilt or anxiety, of disquiet or of joy and find some analogous experiences where we do this or say that, and then feel satisfied. To contemplate the depth of the experience of others we must *look into ourselves for some analogous experiences.*

What kind of analogous experiences are these? What is this *understanding* without an hypothesis or theory? Here is the difficulty. We must think out the analogies for ourselves—no shortcuts or bypasses. In so doing we discover that "the religious actions or the religious life of the priest-king [in Frazer's example, or of a Nyakyusa chief in Ruel's example] are not different in kind from any genuinely religious action today, say a confession of sins or ritual baptism. This also can be 'explained' (made clear) and cannot be explained" (RF, 30f.). Wittgenstein points us in a different direction with his examples. He wants *me* to come to some personal satisfaction regarding a disquieting situation—therein lies *my understanding.* He asks what kind of experiences *I have* that may bring my heart and mind to rest. This requires some kind of imaginative transfer of the other's life into my own—some mutual understanding of their and our cultural differences and similarities. Following a lead from Charles Taylor, W. L. van der Merwe says: "In and through this process it may become evident that certain aspects of the other's culture are inadequate and/or that aspects of the one's own are—in which case the understanding of the other may lead to a transformation of one's own." Such attention to the other and to oneself indicates real listening, a real conversation.[28]

When the seriousness of death, for example, impinges on a person or community *any* manner of action(s) may arise within the person or community to enable them to allay anxiety, dispel further fears, or celebrate a new confidence in the ongoing nature of life in death. We all want to keep our family and community healthy and ongoing. In all the emergent rites and commemorative stories, the aim is not to provide an explanation for death, but to express human life in all its paradoxicalness. In the case of East African Kuria people, Malcolm Ruel says, "The worst that can befall a person—man or woman—is for their descent line to be terminated or 'closed.' " We can connect with the hope of keeping our family alive and prosperous and celebrating family passages. Ruel says, "a generous, hospitable man is described as having 'a wide corral entrance.' " Again a common sign of hospitality—an open door—is an act we can easily connect with.[29] Thus we and others express ourselves.

Back to Wittgenstein's example of the strangeness of celebrating by burning a *man*. The sinister impression is carried with the act, metaphorically "carried over" with a host of connections related to the strangeness of one's own natural history. We come to the strangeness and to an understanding of it, says Wittgenstein, as we discover "the *environment* of a way of acting" (RF, 40)—both the environment of the strange happening and our own. In the end, like those who live out the stories and practices, we must acquire the capacity for the understanding; it cannot be given in the theory. We must look into ourselves and to what others are saying of themselves and put together those links from what we have seen and heard, from what we have experienced and already understood. The *understanding* is something that an individual *does* and it is tied to the particular self-reflective "life-view" a person has within his or her own community.[30]

Wittgenstein's way of "finding our feet" or "finding ourselves in" another's way of life is both a more *universal* and more *particular* way of understanding. It is more universal in that Wittgenstein sees the relevance of tying the feelings and actions expressed in one cultural situation to similar feelings and actions in another, namely in one's own. Meaning "is like going up to someone." It is more particular because the psychological phenomenon of understanding itself is deeply tied to a person or community and a particular life-view—though this does not mean it becomes purely subjective. Rather, understanding comes back to an aesthetic point of view—to the *place where I am*—and this place is always surrounded by some common ways of acting formed within and by a shared inherited background: my family and community, my language, my culture, my status, my gender, my uniqueness as a human being. It is against this background that our understanding of another culture arises and that the possibility of resonant chords are struck in us.

Recognizing our own capacities, or lack thereof, helps us discover the lacunae in our own self-understanding. We may lack a developed life-view of our own, have few hopes, have suffered little, and our anxieties may be trivial. Not feeling what is sinister in the fire-festivals, or joyful in an installation of a Shilluk or Asante king, or tragic in Rwanda or in *Lear*, or beautiful and graceful in Namibian rock art, may reflect our own bereft lives; it may reflect our own inability to understand something that is fundamental to others' lives and to our humanness. We may not be, or may never have been, hospitable, and thus fail to understand another's simple (or ritualized) gesture of hospitality. In our own arrogance or power we may overlook or be blind to what is human in others—a characteristic of all forms of imperialism and virtually built into forms of colonialism and neocolonialism. How do we come to recognize these things in ourselves? Our own horizons may be limited and our capacity to understand therefore impaired. In such cases it is better that we come to see our own limitations, the lacunae in our lives—only then would we be prepared to understand others.[31]

The possibilities for misunderstanding or not understanding at all are always present; we may not be open to another's situation or we may have limited capacities in how we "go up to" or approach another person or a different cultural situation. What we have called understanding another culture, as we have said, must not be seen as always being between two distinct larger "Cultures," like African and European. Within a single society, nation, or continent, cultural differences may be multiple and understanding opaque.

We do not have to leave the African context to see a divergence of world views. A good illustration of this is seen in a testimony given on the last day of public hearings for victims of the "Truth and Reconciliation Commission" in the small farm community of Ladybrand, Eastern Free State, South Africa. South Africa is a multicultural society (as are most nations in the African subcontinent) and one must often work hard at understanding even one's neighbor. In these hearings a shepherd, Lekotse, recounts how in May of 1993 his home was invaded in the middle of the night by South African security police. The encounter is between the "cultures" of the rural Sotho-speaking black community and the ruling white Afrikaner power. That night this shepherd's world was invaded and he could not understand why! Lekotse understands "a jackal among his sheep" better than he can understand this invasion of his home.[32]

Antjie Krog, the lead South African Broadcasting Corporations radio reporter for the some fifteen months of victims hearings, gives an interesting interpretation of this particular day of the hearings. She reveals its particular philosophical difficulties and illustrates our problem of the complexity of cross-cultural understanding. Krog writes [and I quote a rather long, but telling, passage]:

> With the entry of the police into the shepherd's space a second leitmotif is introduced: "They did not provide an answer." Lekotse asks several times: "What do you want?" When they refuse to answer, he plagues them with further questions. Will you give me money to take my children to the doctor if they become ill from this cold? Who gave you permission to visit my home? Is this the way you conduct your affairs? How dare you cut open my wardrobes? Do you want beer, drink, boerewors? Are you hungry? Do you want to implicate us by planting dagga and diamonds? When are you going to fix my doors? Who is APLA?
>
>   This kind of questioning is the foundation of all philosophy. How do I understand the world around me? What is right and just in this world? The

fact that none of his questions are answered explains why the day affects him so deeply: his ability to understand the world around him is taken away. . . .

In a desperate attempt to understand the behavior of others, Lekotse imaginatively transplants himself into several other positions. . . . What makes his story all the more poignant is the fact that he can imagine himself in the other characters' positions, but no one seems able to empathize with his own.

His empathy, his ability to think himself into other positions goes beyond the night he is describing. It even includes the people from the Truth Commission. Perhaps, he is thinking, they are struggling to understand fully the destruction that was sown in his house. "It's a pity I don't have a stepladder./ I will take you to my home to investigate. . . ."

Lekotse knows he cannot insist that the Commission visit his house: but if only he had a ladder that he could set up, perhaps they could see his hut from the top of it, with its newly-mended door. It is a yearning to be understood; to give the people in front of him a perspective on the impossible. A ladder would give the Truth Commission insight, it would raise his story from one plane to another, from the unreal to the real, from incomprehension to full understanding.[33]

The police not only invade Lekotse's world, but they refuse him access to theirs. By so doing his world is negated and he is made nothing. Lekotse was never "seen" as the "human being that he is." In the African's world "there is diversity, the ideal is diversity, not symmetry," says the Zulu poet Mazisi Kunene.[34] That diversity must be respected and acknowledged. Because of this diversity a continual conversation is essential so that "I" may come to my own sight of the other.

I want, finally, to make a comment on what is here understood as *a procedure from an aesthetic point of view*. Wittgenstein situates us in life and shows how the writing or speaking about life becomes part of it. I come to know my surrounding world as "I go up to it" and as it impinges upon me, instructs me. In my approach and response come my level of comfort in it, i.e., how I come to understand it given my own limitations. I continually try to bring concepts to what I see or experience and, in Wittgenstein's terms, the concepts linked to what I see "spread an ordering veil over the objects."[35] I bring what I see and experience within a range of my understanding without "exhausting" or "exactly rendering" the object "as it is"—however, the "ordering veil" of my reading or interpretation renders the object (a ritual practice or strange piece of drumming, or a shepherd's world invaded, for example) as close to "what it is" as is possible in the seeing and hearing. I am now "in touch with" the object of my experience. I am, in this instance, "seeing an aspect," as Wittgenstein says, of the ritual practice or piece of drumming as it is being used by human beings for the purposes and communications that is peculiarly theirs. In these cases it could be said, with Wittgenstein, that what is enacted or communicated "has a definite sense and I perceive it."[36] These are all part of our "natural reactions," antecedent to whatever views or theories might subsequently arise. It is our *presentness to one another* that is most important and this, first of all, is a matter of perception.[37] I might be able, then, to go on and describe or interpret what this definite sense is more fully by "moving around in the grammatical background,"[38] of those whose practice it is, and by moving around in the familiar background that is my own.

It is here that the concept of "narrative" becomes important in our (a non-African's) understanding of "African" philosophy. Lekotse's story is a narrative of his world invaded and Krog's retelling of it helps us see the impasses and moves made by Lekotse and Krog, an Afrikaner. This helps us understand and make sense of this cultural clash. The point of departure of an African's *seeing* of her world is different in many ways from my own. Both the inherited background (the social history surrounding the slave trade and manifest forms of colonialism) and the postcolonial reality that shapes Africa's current social and moral environment must be made accessible to me if I am to claim an understanding of it. There must be ways in which I can listen to and hear the voices of Africa and connect them up with my own understanding.

First-hand written accounts and critical reflections on Africa's experience are largely available to us only in recent literature—in the anthropological literature of Western scholars from the early to mid-twentieth century and a growing body of African fiction (stories, novels, ritual drama, poetry— most from the 1950s onward). Preceding the fictional literature by Africans is a long tradition of oral narratives and forms of iconic expression (visual arts connected with ritual practices and masquerades, music and dance). All of these give first person voice to what Africans have experienced around them, year in and year out, connecting their lives and critical reflections in self-conscious ways.

As a primary source of conscious self-expression, such "narratives" have significance for enabling us to *see and hear* the realities that *are* Africa; narratives are an aesthetic entryway into the African experience "as it is." These narrative forms enable non-Africans to encounter "an aspect of" that experience. In such narratives I am, as Wittgenstein noted, presented with "a definite sense" of what an African self-expression is and "I perceive it." In these narratives I may become "present to" how an African gives voice to the truths of her world. Thus I believe it is crucial for understanding African philosophy, in addition to what contemporary or recent "professional" philosophers have said is relevant to philosophy *in* Africa, that its literary (oral and written) and artistic (iconic) traditions should play a substantial role in helping us discern and understand the truth *in situ* of African life.

Such literary and artistic forms are a kind of "instrumental inflection" for seeing the truth as we shall show throughout this study.[39] Novels, short stories, oral narratives, and other iconic forms are local expression of a culture, of how the author and performer/artist/ community see their local world. But the "local" world is not necessarily provincial; it has been shaped and reshaped by an invasive history that extends beyond its geographic location. I concur with this view of South African literary critic, Annie Gagiano:

> [T]he African settings or African characters depicted in the novels [or stories] ... tie them down to earth in a way that theory [or abstract philosophy] often fails to achieve. The imagined actuality of prose literature works toward qualities of vividness, immediacy, and the convincing force of something more akin to testimony than it is in the nature of most theoretical writing to be.[40]

The novels she discusses—and examples we shall use to "instrumentally inflect" the philosophical—"project ... the anguish of the actual in a way that the theoretical discussions of the same issues cannot achieve, making possible a kind ... of understanding not ... accessible by other means— something *akin to* a 'participatory' understanding...."[41] By seeing Africa through the eyes of its multiple ways of "picturing" itself and hearing its own many voices, understanding of African reality will be more than just hearing my own voice; I will be able to participate in it and respond to it.

This is all related to what it means to approach the very nature of our understanding from *an aesthetic point of view*. The very order of being in the world is like an intricate weave of perception and response, of reacting and embracing the world we see, and familiarizing ourselves with (or reading) the grammatical background found in the particular experiences of our life. This is, in itself, a philosophical conception of the world, and how we go about understanding it will be at work throughout this book. It shows the reflexivity of our human being and the dialogical nature of our knowing and understanding of the world however "strange" it may appear to us.

"Found in Translation"

Now, it may be true that "ascribing" what is sinister or celebrative in another's acts from "an experience in ourselves" or the concepts we find to order another's practices is not to describe the other's actions at all, but only to impose our views on theirs! Although this may be the case, if I am the one who wants to do the understanding then there must be a connection made "in me." If some meaningful "translation" of the other's acts is to be made it must be made meaningful to me. There is no such thing as "an understanding of something" apart from the one seeking the understanding. Also, as said earlier, *I must be receptive to the others' ideas— prepared to have new ideas challenge the one's I have*. Such challenges are built into the whole enterprise of cross-cultural understanding and the particular issues in understanding African philosophy.

In approaching another culture there are at least three kinds of "translations" that take place. First is translating what you see and generally experience on the aesthetic level. This is what is often called an "eye witness" account—something is "taken in" then an account is given in one's own language. There is considerable room for multiple "readings" and "reportings" here and misunderstandings relative to one's degree of familiarity with the thing observed and the familiar landmarks one can find in one's own surroundings. Anthropologists have cultivated this skill in a way that tries to minimize differences in readings and limit misunderstandings. For the trained "reader," as a culture's "background" presumably becomes familiar, greater clarity and precision—even understanding—can be rendered to the reading.[42]

A second kind of "translation" is the detail and art of actual language translation. Here again, the linguist and ethnologist have trained themselves to listen to and learn the native language of the other, then render "a translation" into their own language—for example, from Wolof or !Xhosa or Yoruba to English or French. There is here, still, much room for difference and variation; there is a significant degree of what W. V. O. Quine called "indeterminacy" in this process, and what we have been calling "understanding" is far from guaranteed.[43] Barry Hallen writes of Quine's "indeterminacy thesis": "Quine *is* advocating a degree of *skepticism* about *purportedly* rigorous, objective, detailed analyses of alien abstract ideas *in translation*." Hallen concludes:

> From the standpoint of indeterminacy, studies of African abstract meanings in translation are built upon a more fragile basis of interpretation than their rhetoric implies. This needs to be recognized more widely than it is—especially when such studies serve as an empirical basis for attributing oddities in reasoning and/or theoretical understanding to an African conceptual system.[44]

Although the colonial heritage in Africa has led to much philosophy being written or expressed in English or French, there are literally hundreds of indigenous languages that are the natural languages of vast numbers of African people. To "uncover" and understand any expressions of their lives that may be deemed "philosophical" requires some "radical" translation.

A third kind of "translation" is what was the core of our discussion in the first two sections of this chapter. It is what takes place in an individual's understanding—the understanding *in us* that renders the acts observed or read (by observation or through a linguistic translation, or both) meaningful in a "first person" way. In Geertz' words, this shows "how it is that other people's creations can be so utterly their own and so deeply part of us."[45]

Let us return to our second kind of "translation" with the help of Hallen and Sodipo's study of "knowledge" and "belief" among a regional group of Yoruba people and Hallen and Sodipo's appropriation of Quine's "indeterminacy thesis." There are many problems associated with "a radical translation situation," say Hallen and Sodipo, "[where] there has never been any significant communication between the two languages concerned," and where there are few accounts of what the sounds of one language used by its speakers may be.[46] In such cases, the fear is, as Quine and others would argue, that meanings are more likely to be "created" than "communicated."[47] If, for example, a regional native language is to be translated into English, the translator will naturally try to find some corresponding English word(s) to render the native word(s) intelligible. The risk of imposing the logic of the translator's language and culture on the other is very great.

Another worry about this project led African philosopher Paulin Hountondji to reject most renderings of what he called "tribal" thought *as a legitimate source for philosophy. This is, according to Hountondji, at best a bit of *ethnophilosophy*—folk ideas emanating from traditional life.[48] Although, as we will see later, Hountondji is not totally against such native language translation or oral transcription enterprises, he wants to place major qualifications on their usefulness *for philosophy*.

Aspects of Hallen and Sodipo's "experiment" are, however, interesting to discuss since some conceptual and, I would say, philosophical features of Yoruba life are found in their particular approach to translation. They approach their project with some skepticism, but try to build in numerous safeguards to avoid the worst problems; they are determined to "communicate" the regional Yoruba community's ideas and not "create" ideas for them. They are also focused on native correlates to the ordinary English use and meaning of the concepts "know" and "believe"—limiting their translation exercise to two good philosophical candidates for comparison. Their enterprise itself is "conceptual analysis" and they are African philosophers even if the Yoruba sage speakers interviewed are not philosophers strictly speaking.

They believe their project to be "crucial to the entire enterprise of African philosophy." Hallen says:

> For African philosophy, insofar as it may deal with the *analysis* of African languages (or meanings) and the *evaluation* of African beliefs expressed in these languages, will not even be in a position to *begin* until we are assured that such meanings can be correctly understood and translated in a reasonably determinate manner.[49]

After all, notes Hallen, "in 1975 [shortly after his project was underway] no philosophy department syllabus in Nigeria listed a course in African philosophy."[50] One university had a course in "African Traditional Thought" that reflected more the influence of anthropology than anything recognizably philosophical. Granted, his method was to borrow from Western linguistic philosophy, but it would be descriptive and seek to find the meaning only of those concepts deemed to be philosophical and would be applied strictly to African communities and how they saw and critically reflected on their being in the world.

An underlying premise of what may be found in translation from one culture's language to another is that there are some "cultural universals"—common ways in which humans dispose themselves in the world and that their respective practices reflect those common dispositions. This becomes problematic when the practices observed with their attached sounds are exotic or alien to the observer as in the case of the Danish seaman's report of the practice of *suttee* in Bali or E. E. Evans-Pritchard's attempt at "translating" the practices of Zande witchcraft.

We will not go into the details of Hallen and Sodipo's investigations of knowledge and belief in the Yoruba community they studied—see their chapter 2: "An African Epistemology: The Knowledge-Belief Distinction and Yoruba Discourse"—but we will note some interesting implications that can be drawn from that study. Although they found some correspondence in *uses* of the English term "know" with the Yoruba "mo," and the English "believe" with the Yoruba "gbagbo," their *meanings* are significantly different. From this they concluded, among other things,

- that propositional attitudes are not universal. It is therefore hazardous to take the propositional attitudes of one language as paradigms for the propositional attitudes of the other languages.

- that the conceptual systems of alien languages—including those of so-called "traditional" cultures—have implicit in them alternative epistemological, metaphysical, moral, etc. systems that are of philosophical interest in their own right.[51]

These are important findings since most Western analytic philosophers assume that "propositional attitudes" are the same everywhere, that is, they state what is the case (or claimed to be true) of the world they are said to assert in a more or less direct manner. Hallen and Sodipo do not, however, conclude that because of these differences, the two conceptual systems are incommensurable; they have, in fact, illuminated the Yoruba system for the English reader and surfaced matters of real philosophical interest in the Yoruba system—matters that English speakers might find of value to their own lives and the way they see their world.

Furthermore, I think what they have shown, contrary to the criticism that their experiment is another "bit of ethnophilosophy," is that at the least they were trying to get to the core of African self-expression in the only way possible if one is to try and render it "reasonably intelligible" to non-Yoruba speakers. At its best, their experiment provides non-Yoruba speakers with a glimpse of how Yorubas give meaning to their life and how what may at first seem strange becomes less so in the light of the "translation"—however indeterminate or approximate those translations are to actual Yoruba life.

They were specifically trying to avoid "refashioning" African thought systems according to "Western" logical thought patterns. They were both skeptical and cautious, aware of the very indeterminate nature of their translations. As Hallen states: The philosophical intention in such attempts at "translations" is "to understand" and "to assess." Hallen concludes:

> I would opt for, as a further step toward responsible cross-cultural compara-
> tive research in African philosophy, aiming at a better understanding of *why*
> a specific conceptual network with its peculiar (possibly unique) conceptual
> components may be suited to a particular African cultural context. The
> conceptual network of any natural language does not explain or justify itself
> in the didactic argumentative manner that has become conventional to acad-
> emic philosophy. Such reasons must be educed from the language by siting
> it [possibly imaginatively] in its wider cultural and social contexts. Some may
> object that this sounds more like the sociology of language than philosophy,
> but it is another facet of the comprehensive understanding academic philoso-
> phers are obliged to attempt before they pass comparative judgments.[52]

Part of Hallen's message and the message of cross-cultural philosophical understanding is not to pass comparative judgments that reflect the moral or ideological—even epistemological—biases that are a part of anyone's point of view. Keeping those possible biases in mind and *situating another's language and life "in its wider cultural and social contexts" are essential.* Only then is the reciprocity of understanding possible; that "I" may be open and receptive to the "other's" being in his or her world. Furthermore, such openness and receptiveness imply that I listen and see the other as a partner in dialogue. Paulin Hountondji reminds us that African ideas and thinkers must be dealt with "as the subject of a possible discourse," and not be treated "as a voiceless face under private observation."[53] If this is done as a matter of course, then understanding another way of life, as Winch said, will necessarily extend our own.

In the end there is no way around the issue of translation. Whatever is found and understood about another culture—about Africa (or its many cultures)—will be found in translation. Kwasi Wiredu says it bluntly and in a way few can challenge because virtually all of what is included in the class of "African" philosophy is either done in or immediately translated to one or another "metropolitan" language. Wiredu says:

> The foreign origins of the institutional education of contemporary African
> philosophers ... makes earnest conceptual soul-searching obligatory for all
> of us. Philosophical nurture in a second language automatically converts it
> into a first language for the purposes of meditation. African philosophers,
> accordingly, think philosophically in English or French or German or
> Portuguese or some such language. Fundamental categories of thought in
> these languages begin to seem as natural to them as they do to native
> speakers.[54]

This being the case, Wiredu draws two interesting conclusions from this: First he does not think "that any contemporary African philosopher can claim total innocence of the colonial mentality. "That comes with the foreign language. "But we can," he continues, "try to liberate ourselves from it as far as is humanly possible." This, in itself, is one of the issues embedded in what is called "African" philosophy. He suggests "the next desideratum" be "to try to test philosophical formulations in a metropolitan language in our vernacular to see if they will survive independent analysis. To do this is to try to decolonize our thinking."[55] This is a kind of reverse translation; an attempt at resituating the concepts of concern. Such "testing" of philosophical ideas in "African" waters—whether those be a particular vernacular or the particular historical and lived realities of its people—is the overall agenda at hand.

From this an interesting philosophical consequence follows—and this is Wiredu's second point. He says that "in confronting the conceptual problems arising out of the fact that African philosophy has been done, and will continue for quite some time to come to be done, in foreign languages, the African philosopher may be making contributions to general conceptual understanding. In other words, the universal may arise out of concern with the particular."[56] African philosophy's designator *as* African derives its meaning from the particular concepts that are its history: those embedded in its cultures and the concreteness of its lived realties. *To see these concepts clearly and express them as they are will render them as a matter of universal discourse and place them into the larger stream of the cross-cultural conversation.*

What has been called the "African reality" for the philosopher includes some critique of the larger "postcolonial" situation as well as its myriad cultural specific features, and these are part of the recent landscape that philosophers have found of particular interest in the current discussions. There is not, of course, a completely value-free point of view, but if one's relationship is dialogical, then from listening the possibility of mutual understanding is enhanced. If and when a non-African brings herself to Africa, encountering Africa's historical and lived particulars, an understanding may be evoked that is as distant or as close as her own self-understanding will allow. We will now turn to some particulars—to those language and culture-specific features of Africa and to aspects of its postcolonial reality that pervade the current philosophical debates.

2.

Foundations
of Modern African Philosophy

[T]he set of problems perceived by an earlier generation of African and
black intellectuals is now being supplanted by a new set of problems,
raised by the younger generation.... There is beginning to be a redefinition of what one might call the "African problematic," and this redefinition appears to be related to the changed realities of the contemporary
African situation in the post-colonial era.

—Abiola Irele[1]

There are some important critical developments in recent African philosophy, "raised by the younger generation," which are found across the
African subcontinent. They are, more or less, universal in character but
are identified with the African context in particular. To capture the nature
of these philosophical debates we will engage a selection of concepts
linked with these critical developments. First, in this chapter, we will
explore the inherited background, "perceived by an earlier generation,"
of modern African philosophy in the form of ethnophilosophy and the
"negritude" movement. That will help make sense of the "redefinition"
of philosophy as "critical" and "scientific" as characterized by "the
younger generation." Part of the "redefinition," however, links Africa's
past to the present and lays claim to aspects of an oral tradition thought
to be "sagacious" in nature. In the end, we will discover that both the
"critical, scientific" and the "sage" traditions have at least one foot on the
same platform in the current evolution of what is African philosophy.

By far one of the most engaging and controversial books covering a
wide spectrum of issues discussed by African philosophers is Paulin
Hountondji's *African Philosophy: Myth and Reality*. Hountondji is one
of several younger generation "professional" philosophers of African
origin who will frequent center stage throughout this reading of African
philosophy. His ideas set much of the current philosophical agenda when
it was first published in 1976 as *Sur la philosophie Africaine*, and it
continues to command attention among both African and non-African
thinkers in the postcolonial context.[2] Hountondji's critique of ethnophilosophy and his ideas that philosophy be critical, scientific, and written
will serve as a foil for opening our first issues.

Over and against Hountondji's concerns, and in spite of his criticisms, a distinctive philosophical movement was taking shape, emanating from research in the mid-1970s by Hallen and Sodipo in Nigeria and the work in East Africa begun by H. Odera Oruka. This is known as "Sage Philosophy"—so named by Odera Oruka. As this developed Odera Oruka recognized extensions—or what he calls other "trends"—to what is strictly "Sage Philosophy." One such extension, or "trend," as noted by Odera Oruka, includes critical aspects of certain oral traditions as well as some artistic and literary works of Africans. This "trend" was first introduced in my essay "Narrative in African Philosophy" and will be discussed separately in later chapters.[3]

These two traditions—critical, scientific and sage philosophy—not only stand in significant contrast with one another, they represent the story of how African philosophy has dialectically developed over the past quarter century. Our first section takes a long route round to tell this story. It also provides us with a brief look at the historical background to many of the developments in recent African philosophy that will be discussed throughout this book.[4]

Ethnophilosophy and the "Negritude" Movement

The debate on the "critical" aspects of African thought is a highly self-conscious one among "professional" philosophers in Africa. It has been pursued in part in order to shed the unwanted burdens produced by a generation of so-called ethnophilosophical reflections, the legacies of the "negritude" movement, and the neocolonial aspects of what is called "African humanism" or "African socialism." These are all part of the inherited background of modern African philosophy and provide the context for "critical, scientific philosophy" and its recent reformulation in current debates. African humanism or socialism, because it is the heart and soul of modern African political philosophy, will be looked at more closely in chapter 3.

During the first half of this century there were attempts among Europeans in Africa—mostly theologians and anthropologists—to articulate what they understood to be an identifiable outlook among Africans that was in some sense philosophical. This "apologetic" literature—or literature in defense of an African way of thinking and seeing the world that was different from a European way of seeing—is now called "ethnophilosophy." Some of these were an extension of the nineteenth-century Hegelian philosophical notion that there was a "unity of being" that gave coherence to the natural and human order that could be expressed in some universal way in a single underlying principle. The famous book of the Belgian priest Placide Tempels, *Bantu Philosophy* (1945), is the most important work in this early genre of "ethnophilosophy."

Tempels posited the notion of a "vital force" as foundational to the world view of all Bantu-speaking peoples of Eastern and Central Africa. "The attraction of Tempels' work," writes Abiola Irele, "resides not only in its apparent vindication of the African claim to an elevated system of thought but also in its providing a conceptual framework for this African mode of thought. The vitalist emphasis of Bantu philosophy ties in very well with the epistemology implicit in Senghor's *Négritude*."[5] In the early "market place of ideas" about African thought, Tempels' "Bantu philosophy" became a contender for the throne of "The" primary African philosophical world view—it still retains a certain magnetic quality about it. What has come to be called the "animistic" world view—which is often applied universally and indiscriminately to all of African thought patterns—is traceable, in part, to Tempels and this ethnophilosophical view.[6] We will see this strain of universalism in African thought appear periodically throughout the book.

A second strain of ethnophilosophy is more *pluralistic* in nature. The pluralistic analysis has as one aim to show that cultures differ—specifically cultures within sub-Saharan Africa—and that each has its own coherence and distinctive truth-functional way in which it conceives of and expresses its world. The "philosophy" of one culture is not to be extended to another—though there may be a number of family resemblances between cultures. Thus the Dogon and Yoruba, the Samburu and Dinka, the Kuria and Bambara, the Zulu and San have differing cosmological, ethical, and social systems that may be seen to be coherent world views in their own right. Some argued that each is to be equally valued with the world views of non-African societies. This strain is largely the product of Western anthropologists, and is clearly associated with the rise of cultural relativism.[7] Of this relativism, Melville Herskovits, an early pioneer of African Studies in the United States, says:

> The very core of cultural relativism is the social discipline that comes of respect for differences—of mutual respect. Emphasis on the worth of many ways of life, not one, is an affirmation of the values in each culture. Such emphasis seeks to understand and to harmonize goals, not to judge and destroy those that do not dovetail with our own. Cultural history teaches that, important as it is to discern and study the parallelisms in human civilizations, it is no less important to discern and study the different ways man has devised to fulfill his needs.[8]

Both the pluralistic and univeralistic ethnophilosophy have been at the heart of French and British anthropological literature for the past fifty years or more, and have generated a host of philosophical problems centering around the concept of relativism (moral, cultural, and cognitive relativism) and "unanimism" and the possibility of some cross-cultural rationality. Both forms of ethnophilosophy were primarily aimed at a non-African audience and largely used African societies as a laboratory for cross-cultural studies. As noted earlier, Hountondji's fear was that ethnophilosophies dealt with African societies "as a voiceless face under private observation, an object to be defined and not the subject of a possible discourse," i.e., not the subject of a two-way conversation.[9]

In neither form of ethnophilosophy (universalistic or pluralistic) was there a large amount of actual African philosophical literature generated, that is, philosophy written by Africans—Alexis Kagame's work being one notable exception. Ethnophilosophers and anthropologists have, however, identified and, to a significant extent, transcribed into a written literature some of the oral accounts of traditional world views (their stories, songs, and mythologies) and given us detailed ethnographies of ritual practices of African people. In this way it has helped "picture" Africa's past and contributed toward the conversion of African self-understanding from an oral to a written mode. The importance of this latter point will be discussed later.

The concept of "negritude" has different origins from, but is not unrelated to, ethnophilosophy. They both ended up serving some common ends in the formation of African identity during the period of independence struggles against colonial rule. What is called the "negritude movement" was launched by a handful of young, black students—Africans and Afro-Caribbeans in the early to mid-1930s in the Latin Quarter in Paris. A number of writers are quick to point out that the "negritude movement," as identified with African nationalist poets and politicians in both Paris and the French West Indies, recognized and drew inspiration from the larger black consciousness writings of the African-American "Harlem Renaissance"— writers such as W. E. B. Du Bois, Langston Hughes, Claude McKay, Countee Cullen, Sterling Hayden, Paul Vesey, and James Weldon Johnson.[10]

Negritude shares the universalizing tendency with some ethnophilosophy in identifying common, fundamental cultural characteristics that were thought to be specifically African or "Negro." The leading spokesman for the "negritude movement" was Léopold Senghor. He emphasizes the uniqueness of racial and cultural consciousness. The particularity of the African racial and cultural consciousness contributes to the idea of its singular cultural identity. In a rare glimpse of the personal origins of "negritude," Senghor wrote the following account very late in his life:

> It was in 1936 ... in the middle of the Latin Quarter in Paris. We had no lack of arguments with which to attract our fellow Africans and Negroes of the Diaspora to the Renaissance of Black Culture. There were jazz, blues, and dance, but above all there was Negro art, expressive force of which had struck Picasso and artists from the Paris School—Tristan Tzara and certain surrealist poets—like an illumination. Yet we began to seek other even more striking arguments after we encountered Leo Frobenius.
>   His interest piqued by a review he read in the journal *Les Cahiers du Sud*, Aimé Césaire bought one of Frobenius' major works, *Histoire de la civilisation africaine*. It was a translation, published by Emmanuel Gallimard, of

Kulturgeschichte Afrikas. After having read it, Césaire passed it on to me, and I still have that copy with his name on it in my library. To understand the joy which took hold of us as we read this book, it is necessary to go back in time—to the instruction given in all the "white man's schools," public or private, in the colonies.[11]

The "white man's schools" had taught Senghor a rather colorless "rationalism"—a la Descartes—and that they should "distrust the imagination and particularly the emotions: everything that distracted or beguiled rational thought." But Senghor had retained three essential elements of what he called "the Negro-African aesthetic" from his childhood. Those elements were: "the symbolic image; the melody of forms and movements, sounds and colors; and, finally, the rhythm of asymmetrical parallelisms."[12] He challenged his white teachers and was expelled from his Catholic secondary school. The result here is that Senghor and others of the "negritude movement" found in 1936 in Frobenius a critical form of German romantic thought that allowed them to translate their African aesthetic into a new expression of their cultural heritage. They could begin to argue for what Senghor said would be "a new world of harmony and equilibrium, a world where each continent, each race, each nation, and, above all, each culture would contribute its own irreplaceable virtues."[13]

Senghor is full of poetic allusion when he talks of *Negritude*. It is rooted in the "Negro-African aesthetic;" its end point is the rediscovery of the black African's "fervent quest for the Holy Grail, which is our *Collective Soul*;"[14] it is based on "our continent's genius: *our need to love*;"[15] and that the coming of a "civilization of the universal" would be possible only "by pouring into it the burning lava of our Negritude."[16] Negritude was always seen as the intuitive or romantic counterpoint to the West's sterile rationalism and scientific, material society.

Senghor's version, however, complicates the matter by arguing for a *collective* African consciousness, thus neutralizing the significance of the plurality of African cultures. It contrasts collective racial and cultural traits of Africans with specific traits of other collective cultures, e.g. Europeans or Chinese. In a word, Senghor identified the collective trait of Africans as "Emotive sensitivity." "Emotion," he said "is completely Negro as reason is Greek ... Yes, in one way, the Negro is richer in gifts than in works."[17] In sum, Abiola Irele says "the specific contribution of negritude to [the development of nationalism in Africa] was to articulate, in the form of an all-encompassing concept of black identity, the sense of the African's separate cultural and spiritual inheritance."[18]

There is an important difference to be noted in Senghor's concept of negritude with Jean Paul Sartre's definition of *Négritude* in his widely read *Orphée Noir* (Black Orpheus). Irele concisely characterized this difference: Sartre defined "negritude as 'an attitude to the world'—a subjective disposition expressive of the black man's total apprehension of his peculiar situation. . . . he went on to give an active significance to the black *prise de conscience,* seeing in this the passage from an unreflected to a reflected mode of experience."[19] Senghor called Sartre's view "subjective *Négritude*" while his own view was "objective *Négritude.*" The objective concept "designates an *attribute* [not an attitude] of the black man . . . *a unique racial endowment of the black man.*" "For Senghor," says Irele, "culture has a racial character to the extent that culture is the effect of a total response by man to his environment, a response that involves his total being, including his organic constitution."[20] We will return to this connection between race and culture in chapter 3.

Although negritude became a significant force for African "race recovery" and independence movements—providing them with their own "irreplaceable virtues"—and was lifted up as a virtue powerfully expressed in nationalistic poets such as Aimé Césaire, it was also a most unhappy platform upon which to stand once independence was achieved. It had a most unfortunate by-product, argues Wole Soyinka, leading to "an abysmal angst of low achievement." "Negritude," Soyinka said, "revealed to them [Africans] the very seductive notion that they had to search for their Africanness. Until then, they were never even aware that it was missing." Most devastating about the theory, said Soyinka, is that

> Negritude trapped itself in what was primarily a defensive role, even though its accents were strident, its syntax hyperbolic and its strategy aggressive. It accepted one of the most commonplace blasphemies of racism, that the black man has nothing between his ears,. . . .[21]

The negritude movement is generally understood by recent African thinkers as a form of universalistic ethnophilosophy. Ethnophilosophy and negritude both "appear as a byproduct of underdevelopment, a consequence, among many others, of cultural amnesia," said Hountondji.[22] Partly in reaction to these ideas comes the call for both a more "critical, scientific philosophy" and a more revolutionary one so that philosophy in Africa can shed itself of the more "colloquial" and "stereotypical" image it had inherited and created for itself.

Critical, Scientific Philosophy

What is critical, scientific philosophy and how does this duo of concepts arise in the African philosophical discussion? Philosophy as a critical enterprise is an active process of questioning and self-criticism. It engages in this activity to identify the biases of one's thought and to transcend or logically alter those thoughts for ones that more accurately reflect our natural and human world. This process never ends because it is continually experiencing new realities embedded in our world. Each new reality we encounter or create calls for new criticism. Included in the critical aspect of philos-

[handwritten marginalia: Philosophy (re of language focusing) focus on concepts in language (call for problem) concepts which call for ...]

ophy is conceptual clarification, whereby the meaning and the use of concepts in our language are the focus of critical investigation. There is, therefore, "development" in philosophy and this is no less true in the African setting.

There are two currents in "critical" philosophy in the African context, the universalistic and the dialectical. The universalistic current is most strongly advocated by P. O. Bodunrin, Kwasi Wiredu, and Odera Oruka,[23] whereas the dialectical current is favored by Hountondji, Eboussi Boulaga, and the more ideological Marxists such as Marcien Towa and Amilcar Cabral.[24]

The starting point for the more universalistic approach is the rejection of ethnophilosophy and a stand taken with philosophy as practiced by the main line of the Western philosophical tradition inherited from the ancient Greek philosophical context. Philosophy for Bodunrin is "criticism." He argued that as with the Greek context where Socrates and Plato were opposed to popular beliefs and opinions, so, too, must African philosophy be opposed to traditional cultural beliefs and the popular folk behavior. "Criticism," says Bodunrin, is "rational, impartial, and articulate appraisal whether positive or negative."[25] Wiredu is not as narrow in his conception as is Bodunrin. Wiredu says that the philosopher, regardless of their culture, must proceed "in the spirit of due reflection, being always on the lookout for conceptual snares" and that an *African* philosopher should combine insights gained from either East or West (or both) "with those gained from our own indigenous philosophical resources to create for ourselves" something from which *all* might learn.[26] For these thinkers the point is to lift the philosophical enterprise by "due reflection" and self-criticism to the universal level of discussion, then to turn to the specific existential conditions and priorities of the African social and political context, combining these in search of truth.[27]

A recent example of critical philosophy in the analytic, conceptual analysis tradition turned to specific existential conditions and priorities in Africa is found in Augustine Shutte's book *Philosophy for Africa* (1993). Shutte is a white South African, who, as a philosopher, had struggled with the relevance of his discipline for the lived situation of apartheid South Africa. He is very much aware, as is the focus of "postcolonial" African philosophy, that "the present struggle in South Africa is partly a struggle between Africa and Europe" and the degree to which his mind has been colonized.[28] In the context of the "new" South Africa, Shutte's questions probe how philosophy should be *applied*. He writes, how are we to define "new" in our context:

> As democratic? . . . Socialist? Liberal? Capitalist? Whichever terms we choose to describe our future we had better define them carefully. The same is true if we choose to define the predicament from which we are struggling to free ourselves. What are we fighting against? Racism, poverty, non-participation,

inhumanity, underdevelopment, sexism, alienation, communism? Imprecise language in this sphere can be very dangerous. There is a job for philosophy here, a job for which its tools of conceptual analysis and rational criticism are necessary.[29]

Shutte's approach is an exercise in critical conceptual analysis—an exercise we will take up further in our analysis of the concept of race in chapter 3 and in discussing moral issues such as community and democracy, poverty, reconciliation, and justice in chapters 4 and 5. Shutte, himself, analyzes the uses of the concepts of "work" and of "gender" (among others) in the South African context.

The universal view does not go nearly far enough according to Paulin Hountondji, and at the same time it goes too far. It goes too far in risking African philosophical identity to the Western bias—using Western philosophy as the measure of all philosophizing—and it does not go far enough in limiting the discussion to the specifics of the African context itself. Like most African philosophers, Hountondji wants a fresh start—a break from ethnophilosophy and other "intellectual impediments and prejudices." But he also wants to carve out a more specific channel for African philosophy. So although both of these currents, universalistic and dialectical, share some common goals, he believes the dialectical current of critical philosophy is more closely bound to the political struggles and intellectual history of contemporary Africa. Hountondji sees philosophy as "a perpetual movement, a chain of responses from one individual philosopher to another across the ages."[30] In this sense the literature of ethnophilosophy and the "negritude movement" *could be considered* philosophical texts of an earlier age—"texts" to be criticized and dialectically "taken up" into a new stage in an ongoing dialogue.

Hountondji establishes what could be identified as four criteria for philosophy in the African context. A review of Hountondji's thesis will serve to critique the critical-dialectical view and will provide us with both a clear contrast to and an opening toward "Sage Philosophy," and will thus carry us to the next move in our argument. These four criteria are also the grists for a large portion of the African philosophical mill from 1976 to the early 1990s. His four criteria are as follows.

1. *That philosophy be written.* Philosophy, Hountondji says, is "critical reflection *par excellence*" and cannot develop fully unless it " 'writes its memoirs' or 'keeps a diary'."[31] Philosophy is a "set of texts written by Africans and described as philosophical by their authors themselves."[32] Prior to his revision of this definition in 1996, as noted earlier, this seemed to rule out what Odera Oruka had called "philosophic sagacity" or the oral reflection of Africans reputed for their wisdom and insight. Such sagacity, Hountondji says, is mythological discourse rather than philosophical discourse.[33]

Houndondji's argument here is very interesting and the pros and cons of this point are widely discussed in both African and non-African philosophical and literary critical circles. To give just a flavor of his argument I will provide a lengthy passage.

> Oral tradition favours the consolidation of knowledge into dogmatic, intangible systems, whereas archival transmission promotes better the possibility of a critique of knowledge between individuals and from one generation to another. Oral tradition is dominated by the *fear of forgetting*, of *lapses of memory*, since memory is here left to its own resources, bereft of external or material support. This forces people to hoard their memories jealously, to recall them constantly, to repeat them continually, accumulating and heaping them up in a global wisdom, simultaneously present, always ready to be applied, perpetually available. In these conditions the mind is too precoccupied with *preserving* knowledge to find freedom to *criticise* it. Written tradition, on the contrary, providing a material support, liberates the memory, and permits it to forget its acquisitions, provisionally to reject or question them, because it knows that it can at any moment recapture them if need be. By guaranteeing a permanent record, archives make actual memory superfluous and give full rein to the boldness of the mind.[34]

This is a much disputed point in the discussion among African thinkers and Hountondji's view leaves only a slight crack in the door for oral tradition when he says that moral tales, legends, proverbs, etc., may prove philosophical only when they are transcribed. Only then, as texts, are they subjects for critical reflection.[35] This does allow some of the transcriptions provided by ethnographers and literary scholars of African culture to become the subject matter of philosophical reflection, but the oral tradition as such cannot qualify as philosophy. Although he later softens his tone a bit, his basic principle remains.[36] We would have to interrogate Hountondji further on the full implications of his 1996 revision when he says "By 'African Philosophy' I mean the set of philosophical texts produced (*whether orally or in writing*) by Africans" (p. xii, my emphasis). One could read this to mean that a "text" could be produced "orally." Hountondji still qualifies what kinds of orality may become a "text" *for* philosophy.

Marcien Towa, whose views generally agree with Hountondji, breaks with Hountondji on this point and has a less rigid view of the possible philosophical role of traditional folk tales or orally produced texts. Irele writes of Towa's position:

> The very fact that a major segment of these tales dramatizes social and moral conflicts gives them a critical function within the context of traditional life; hence, they become the mode of expression of an intelligence that constantly calls into question established values and institutions, including religious beliefs. Their philosophical value and status, reside, therefore, in their function as a critical interrogation of the natural world and of social facts.[37]

2. *That the Literature or Discourse be "Scientific."* Related to the first criterion, Hountondji makes a distinction between what he calls "artistic literature" and "scientific literature."[38] Philosophy belongs to the latter. The "sagacity" of an expressed mythology or folk tales, or poetry, or the visual arts (the iconic traditions of a culture) as "artistic literature" is contrasted with a way of thinking more akin to the natural or theoretical sciences, i.e., "mathematics, physics, chemistry, biology, linguistics."[39] Furthermore, scientific discourse is historical, says Hountondji; it has an "intrinsic historicity of a pluralistic discourse," while "the discourse of a man like Ogotemmeli ... opts out of history in general and, more particularly, from that groping endless history, that unquiet, forever incomplete quest we call philosophy."[40] Hountondji's distinction between "artistic" and "scientific" literature is highly problematic as a way of dividing philosophy from other literary/cultural forms of expression, as we shall argue in chapter 6.

For there to be an African philosophy, Hountondji believes there must first be an African science. "It is not philosophy but science that Africa needs first." This, he says, will get us away from "metaphysical problems," "the meaning of life," and problems of "human destiny" and "the existence of God."[41] Only when we rid ourselves of such problems could a scientific philosophy be developed. This may be one of Hountondji's most contested points. Few "African" philosophers, not to mention philosophers of any "geographic" designation, have given up on metaphysical, moral, and religious questions as legitimate subjects for critical reflection. It would seem to many philosophers in and out of Africa that if such problems cannot be included as philosophy, then we have made a radical shift in the meaning of the term "philosophy" altogether. Few feel constrained by Hountondji's narrow conception of philosophy as "science."

3. *That the Discourse be Exclusively of African Geographic and Ethnic Origin.* Not only does Hountondji rule out most oral discourse and virtually all "artistic literature," but most of the so-called ethnophilosophical literature can only be an occasion for African philosophy since the vast majority of it is written by Europeans and North Americans. African philosophy is restricted to "scientific" texts by Africans—texts "signed by Camerounians Eboussi-Boulaga, Towa and N'johMouelle, by the Ghanaian Wiredu, by the Kenyan Odera. ..." Along with Hountondji himself, these thinkers, he says, "announce and delineate a new theoretical structure in the history of our philosophy."[42] This, of course, is precisely what is meant by "recent" philosophers and their philosophy, and is part of a defining feature for what is meant by "African" philosophy.

Hountondji further acknowledges that some past literature could qualify as African philosophical discourse, e.g., some works of the eighteenth-century Ghanaian Anton-Wilhelm Amo and the mid-twentieth-century works of W. E. Abrahams as well as such political leaders as Kwame

Nkrumah. And, since he first published *Sur la philosophie Africaine,* he is heartened by new works in the history of African philosophy.

> In the wake of Cheikh Anta Diop's writing, scholars such as Pathé Diagne and Théophile Obenga drew attention to the antiquity and historical depth of African philosophy. This direction of research seems to me particularly exciting. It allows us to put the colonial and late pre-colonial period into perspective and to probe more deeply into Africa's past. It encourages us to look beyond the era of the slave trade.[43]

To "put the colonial and late pre-colonial period into perspective" is itself part of what contemporary philosophers mean by "postcolonial" philosophy. This contributes to a more complete picture of building a tradition of African philosophy, a tradition that critically understands itself in the situation of its "postcolonial" reality. We must add to this the recent translations and availability of Ethiopian *written philosophical texts* from as early as the third century BCE, the important texts of the early sixteenth century, *The Book of the Philosophers,* and from the seventeenth century, *The Treatise of Zär'a Yacob and of Walda Heywat.*[44]

4. *That the Internal Texture of Philosophy Be Purely Dialectical.* This is the most far reaching and the most promising of Hountondji's criteria.

All learning, Hountondji says, appears as "an event in language, or more precisely, as the product of discussion."[45] African philosophy must develop in the context of a "constant free discussion about all problems concerning its discipline."[46] Paradoxically by such an "internal discussion" among Africans, Hountondji believes that African philosophy will develop beyond narrow ethnic boundaries and become universal. This is not unlike Wiredu's remark that the universality of African philosophical reflections "will arise out of concern with the particulars." This, of course, is how the concepts being discussed in any cultural context concerning issues of our human being in the world *become* philosophical, i.e., are of concern to the very meaning and critical life of humans everywhere.

Philosophy as this dialectical event in language must secure for itself "freedom of expression as a necessary condition for all science, for all theoretical development and, in the last resort, for all real political and economic progress...."[47] After securing liberty for criticism, philosophy may then begin its more concrete task of developing its own theoretical course; it may take on its own history in the African context. In the course of developing his dialectical view of philosophy, Hountondji makes this Socratic point: that "truth is the very act of looking for truth, of enunciating propositions and trying to justify and found them."[48] Socrates, Hountondji concludes,

> was able to enter the theoretical history of Greece because his disciple or fellow citizens took the time and trouble to write down his thoughts, to discuss, sometimes to criticize and often to distort them. Similarly, we Africans can probably today recover philosophical fragments from our oral

literature, but we must bear in mind that so far as authentic philosophy goes, everything begins at the precise moment of transcription, when the memory can rid itself of cumbersome knowledge now entrusted to papyrus and so free itself for the critical activity which is the beginning of *philosophy*, in the only acceptable sense of the word.[49]

There are seeds in Hountondji that point us in the direction of what Odera Oruka has called "Sage Philosophy." There are also formidable constraints that, in the end, lead Hountondji to reject such an idea.

Sage Philosophy

When Hountondji said that "truth is the very act of looking for truth, of enunciating propositions and trying to justify and found them," he concisely states a Socratic vision of philosophy. What he failed to accept, however, and what his first criterion disallows, is that Socrates himself *is* a philosopher—an oral and sagacious philosopher. Socrates' dialogues with his fellow Athenians were neither simply for the sake of stimulating public discussion nor were they to recollect Athens' past history. Socrates sought to elicit and challenge alternative views on issues of moral and civic importance; he pushed for resolution to disputes and just solutions to expressed human concerns—to clarify the meaning of justice itself was an aim of his dialectical bouts. For him, each new situation that forced dialogue in a critical fashion was the narrative "stuff" of philosophy. We will return to this last dialectical, Socratic point of Hountondji when we discuss the importance of the transitions from oral to written literature in the African context in chapter 6.

We earlier had a glimpse of an African sage tradition in Hallen and Sodipo's critical exploration of Yoruba "sages"—that is, a look at whether the *onisegun* seemed to be able to differentiate between opinion or "belief" and more certain "knowledge." Hallen and Sodipo began their research with the assumption that there might be "philosophy" encased in traditional wisdom, not just folk mythology and stories. Could they in some meaningful translation determine whether this traditional wisdom was at all critical or reflective; could this wisdom be "tapped" *for philosophy*? Or could it be called "philosophical" wisdom in itself? Hountondji is very skeptical but concedes "the possibility of an oral philosophical literature (a philosophical 'orature')" and he came to qualify his appreciation of Griaule's approach in recording the wisdom of Ogotemmeli as a "starting point of a critical discussion . . . rather than as a reconstruction of implicit philosophy."[50] This, too, is essential to Odera Oruka's conception of "Sage Philosophy."[51]

In the introduction to Odera Oruka's *Sage Philosophy* he says that this book stands in "contrast [to] the claim that philosophy is and can only be a 'written' enterprise."[52] He also says that any claim that "illiterate" philosophy is "non-scientific" or "mythological" is false. Odera Oruka does not, on the other hand, want to say that philosophy must be illiterate, but that some cultures have critical, reflective philosophers who never wrote anything; their thoughts or wisdom is only spoken—and he reminds us of Thales, Pyrrho of Elis and Socrates, Lao Tzu, Buddha, and Jesus. *What* these sages said was itself the result of a dialectical and dialogical tradition that was both critical and reflective; what was said did not depend on it being "written" (even though it may later have been written down by others) in order for it to be "philosophical."

Odera Oruka says the objection to philosophical sagacity by Lansana Keita "that it purports to be unwritten" and thus not accessible, and if it is accessible it *is* written, therefore writing is a necessity for philosophy, is little more than a bit of logical sleight of hand. Odera Oruka responds:

> Keita needs to be reminded that Socrates' philosophy, for example, did not exist just because Plato and others gave birth to it through their pens. Plato and others wrote it down (even if they distorted much of it) because it existed in the first place. And such is the case with Sage philosophy in Africa. It exists independent of Odera Oruka or anybody else, so we search for it and write it down as this is the modern practice of keeping thought.[53]

Strictly speaking, Odera Oruka distinguishes two other trends in African philosophy which are often thought to be variations or extensions of Sage Philosophy. They are "the hermeneutic trend and the artistic or literary trend."[54] The former includes those who start from the interpretation of the concepts of ordinary language such as Hallen and Sodipo and Wiredu's analyses of Akan language. The "philosophy" here, however, is not so much in *what* is said but by *how* it is interpreted. Although it looks at first-order speech, what is philosophical is the second-order critique of that speech and that, of course, is written.

The latter trend, the artistic and literary, Odera Oruka notes, consists in what I have referred to as "the *narrative* element in African philosophy." Here, the material that may qualify *as philosophy* is either written or iconic, but its use is both expressive, reflective and critical of the lived reality of Africans; it "constantly calls into question established values and institutions," as Towa suggested.[55] I see these two trends also as distinctive and they will be explored separately from Sage Philosophy.

In his more explicit statements on what is philosophic sagacity, Odera Oruka says that it is a form of "culture wisdom" but not just folk wisdom or an expression of a communal world view. Rather:

> Philosophic sagacity . . . is often a product and a reflective reevaluation of the culture philosophy. The few sages who possess the philosophic inclination make a critical assessment of their culture and its underlying beliefs. Using the power of *reason* rather than the celebrated beliefs of the communal consensus and explanation, the sage philosopher produces a system within a system, and order within an order.[56]

The *philosophical* sage must be a *thinker*, not just a storyteller. This sage has shown a capacity to critically reflect on the first order stories or myths, and

> in many cases, it is a critical rebellion against the first order conformity and anachronism. While the first order glorifies the communal conformity, philosophic sagacity is skeptical of communal consensus, and it employs reason to assess it. While the first order is purely absolutist and ideological, the second order is generally open-minded and rationalistic. Its truths are given as tentative and ratiocinative, not as God-sent messages.[57]

An interesting example is given by Odera Oruka to differentiate first-order from second-order sages. The Dogon sage, Ogotemmeli, says the following of women: "After God made woman, he gave her bad blood, which has to flow every month," while Paul Mbuya Akoko, a Luo from Kenya, knowing what his community thinks of women, nevertheless makes his own rational assessment. Mbuya argues: "A man has the physical capacity to run faster than a woman. But on the other hand, a woman has the physical capacity to undergo the pains of carrying and bearing a baby which a man lacks. So we cannot correctly say one is superior or inferior to the other. . . . In truth . . . the two sexes are naturally equal or balanced."[58]

This is the crucial distinction for Odera Oruka that enables him to differentiate types of sagacity—"folk" or "philosophical." He classifies the Dogon sage as a folk sage only. He also says of Hallen and Sodipo's *onisegen* that they are only folk sages even though he believes that Hallen and Sodipo's interpretive method is a promising second-order philosophical exercise, a hermeneutical one. Kwasi Wiredu says of this overall enterprise that the work in Sage Philosophy undertaken by Odera Oruka—and this would apply to others—is "one of the most important developments in post-colonial African philosophy," and that such *sages* as Odera Oruka discerns as philosophical "are the present-day exemplars of our ancestral philosophers." Furthermore, he believes that in taking these ancestral philosophers seriously that we "should be not just expository and clarifying; [but] should be reconstructive as well, evaluating our heritage in order to build on it."[59]

This debate in recent African philosophy is ongoing with strong voices supporting both sides, i.e., the side that philosophy must "write its memoirs" and "keep a diary" (Hountondji, Dismas Masolo, and Bodunrin) and those who line up along with Odera Oruka's Sage Philosophy (Towa, Wiredu, and Kwame Gyekye). It is believed that one of the best ways to preserve and show the critical value of "traditional" thinking is to legitimize its "thinkers" as a kind of philosopher. In both, however, the importance of dialogue and an ongoing critical discussion or conversation is essential and common. Important elements of this discussion will be revisited in chapter 6.

One sees in Hountondji's fourth criterion on the internal dialectical structure of philosophy or philosophy understood as conversation, and in Odera Oruka's emphasis on "reflective reevaluation of culture philosophy" or that the *philosophical* sage must be a *thinker*, a convergence of the meaning of African philosophy in the direction of a dialogical enterprise. As a conversation philosophy reflexively presents and re-presents the story of Africans' being in the world—that "chain of responses" to its lived reality. That being is complex; it is tied to Africa's traditional past, its intervening colonial history, its harsh environments, and its internal human struggles. These have all been "voiced" by Africa's sages, by its politicians and writers, and now by its literary critics, social theorists, and philosophers. These make up the particular texts for Africa's philosophy that its recent philosophers are critically examining for their universal significance.

3.

Liberation and Postcolonial African Philosophy

"We had achieved socialism before the coming of the European."

—Léopold Senghor

African Humanism and Socialism

Owing, in part, to the background of the concept of negritude, African humanism is identified with movements of national independence and with the development of collective African identity. The more political side of African humanism is also referred to as African socialism. The broader base of African humanism and socialism, however, includes the ideological works of Franz Fanon, a particular style of socialism or communalism, and the inspiration of such founding national leaders as Kwame Nkrumah, Julius K. Nyerere, Léopold Senghor, and Kenneth Kuanda. The social and political writings of Nkrumah and Nyerere are of particular importance in formulating the basis for African socialism. Among important philosophical and social concepts are "consciencism," "negative and positive action" (Nkrumah), "villagization," *ujamaa* or "familyhood," and "education for self-reliance" (Nyerere), and the aspect of "spirituality" in Senghor's "revised humanism."[1] Both African humanism and socialism were used to underscore the values of a common African heritage and the inherent struggle left to a people who were exploited by colonial powers.

It became clear to many African leaders after World War II that sustaining Western colonialism was seriously undermining, if not destroying, the African social infrastructure based on traditional humanistic values. It was thought by Nkrumah, Senghor, and Nyerere that "capitalism" was incompatible with African culture and that the colonial heritage was equated with capitalism. It was at this time that the growing appeal and spread of Marxism or revolutionary socialism was being exported and seemed to "dovetail" with notions of African humanism. The new revolutionary ideology could lay some claim to being more compatible with African humanism or communalism than was capitalism. As Senghor said: "we had achieved socialism before the coming of the European." Nkrumah, too, noted that Africa's socialism was "more in tune with the original humanist principles underlying African society."[2] And

Nyerere said: " '*Ujamaa*', then ... describes our Socialism." "Our socialism" is the recognition of society as an extension of the basic family unit; it was an attitude of mind for Nyerere that reaches back to "tribal days." But, he says, "the family to which we all belong must be extended yet further—beyond the tribe, the community, the nation, or even the continent—to embrace the whole society of mankind. This is the only logical conclusion for true Socialism."[3]

It has been argued that during the post–World War II struggles for independence and in the immediate period after independence the only relevant philosophy for Africa was a politicized "liberation philosophy"—one of resolute revolutionary self-assertion and self-reliance. From the 1950s, with the political awakening of black Africa, says V.Y. Mudimbe, "Marxism appeared to be the inspiration for the renewal of the continent ... Marxism seemed to be the exemplary weapon and idea with which to go beyond the colonialism incarnated and ordained in the name of capital."[4] Mudimbe goes on to say that the key concepts of negritude, black personality, and authenticity "all hail in one direct line from the Marxian presupposition of the centrality of the individual as historical actor."[5] Transposed to African soil "the individual" actor became the collective notion of a people acting. The regimes, the progressive movements, and their leaders were Marxist— if not Marxists they "wielded a syntax that had a Marxist aspect."[6] Let us look at Senghor's way of "wielding" the Marxist syntax.

Senghor is very explicit about how Africa's socialism is both linked to and diverges from Marxist socialism. This is laid out in his lecture at Oxford referred to earlier. Senghor believed that the Marxist theory and the Soviet practice of socialism stressed "material" development at the cost of "spiritual" development, and that African socialism based on its humanism will fill the spiritual breech. "*Revised humanism*," according to the "living experience" of Africans, he says, will include "*revised Negritude* which, ... is a form of *Humanism*."[7]

In brief Senghor's program of African socialism—its *material* and *spiritual* features —is characterized as follows:

> The specific object of African socialism, after the Second World War, was to fight against foreign capitalism and its slave economy; to do away, not with the inequality resulting from the domination of one class by another, but with the inequality resulting from the European conquest, from the domination of one people by another, of one race by another.
>
> ... Here it is not only a matter of suppressing private capitalism, it is a question of replacing it. ... The workers in field and factory must take over the means of production and organize them more rationally, that is, more efficiently, thanks to help from the state, and the new hope roused in them by their re-won freedom, of which they now have a *living experience*.[8]

And its spiritual side is deeply embedded in Africa's community-based society. He writes:

The satisfaction of the spiritual needs which transcend our natural needs has to be achieved. This has not yet happened in any European or American form of civilization: neither in the west nor the east. For this reason we are forced to seek our own original mode, a Negro-African mode ... paying special attention to ... *economic democracy* and *spiritual freedom.*

... Our Negro-African society is a classless society, which is not the same as saying that it has no hierarchy or division of labour. It is a *community-based society*, in which the hierarchy—and therefore power—is founded on spiritual and democratic values: on the law of primogeniture and election; in which decisions of all kinds are deliberated in a *palaver*, after the ancestral gods have been consulted, in which work is shared out among the sexes and among technico-professional groups based on religion. This is a community-based society, *communal*, not collectivist.[9]

On the spiritual side, Senghor draws heavily on the writing of French paleobiologist and theologian Pierre Teilhard de Chardin and his form of theistic-evolutionary humanism. For Teilhard de Chardin and Senghor, Marx's matter becomes "Holy matter ... subtended by a *radial* energy of a psychic nature. And this, paradoxically, is how Negro-Africans have always thought of matter."[10] The sources of this "radial energy" for Senghor in a poetic metaphor is "the burning lava of our *Negritude.*"

As it turned out the Marxist based socialism that was "infecting" African liberation movements was just another kind of "neo-colonialism"—an extraneous kind of "communalism" imposed from the outside for economic and ideological considerations. Africa was only a "theater" for the larger "cold war" drama. Marxist socialism was theoretically based on an industrialized class-based economy, not a rural communal-based one. For example, given all of Nyerere's good intentions, Tanzania's failed experiment in forced collectivization—"villagization"—illustrates why such a "Soviet"-imposed ideology simply could not work.[11] Senghor might blame the failure of revolutionary socialism in Africa on its lack of a spiritual dimension or on his *mis*calculation that "after some sixty years of colonial rule, no economic bourgeoisie is to be found in the majority of the Negro-African states promoted to independence."[12] With independence, a new economic bourgeoisie, if not already present, rapidly arose to unsettle the ideals of African socialism.

With the collapse of the Soviet Union in 1989, and the independence or move to majority government of nearly all African States by 1994, the character of "revolutionary" tensions changed dramatically. There is now one predominant economic ideology in Africa, "development" under some variation on the theme of capitalism—even though this is sometimes an unfamiliar theme. There are few exceptions to this—and fewer still as pressures continue to join the tide of economic globalization. The revolutionary rhetoric, however, still lingers in many postcolonial governments.[13]

Although the literature of African humanism and socialism—ideological essays, political party credos, major addresses aimed at the international community—provides a rich source for philosophical reflection and criticism, not all Africans see its effect upon an African philosophy as wholly positive. Hountondji and Towa, for example see this literature as an ally of ethnophilosophy and neocolonialism.[14] For Hountondji, for example, as literature it does provide an opportunity for philosophers to critique it and to transcend its limitations in an ongoing search for truth. As a part of African literature it is an occasion for dialogue, but should not be taken as philosophical truth in its own right. In spite of Hountondji's qualifications, this political literature linked to African humanism and socialism has produced a rich and interesting set of written texts that I believe *are philosophical* as well as of social and political value.

Before leaving this subject we should step back again and look more closely at one of the most philosophically original pieces of literature to come out of Africa by one of its most prominent national leaders. Kwame Nkrumah's *Consciencism* is both a piece of political philosophy and an ideological treatise. It helped to define and clarify the concepts of African humanism and socialism as tools to justify the liberation struggle. These concepts were thought by Nkrumah, Nyerere, Senghor, and others to be part of Africa's precolonial heritage—a kind of grassroots humanism embedded in traditional society.

African humanism is quite different from the "Western, classical" notion of humanism. The Western, classical notion of humanism stresses a particular concept of education and civilization; it is premised on ancient Greek ideals such as balance of the arts and sciences, cultivation of individual virtues, and the exercise of rational self-control. It places a premium on *acquired individual skills*, and favors a social and political system that encourages *individual freedom and civil rights*. The Renaissance elevation of humanism, whereby the individual person is measured by achievements, is celebrated in such figures as Leonardo, Vico, Erasmus, Thomas More, and John Calvin—all "Renaissance Men"—champions of secular and ecclesiastical freedoms and cultivators of human moral, artistic, and intellectual achievement.

African humanism, on the other hand, is rooted in traditional values of mutual respect for one's fellow kinsman and a sense of position and place in the larger order of things: one's *social* order, *natural* order, and the *cosmic* order. African humanism is rooted in *lived dependencies*. Where life's means are relatively minimal and natural resources are scarce, the individual person must depend on his or her larger community. Nkrumah says, "Our philosophy must find its weapons in the environment and living conditions of the African people."[15]

African humanism is linked to larger discussions of "communalism" in Africa, though not to radical communalism. There is a certain "self-interest" among men and women but that self-interest is subordinated to communal well-being. Kwame Gyekye defines the concept of African humanism as follows: "a philosophy that sees human needs, interests, and dignity as of fundamental importance and concern. For, the art, actions, thought, and institutions of the African people, at least in the traditional setting, reverberate with expressions of concern for human welfare."[16] This he sees as the "fundamental concept in African socioethical thought generally." This basic socioethical humanism is the underpinning of African *socialism* in the post-World War II period.

The attempt by Nkrumah in his *Consciencism*, and put in practice with his newly won independence from Great Britain in 1957, was very promising. He sought to develop a new kind of socialism "in tune with the original humanist principles underlying African society."[17] This he called "philosophical consciencism." Nkrumah, in his "African Socialism Revisited," said, "the aim is to remold African society in the socialist direction; to reconsider African society in such a manner that the humanism of traditional African life reasserts itself in a modern technical community."[18]

One of the key concepts in philosophical consciencism was "positive action." For Nkrumah positive action is the revolutionary arm of philosophical consciencism, it balances the forces of "negative action" that were embodied in the social, political, and economic forces of colonialism. Originally Nkrumah had drawn his notion of positive action partly from Gandhi to analyze social and economic conditions and bring about change nonviolently (a modification of Marxist–Leninist doctrine). "Positive action," says Nkrumah, "will represent the sum of those forces seeking social justice in terms of the destruction of oligarchic exploitation and oppression. Negative action will correspondingly represent the sum of those forces tending to prolong colonial subjugation and exploitation. Positive action is revolutionary and negative action is reactionary."[19] Positive action requires increased *self-awareness* through constant political education, for example, awareness that one aim of colonial governments was "to treat their colonies as producers of raw materials, and at the same time as the dumping-ground of the manufactured goods of foreign industrialists and foreign capitalists."[20] Self-awareness exposes the negative action at work in colonialism. The second feature of positive action is *self-reference*. Self-reference is the means by which the African personality can penetrate every aspect of society. This requires a systematic elimination of the residues of colonialism found in neocolonial governments— what he called exposing the wolf in sheep's clothing. In a rhetorical flare, Nkrumah says that self-reference is the activation of the "powers of self-motion" that represents the very life forces within the "materialistic universe." Such powers are released through the dialectical tensions created when positive action is asserted against negative action—only then, he thinks, will the African personality be enabled to emerge.[21] Initially Nkrumah was against armed revolution. He thought that through *self-awareness* and *self-reference* the powers of "positive action" could transform the inherent values of communalism to a form of revolutionary socialism. What was required was "a restatement in contemporary idiom of the principles underlying communalism." Nkrumah had chosen the language of Marxism as his "contemporary idiom" to draw out what he called "the cluster of humanist principles which underlie the traditional African society."[22]

Once again critics like Hountondji cry "foul" when thinking about the philosophical implications of such views as Nkrumah's or Nyerere's. These views, Hountondji argues, rely on the acceptance of a unified thesis of African cultural identity—the "African personality" or "communalism" or "familyhood" (*ujamaa*)—and gloss over the fact of African pluralistic reality. Hountondji stresses that Africa is not a closed system of values, but embraces many values. These criticisms are largely aimed at Nkrumah's first edition of *Consciencism* (1964). In the later revised edition (1970), Nkrumah had made some major revisions that reflected the changing African reality, at least in terms of what he saw happening with the newly independent states. A brief look at Nkrumah's later analysis of the changing African reality is instructive in seeing how the concept of the "postcolonial" in recent philosophical discussions was changed from a descriptive term—"post" referring to the period following colonial rule with the indigenous self rule of Independent African States—to a more highly theoretical notion that "the postcolonial" itself was a new and distinct problem to be analyzed and dealt with; "the postcolonial" had somehow been transformed from a descriptive historical term of reference to a highly complex philosophical concept used in the analysis of the contemporary African situation itself.

Nkrumah, himself, provides us with a good example (and one of the earliest examples) of postcolonial criticism in identifying one of the central weaknesses in self-rule that leads to its own destruction—a weakness that should, itself, come under the scrutiny of "positive actions." Nkrumah, in an author's note to the 1970 edition of *Consciencism*, writes:

> Since the publication of the first edition of *Consciencism* in 1964, the African Revolution has decisively entered a new phase, the phase of armed struggle. In every part of our continent, African revolutionaries are either preparing for armed struggle, or are actively engaged in military operations against the forces of reaction and counter-revolution.
>
> The succession of military coups which have in recent years taken place in Africa, have exposed the close links between the interest of neocolonialism and the indigenous bourgeoisie. These coups have brought into sharp relief the nature and the extent of the class struggle in Africa. Foreign monopoly capitalists are in close association with local reactionaries, and have made use of officers among the armed forces in order to frustrate the purposes of the African Revolution.[23]

Even with the highly charged Marxist rhetoric, Nkrumah's brief description here is on the mark. "Neo-colonialists and the indigenous bourgeoisie" had economic interests to protect and the Western democracies that control these interests were going to do whatever it took to keep Soviet communism at bay in Africa. Again it was external forces who were in charge. Since 1970 that pattern has changed in only one major way. Soviet communism is no longer the threat it was, but the indigenous African regimes are still trying to protect their personal interests that are linked to external transnational economic forces, and these regimes continue to "frustrate the purposes of the African Revolution"—assuming the purposes were originally aimed at self determination, equality, and the overall general welfare of the people. In Nkrumah's revised edition the possibility of *a natural transformation* from communalism to socialism no longer seems viable. The interjection of "class struggle" changes the plausibility of his overall thesis.

Hountondji has a very good analysis of this change in Nkrumah's thought. Hountondji has, however, a more telling criticism based on his general criticism of the unanimism of Nkrumah's larger thesis. Hountondji asks, what is the meaning of Nkrumah's philosophy of *consciencism*? Nkrumah would like to overcome (or synthesize) the three competing ideologies in Africa, precolonial African traditional ideology, Euro-Christian and Muslim ideologies, with a new "philosophy of consciousness." Hountondji writes: "Consciencism is a classic philosophy of consciousness, in that it aims at restoring the lost unity of African consciousness and at articulating three separate ideologies into a single, unified system of thought."[24] Consciencism therefore seeks an "ideological unity." Hountondji says that Nkrumah believed that his "consciencism" would, one day, "be the collective philosophy of Africans, the African philosophy."[25] A major flaw in Nkrumah's philosophy of consciencism is "the idea that there were no ideological conflicts in precolonial Africa on the one hand and, on the other, that this illusion should be valorized by making theoretical unanimity into a value to be struggled for. Let us call this the unanimist illusion."[26]

Combining the earlier discussions of "unanimism" in the "negritude" movement and in universalists forms of ethnophilosophy (a singular Bantu ontology, for example) with the "humanist-socialist vision of a collective African personality" and we have one of the biggest stumbling blocks in the development of African Philosophy—the drive for a "singular" philosophy, "*the* African philosophy"—the chasing of a chimera. Identifying some of the difficulties in such a chase is part of what is at the heart of the question "What is African Philosophy?" The growing consensus is that there is no single "African" philosophy, partly because African culture is highly pluralistic and partly because the nature of philosophy itself is such as to divert attention from singular and simple solutions or unitary systems to particular problems. We have already discussed a number of issues in this debate in our previous chapters. We will now turn to what is called "postcolonial African philosophy," which we will discover is not *one thing* either but a multiplicity of things.

Postcolonial African Thought

Abiola Irele reminds us of the "irreversible nature of the transformations the impact of Europe" has made on Africa, and how these transformations have become the defining "frame of reference of [Africa's] contemporary existence."[27] In only our brief discussion of liberation themes and of the role of African humanism and socialism in the development of political philosophy in Africa, we have had to account for at least two critical factors: (1) that political philosophy explicitly grows out of the independence and liberation movements against colonial rule in Africa, and (2) that much of the discussion engages Marxist philosophical themes as these are thought to intersect with traditional African socioethical values or with the dialectical and material unfolding of revolutionary struggles in themselves. Thus *colonialism* and *Marxism*—distinctively Western ideas—define to a substantial degree the "frame of reference" of African political philosophy from the 1930s through the twentieth century.

It is all too clear that African philosophy cannot escape its being intertwined with European colonialism of the nineteenth and twentieth centuries, or with the legacy of slavery and other forms of Western imperialism for the past 500 years, or with the questions of "modernity" and its challenges to the development of present-day Africa itself. In Emmanuel Chukwudi Eze's introduction to his collection, *Postcolonial African Philosophy: A Critical Reader*, he writes: *"The single most important factor that drives the field and the contemporary practice of African/a Philosophy has to do with the brutal encounter of the African world with European modernity*—an encounter epitomized in the colonial phenomena."[28] As important and central as this theme is, it can become formulaic or deflect too much attention away from the conditions of the postcolony and its needs to move forward. A larger and more general point that embraces "the brutal encounter of the African world with European modernity" is the fact that Africa has not just *encountered* modernity, but Africa has actually *interpenetrated* it and stands as a challenge to be taken seriously. A leading postcolonial theorist, Gyan Prakash, makes this larger point: "The third world, far from being confined to its assigned space, has penetrated the inner sanctum of the first world . . . arousing, inciting and affiliating with the subordinated others in the first world. It has reached across boundaries and barriers to connect with minority voices in the first world: socialists, radicals, feminists, minorities, etc."[29] Or put more succinctly by Trinh T. Minh-ha: "There is a Third World in every First World, and vice versa."[30] We must look at how African philosophy speaks beyond its "assigned space" as well as within it for that is what the contemporary notion of the "postcolonial African philosophy" is all about.

A primary factor that entwines Africa with European modernity is the philosophical shaping of the concept of "race" by three of the most prominent modern European philosophers: Hume, Kant, and Hegel—each of whom, perhaps unwittingly, established a rationale for conquest and subjugation of people of the black race. Hume took the lead in his essay "On National Character" with this comment: "I am apt to suspect the Negroes to be naturally inferior to the whites. There scarcely ever was a civilized nation of that complexion, nor even any individual eminent in action or speculation. No ingenious manufacturers amongst them, no arts, no sciences. . . . Such a uniform and constant difference [between the white and Negro race] could not happen . . . if nature had not made original distinction betwixt these breeds of men. . . ."[31] And Hegel had written off Africa south of the Sahara (the rest of Africa he somehow links to Europe) as being of any "universal" and "historical" significance. "The Negro," he says, "exhibits the natural man in his completely wild and untamed state. We must lay aside all thought of reverence and morality—all that we call feeling—if we would rightly comprehend him; there is nothing harmonious with humanity to be found in his type of character."[32] This alone provides a rationale for not treating Africans in any morally significant way, nor to revere their cultures in any way. Eze writes that given these assessments of African humanity: "It is for good reason that 'the critique of Eurocentrism' has become a significant, if 'negative,' moment in the practice of African philosophy."[33] With this eighteenth and nineteenth century groundwork on the idea of "race," colonialism had its "rationale" to "civilize" and economically exploit the "inferior breed,"—those for whom one can "lay aside all thought of reverence and morality." In the wake of such extraordinary ideas, the subsequent colonization, the anthropological study of black cultures, and the rise of ethnophilosophy seemed to naturally follow.

Another concern within what is called postcolonial African philosophy is the issue of interpretation and understanding, or *hermeneutics*—of which this book is, overall, an example—whereby the interpretive method(s) of one philosophical tradition is used to apply to and understand some subject matter or another. Although interpretive theory goes back a long way, historically, I am thinking of theories or methods that have arisen since World War I and are now taken up in the perennial search for truth. The uses of such interpretive methods are universalist at heart since the cross-fertilization between theories or philosophies are, and have been, standard practice within the disciplines of philosophy and critical theory. For example, use of analytic or phenomenological philosophical methods cross between Continental, British, American, Asian, and African thinkers as they apply to specific problems being worked on by philosophers in those regions. Or one might think of the use of a major philosopher from one tradition applied to tackle problems being pursued in a different setting, e.g., Wittgenstein applied to understanding Buddhism or theories of justice, or Heidegger and Gadamer's ideas used as an "hermeneutical" tool for the interrogation of a problem embedded in a particular culture, as in Heidegger's analysis of Western technology, or Gandhian ideas to critique oppression.

Many identify the origins of what is called "postcolonialism" with the utilization of Foucault's "archaeological" methodology to subvert conventional historical criticism and to analyze forms of knowledge as power, or with the psychoanalytic methods of Jacques Lacan in the interrogation of self-identity, history, and literature. Each of these philosophers or philosophies and their methodological implications has been applied by one thinker or another on virtually every continent. It seems in the nature of *hermeneutical* (interpretive) analysis that it has become highly cross-disciplinary and multicultural.

Tsenay Serequeberhan, for example, appropriates Heidegger and Gadamer in order to critique the contemporary African situation.[34] Serequeberhan lays claim to having discovered *hermeneutics*, as if for the first time, as a method to apply to Africa's "postcolonial" situation. With this "new" tool in hand, he says that "Contemporary African philosophy [becomes] an added critical questioning voice in the varied current discourses of philosophy. It is the questioning voice of those whom the modern European world compelled into voicelessness in the process of its own violent and self-righteous establishment."[35]

We have already seen Marxist analysis applied to social and economic oppression resulting from colonialism in Africa, and the neo-Hegelian writings of Louis Althusser dialectically driving the "scientific, critical" philosophy of Hountondji. We have also seen an example of the strict analytic-linguistic method of W. V. O. Quine applied to the analysis of Yoruba *onisegen* sages and the "indeterminacies" inherent in the translatability of their concepts to a metropolitan language. This cross-cultural fertilization in the name of *hermeneutics* or interpretive theory is not about to stop, nor should it, as the very task of philosophy is the search for truth—as a pragmatist philosopher following William James might say—by "all" means.

On the question of "Postcolonial" Studies, which has emerged as a discipline all its own in the Academy, the main architects are thought to be Edward Said with his book *Orientalism* (1978), Gayatri Spivak, *In Other Worlds: Essays in Cultural Politics* (1987), and Homi Bhabha, *The Location of Culture* (1994). Interestingly, none of these theorists is African, but all have roots in former or present colonized nations. These and other works have spun a new rhetorical web dealing with how to reclaim the identity of what were called "third-world" cultures (the products of Western colonialism) and have developed a new critical discourse to critique colonialism from their own postcolony perspectives. Perhaps the most unique feature of Postcolonial Studies is its interdisciplinary nature. As such, "postcolonial *philosophy*" could be understood as a branch, therefore, of the larger "studies." A helpful book to guide one through the maze of "postcolonialism," especially as applied to African thought, is Ato Quayson's *Postcolonialism: Theory, Practice and Process* (2000). Quayson has a way of clearly presenting what is often unclear in the theory and practice and reminds us of the following:

> the project of Postcolonialism . . . is always entangled with ethical questions. In other words, it seems to me almost impossible to talk about the negative effects of colonialism past and present without implicitly or explicitly being tied into discussions of the ethical value of the knowledge that is produced. . . . The interdisciplinary model has ultimately to answer to the ways in which it shapes an ethical attitude to reality, in this case to post-colonial reality. . . . [W]e need clear tools by which to understand and struggle against injustice, oppression and even obfuscation.[36]

Quayson's question about assessing the ways in which postcolonial criticism shapes "an ethical attitude to reality" is very important. Any theory (or 'ism') should be used to serve something more important than itself as a critical model; it should help us "to understand and struggle against injustice, oppression and even obfuscation." Too often, however, what goes by the name of "postcolonial" contributes to further "obfuscation." Quayson's moral reminder brings a sharper philosophical focus to the larger "studies," but also makes clear the cross-cultural and interdisciplinary nature of post-colonial philosophy.

The postcolonial theorist, Homi Bhabha, defines postcolonial criticism as follows:

> Postcolonial criticism bears witness to the unequal and uneven forces of cultural representation involved in the contest for political and social authority within the modern world order. Postcolonial perspectives emerge from the colonial testimony of Third World countries and the discourses of "minorities" within the geopolitical divisions of east and west, north and south. . . . They formulate their critical revisions around issues of cultural difference, social authority, and political discrimination in order to reveal the antagonistic and ambivalent moments within the "rationalizations" of modernity.[37]

The fact that postcolonial perspectives emerge from "the discourses of minorities" from different geopolitical regions points to its concern with giving voice to the particular narratives of different minorities or cultures. This discourse of minorities, Bhabba recently called "the right to narrate"—an "ennunciatory right" that gives authority to a peoples' speech acts.[38] There is no *one* minority voice or universalizable disenfran-chised "meta-narrative" that is *the* postcolonial perspective.

Another feature of the postcolonial perspective is that even though it is "voicing" the so-called "otherness" of disenfranchised peoples, this is iron-ically done by applying essentially Western critical tools—for example, using Foucaultian, Derridian, and Lacanian historical, literary, and psychoanalytic analyses. This is one of the paradoxes—if not an Achilles heel—in postcolonial studies. It uses Western forms of critical analysis to disrupt and undermine Western hegemonic control over knowledge and power. Thus the postcolonial perspective uses Western criticism and a metropolitan language to find ways of allowing non-Western critical voices in their own postcolony modalities to redress the West—it does this "in order to reveal the antagonistic and ambivalent moments within the 'rationalizations' of modernity," as Bhabha said. So here we are—east/west, north/south, black/white, rich/poor—thoroughly enmeshed with one another even at the deepest of critical levels. So, too, Western philosophers along with their "third-world" counterparts, in this same postcolonial spirit, seek to find points of vulnerability in Western philosophy and interrogate those points.

In this spirit Robert Bernasconi, in his "African Philosophy's Challenge to Continental Philosophy," announces that his "intention is to begin a discussion among Continental philosophers of the following question: what would it mean to do Continental philosophy in the light of African philosophy?" This will serve, he believes, to make Continental philosophy more critical of its own tradition and thus "become more open to other traditions."[39] Of course, Bernasconi's overall end is to demonstrate that all "Western" philosophies may gain something by listening to the voices of African philosophy. This is a kind of turning of the hermeneutical tables back upon its European originators.

Until recently Continental philosophy, up to and including some of the post–World War II writings of Heidegger and Levinas, had totally excluded Africa—historically, culturally, philosophically. They were thought to be nonassimilable to "Western" thought. The Eurocentricism of Continental philosophy with regard to Africa was almost total.[40] To illustrate this Bernasconi cites this remark of Levinas: "I always say—but in private— that the Greeks and the Bible are all that is serious in humanity. Everything else is dancing." And, of course, Heidegger's project focuses on a retrieval of the concept of "Being" from early Greek philosophy. Bernasconi wants us to go "dancing" with African philosophy! Remarks like Levinas' are, of course, one reason that the "negritude" movement *could* make a dent into Euroconsciousness. Negritude was so designed as to *not interfere* with European rationality—it was so much "dancing" in Levinas' sense. Things African were cast as "other": "Emotion is African, as Reason is Greek" (Senghor).

In another ironic turn, Bernasconi points out how Lucius Outlaw shows that African philosophy has a certain "deconstructive" capacity when placed up against Western Continental philosophy. In the frame of Western Continental philosophy the phrase "African philosophy" not only does not register, it is seen as a contradiction. What this suggests, says Bernasconi following Outlaw, "is that 'African philosophy' as a term functions . . . to expose the limits of the dominant framework as they are enshrined within the double bind, thereby to displace them."[41] If African philosophy as a "deconstructive" tool serves to "expose the limits," or functions as "a wake up call," to Eurocentric thought, then it may also have a "reconstructive," or more positive, function with regard to Continental philosophy. Here is where postcolonial African thought moves beyond its "assigned space," as Prakash said.

Bernasconi makes this comment, which I believe hearkens back to our first chapter and the recognition of lacunae in our own understanding, which suggests the need to be open to the challenges that other cultures may offer us: "It is possible that the basis of dialogue is not the presumption of agreement, but the admission on the part of the hearer that he or she is incapable of understanding. 'You don't know what I'm talking about,' closes the conversation only if the listener wants to control what is said. It can also elicit further response."[42] Bernasconi also cites D. A. Masolo's closing remarks from his *African Philosophy in Search of Identity*: "Philosophy is experience. It is a personal point of view insofar as it is mine, and because philosophy consists not in persuading others but in making our own minds clear."[43] What does it mean to "make one's own mind clear?" This is also Nietzsche's point in *The Genealogy of Morality* where he challenges Western Christianity to clarify what morality has become; he calls us to "ruminate"—to turn a spotlight on ourselves to see our blindness and consider the possibilities of cultural "transvaluation." This very notion of Nietzsche's "transvaluation of values" will be used as a critical tool when discussing the value of African literature and art *for* philosophy.

Finally, Bernasconi closes his essay with these two remarks: "The existential dimension of African philosophy's challenge to Western philosophy in general and Continental philosophy in particular is located in the need to decolonize the mind. This task is at least as important for the colonizer as it is for the colonized." And: "If Continental philosophers would open themselves to a critique from African philosophy and thereby learn more about their own tradition seen from 'the outside,' they would find that the hegemonic concept of reason had been displaced, and they would be better placed to learn to respect other traditions, including those that are not African."[44]

What can we conclude from this exchange that is called "postcolonial thinking"? Let me suggest the following. Africa's interface with European modernity is itself a philosophical text to be read, critically appraised, and understood; it is clearly an item on the philosophical agenda called "postcolonial African philosophy." Because African philosophy is embedded in its postcolonial reality it speaks to Europe and the West out of its lived experience with Europe and the West. This necessitates a two-way dialogue. The very fact of a non-African trying to understand Africa requires engagement of this part of the dialogue and further requires some equipment for the engagement—cross-cultural equipment from an aesthetic point of view like those suggested in chapter 1. And as we have noted several times, the cross-cultural discussion must be a two-way conversation.

The postcolonial African reality is speaking, writing, and artistically expressing a philosophy out of its encounters with European modernity. It is also speaking out of its poverty, suffering, and affliction, and from its own rich heritage of humanistic dignity. The ethical values, forged within these contexts, have given legitimacy to Africa's claims to give voice to issues of justice, the nature of oppression, matters of human character such as patience, hope, forgiveness, and reconciliation—matters on virtually everyone's mind these days. Africa's postcolonial text is being written by Africans, but it is also addressed to a world outside Africa. All of Africa's diasporic millions are voices of the legacy of the postcolonial reality and these voices *are* entwined with North, South, and Caribbean Americans, with Arab and Jew, and with virtually every European who has a colonial history with Africa.

The Question of "Race"

"Negroes want to be treated like men," wrote James Baldwin. In "Fifth Avenue, Uptown," Baldwin says that "[p]eople who have mastered Kant, Hegel, Shakespeare, Marx, Freud and the Bible find this [perfectly straightforward seven word] statement impenetrable."[45] To be treated as human beings is what black Africans (and other dispossessed peoples) were denied. That is what "racism" means—to be denied one's humanity.

"Europe brought racialism into Africa," said W. E. Abraham.[46] The whole issue of race was introduced into Africa beginning with both the Western and Arab slave trade. "The history of civil society in colonial Africa is laced with racism," remarks Mahmood Mamdani.[47] Mamdani goes further to argue that such racism became institutionalized with the introduction of "customary law" where black Africans were set apart and given a different set of "laws" for their customary practices from "civilized society." "Customary law" was, however, the creation of the colonial state and it was the colonial state that oversaw the local or customary authorities. This, in fact, he argues is the precedent to South African apartheid and was well established in both French and British colonial rule long before it was "official policy" in South Africa.[48]

The African-American intellectual W. E. B. Du Bois had prophesied at the beginning of the twentieth century that the concept of "race" would "possess our century." As we exit that century and enter another we are still possessed by the concept. Du Bois' life stretched from before the European colonial powers divided up Africa into its geopolitical states at the Congress of Berlin in 1884, and he witnessed the independence of Ghana from colonial rule in 1957. He called his life story "an autobiography of a race concept."[49] It will be instructive to follow this autobiography of Du Bois' race concept as it parallels the development of colonialism in Africa.

Du Bois first articulated his "race concept" in 1897 in his celebrated essay "The Conservation of Races." He revisited the issue many times, and modified his conception in an essay in the journal of the NAACP, *The Crisis*, in August of 1911. In 1940 he reiterates his views in his autobiography entitled *Dusk of Dawn: An Essay Toward an Autobiography of a Race Concept*. What does Du Bois mean by "a race concept"? In its evolution, his concept of race moves from the nineteenth-century physiological discussions with clear vertical-hierarchical notions of "races" hypothesized to a more horizontal sociohistorical view of "races."

In his address "The Conservation of Races," delivered to the American Negro Academy in the year it was founded by Alexander Crummell, he declared that the "American Negro has been led to . . . minimize race distinctions" because "back of most of the discussions of race with which he is familiar, have lurked certain assumptions as to his natural abilities, as to his political, intellectual and moral status, that he felt were wrong."[50] He goes on, nevertheless, to articulate a concept of race that went against the grain of many conceptions prevalent in the nineteenth century. He noted that at this time "science" had generally agreed that "there were at least two, and perhaps three, great families of human beings—the whites and Negroes, possibly the yellow race."[51] Du Bois was not satisfied with the "final word" of late nineteenth-century "science" because he felt that the "grosser physical differences of color, hair and bone" were less important than more "subtle, delicate and elusive" differences "which have silently but definitely separated men into groups."[52] He went on to characterize these more "subtle, delicate and elusive" differences, which led to his well-known definition of what race means. He said these subtle differences transcend scientific differences and become apparent, rather, to the "eye of the historian and sociologist." Here is his well known definition from his address:

> If this be true, then the history of the world is the history, not of individuals, but of groups, not of nations, but of races. . . . What then is a race? It is a vast family of human beings, generally of common blood and language, always of common history, traditions and impulses, who are both voluntarily and involuntarily striving together for the accomplishment of certain more or less vividly conceived ideals of life.[53]

Thus he moves away from a "scientific"—that is biological and anthropological—conception of race to a sociohistorical one. Du Bois continues:

> The question now is: What is the real distinction between these nations? . . . Certainly we must all acknowledge that physical differences play a great part. . . . But while race differences have followed along mainly physical lines, yet no mere physical distinction would really define or explain the deeper

differences—the cohesiveness and continuity of these groups. The deeper differences are spiritual, psychical, differences—undoubtedly based on the physical, but infinitely transcending them. . . . [Furthermore, the various races are] striving each in its own way, *to develop for civilization its particular message*, its particular ideal, which shall help guide the world nearer and nearer that perfection of human life for which we all long. . . .[54]

For Du Bois, then, the problem for the Negro is *the discovery and expression of the message of his or her race.* He concludes:

The full, complete Negro message of the whole Negro race has not as yet been given to the world. . . .
  The question is, then: how shall this message be delivered; how shall these various ideals be realized? the answer is plain: by the development of these race groups, not as individuals, but as races. . . . For the development of Negro genius of Negro literature and art, of Negro spirit, only Negroes bound and welded together, Negroes inspired by one vast ideal, can work out in its fullness the great message we have for humanity.[55]

Now what does Du Bois's 1897 conception of race boil down to? He says that "race" is not a scientific or biological concept, though he still leans on a few characteristics lodged in the "scientific literature." His conception of race is a sociohistorical concept and as such it has a message for humanity, *a message particular to a distinctive human family created by God, and that the message should come from this group's history and spirit.* His argument went against the notion that we should "minimize race distinctions." That notion was a denial of difference and Du Bois wanted to celebrate, or at least find a way to express, the message of difference. Each group, he thought, had a part to play in the human family; that the white and Negro races are related not as superior to inferior but as complementaries; the Negro message is, with the white one, part of the message of humankind. This as we have seen forms part of the background for the "negritude" movement a generation later. The "message" of negritude would be tailored to Africa's history and spirit under colonialism and mark off the differences that would serve their particular liberation ends.

As the "scientific" debate developed in the twentieth century, the idea of biological differences receded steadily—differences in "blood" and any physical features became so negligible that the very concept of "racial difference" seemed to be a mute one. In 1911, Du Bois wrote: "These physical characteristics are too indefinite and elusive to serve as a basis for any rigid classification or division of human groups." And while pursuing his Pan-Africanism he rejected talk of race as anything other than a synonym for color. His very conception of race shifted more toward a purely sociohistorical and political notion; *his concerns were more with social and economic exploitation of people of color*—Africans, the African Diaspora, and Asians. By 1940 in his autobiography *Dusk of Dawn*, Du Bois writes:

Since [the writing of "The Conservation of Races"] the concept of race has so changed and presented so much of contradiction that as I face Africa I ask myself: what is it between us that constitutes a tie which I can feel better than I can explain? Africa is of course my fatherland. Yet neither my father nor my father's father ever saw Africa or knew its meaning or cared overmuch for it. My mother's folk were closer and yet their direct connection, in culture and race, became tenuous; still my tie to Africa is strong. On this vast continent were born and lived a large portion of my direct ancestors going back a thousand years or more. The mark of their heritage is upon me in color and hair. These are obvious things, but of little meaning in themselves; only important as they stand for real and more subtle differences from other men. . . .

But one thing is sure and that is the fact that *since the fifteenth century these ancestors of mine and their descendants have had a common history; have suffered a common disaster and have one long memory. . . . the real essence of this kinship is its social heritage of slavery; the discrimination and insult;* and this heritage binds together not simply the children of Africa, but extends through yellow Asia and into the South Seas. It is this unity that draws me to Africa.[56]

So, finally, all that is left of the concept of race for Du Bois is *some common social history bound to slavery and oppression and rooted in memory.* Of course if what is common is primarily "discrimination and insult" then by his own account he is "racially" linked to "Yellow Asia" and the "South Seas" as much as to Africa—or for that matter he is linked to ethnic Albanians in Kosovo or Kurds in Turkey or women in Afghanistan as much as to Afro-Caribbeans in Colombia or Tutsis in parts of central Africa or black South Africans. Although a long way from his earlier conception of race, *we are left with something important in this last account of Du Bois* that we must consider more fully in reflecting on the current postcolonial context in which we find ourselves.

Although Du Bois identifies the "heritage of slavery" and oppression and "the discrimination and insult" that accompanies such social disasters, the African-American philosopher Cornell West has made an important criticism of Du Bois' conception of race.[57] West believes that Du Bois is too much the "rationalist" and also one who buys into the Victorian ideal that "exceptional men will save the race." What his conception lacks is a sense of the tragic depths of black suffering. West said that the idea of "black liminality frightened this black rationalist," and that black educated elite like Du Bois and Booker T. Washington had less influence than some contemporary social movements—like the black civil rights movement of the 1950s and 1960s in America. West commented that love of "high" culture is less likely to save than "low" cultural communitarians. But most significant for West was Du Bois' inability to deal with the problem of evil. He fails to wrestle with those writers who dealt with great problems of evil and human suffering; a sense of the tragic is missing completely in Du Bois' understanding of black suffering. West notes that this sense of the tragic and suffering is found in a number of black artists and he cites the music of John Coltrane and the fact that Toni Morrison takes us beneath the veil to reveal the tragic in black life. He also thought that Du Bois would have benefited from reading the great Russian writers Dostoievski, Tolstoy, and Shestov. I believe that West has hit a very important point that should be applied to our understanding of African thought in general—a point that subsequent chapters will amplify in discussions of suffering, poverty, and injustice, and in looking at modern African literature.

There are lessons to take away from Du Bois, however, and we shall come to those in a moment. But first we must make a brief account of two stages that followed Du Bois in response to the question of "race" that are important to African philosophy. The first stage is the articulation of the concepts of "negritude" and the "African personality" from Senghor through Nkrumah, a topic we have already covered. The second stage is found in the writings of Franz Fanon. It is in Fanon's writing that we find a theoretical underpinning for the liberation movements and the revolutionary changes that followed immediately on the heels of independence.

The discussion of "race" within the twentieth century moved from a vulgar to a more insidious kind of "racism"—from an oversimple material, physiological doctrine to a more refined cultural argument. This was traced by Du Bois, but the more important view of the relation of race to culture in the African context comes from Franz Fanon. Fanon says:

> These old-fashioned ["scientific"] positions . . . disappear. This racism that aspires to be rational, individual, genotypically and phenotypically determined, *becomes transformed into cultural racism.* . . .
>
> We witness the destruction of cultural values, of ways of life. Language, dress, techniques, are devalorized. . . .
>
> The enslavement, in the strictest sense, of the native population is the prime necessity.[58]

Given this more open, total, and subtle form of "cultural racism," Fanon asks: How do those who fall prey to racism behave? What are their defense mechanisms? It is in the psychological analysis of the effects of racism on the oppressed that the power of Fanon's work lay. He writes:

> Having witnessed the liquidation of its system of reference, the collapse of its cultural patterns, the native can only recognize with the occupant that "God is not on his side." The oppressor, through the inclusive and frightening character of his authority, manages to impose on the native new ways of seeing, and in particular a pejorative judgment with respect to his original forms of existing.[59]

"Guilt and inferiority are the usual consequences of this dialectic," says Fanon, and to escape these the oppressed does two things: he proclaims "his total and unconditional adoption of the new cultural models," and pronounces "an irreversible condemnation of his own cultural style." Then,

[h]aving judged, condemned, abandoned his cultural forms, his language, his food habits, his sexual behavior, his way of sitting down, of resting, of laughing, of enjoying himself, the oppressed *flings himself* upon the imposed culture with the desperation of a drowning man.[60]

All this having been done, the oppressor has succeeded in enslaving the oppressed without making them equal, without in any meaningful ways accepting the enslaved group into their own. Thus the "acculturized" and "deculturized" continue to come up against their *difference* and thus racism, and see the futility of their alienation and deprivation.

It is at this point that the oppressed sees the illogic of this system. "He perceives that the racist atmosphere impregnates all the elements of the social life. The sense of an *overwhelming injustice* is correspondingly very strong."[61]

Trapped in this "liminality," the oppressed resorts to radical means to overcome the overwhelming injustice. Here is where the revival of tradition surfaces; it is a "falling back on archaic positions." "Tradition is no longer scoffed at by the group. The group no longer runs away from itself. . . ."[62] Fanon sees this as one's "culture put into capsules . . . [and] revalorized." This, in fact, is how he sees the negritude movement as articulated by the radical poets such as Césaire. Abiola Irele notes: "When one considers the effect of Fanon's thought on the ideological temper of [the recent, postcolonial] generation, there is no little irony in the fact that the points of departure for his entire reflection was *Négritude.* . . . Césaire's brand of *Négritude* involves no elaborate theory of blackness in a total and aggressive response to centuries of denigration and humiliation."[63] These poets of negritude were playing out their aggression against their enslavement by colonialism. Irele says that it was Fanon's

> preoccupation with the psychiatric effects of colonial oppression . . . [which] led him to see in the aggressive reaction against this oppression quite simply a therapeutic means of self-recreation for the colonized subject. Through the violence directed at his oppressor, the colonized subject remakes himself as a full human being, without any limiting qualifications to his human status and quality.[64]

Returning to Fanon's own words, he concludes his 1956 address with these observations:

> This rediscovery, this absolute valorization almost in defiance of reality, objectively indefensible, assumes an incomparable and subjective importance. On emerging from these passionate espousals, the native will have decided, "with full knowledge of what is involved," to fight all forms of exploitation and of alienation of man. . . . The logical end of this will to struggle is the total liberation of the national territory. In order to achieve this liberation, the inferiorized man brings all his resources into play, all his acquisitions, the old and the new, his own and those of the occupant.
>
> In the course of struggle the dominating nation tries to revive racist argu-

ments but the elaboration of racism proves more and more ineffective. There is talk of fanaticism, of primitive attitudes in the face of death, but once again the now crumbling mechanism no longer responds. Those who were once unbudgeable, the constitutional cowards, the timid, the eternally inferiorized, stiffen and emerge bristling.

The occupant is bewildered.

The end of race prejudice begins with a sudden incomprehension.[65]

The analysis of the occupant's "bewilderment" and "sudden incomprehension" is an apt description of most colonial powers' retreat and surely applies well to the fall of apartheid in South Africa as we will discuss later.

The result of Fanon's analysis of the problem of "race" rids it of sentimentalities and clichés. He introduces a new realism that exposes not only the colonialists in retreat, morally bankrupt, but also the neocolonial bourgeoisie and nationalistic elites as wearing "a superstructural mask thrown over [their] class interests."[66] This new realism following Fanon is found in such philosophers as Macien Towa and Paulin Hountondji.

Having been in slow retreat now for awhile (and finally "retreating" in southern Africa) colonialists and neocolonial bourgeoisie are gradually losing their grip on Africa. The prospect for developing a new nonracist civic order, however, is daunting. Kwame Anthony Appiah is contributing to such a development by articulating *a third stage* in the current discussion of "race"—a stage that reduces even further than Du Bois did, or rather *changes*, the significance of "race" with respect to cultural difference. Appiah and others move the philosophical discussion toward one of identity and universal human rights and the relative value of "cosmopolitanism." This current debate also examines the moral implications of global citizenship and multicultural civil societies.[67]

What philosophical lessons can be drawn from Du Bois' and Fanon's conception of "race" and the effects of "racism"? The philosophical lessons are largely moral ones rather than epistemological or metaphysical ones.

First we learn that those who suffer from "discrimination and insult"—victims of poverty and affliction—must find their voice and articulate their message in their struggle against all forms of exploitation. When Martin Luther King, Jr. stood in front of the Lincoln Memorial and shared his dream he found a voice for African Americans. When Václav Havel and millions of his fellow Czechoslovakian citizens stood silently in the streets of Prague with lighted candles in 1989, they spoke with one voice that they would no longer live a lie. When 25 million South Africans stood in long lines all day to vote for the first time in April of 1994 they had a message for their minority oppressors that they will never again have their minds colonized nor allow their children to be shot.

The voices of the oppressed—those who suffer from overwhelming injustices—must not remain anonymous and nameless; African and African-American critiques of colonialism and postcolonialism by Fanon, Soyinka, Malcolm X, Ngugi, Aimé Césaire, Cabral, Du Bois, and others must form part of our collective memory. It is through specific voices that great evil is unmasked and a message is conveyed. The voices of protest and suffering, in literature that is self-expressive of the reality of a culture, or the voice of a common silence that says no more lies must be heard. *We must learn how to listen and give detailed attention to the faintest cries of insult and oppression. This requires looking injustice in the eye and developing a capacity to listen to other voices as well as one's own, and cultivating a moral sensibility that goes beyond local thinking, self-interest, and greed. This, of course, is foundational for all cross-cultural understanding.*

Furthermore, beyond listening we must assume responsibility for a sustained critique of cultures—a renewed and revised form of Nkrumah's "positive action"—in order to spot forms of "new colonialisms" in what is called a "postcolonial" era. This may be one of the practical legacies of *postcolonial philosophy*. Some of the following new forms of colonialism are already with us:

- *Economic colonialism* in the guise of "globalization." This is shaped by multinational corporations and the rigid ideological constraints mandated by wealthy nations, the IMF, and the World Bank in controlling the flow of wealth often earned off the backs of the poor who seek a share in return.

- *Cultural colonialism*, which feeds upon the expectation that Levis and Nike shoes are the world's dress code, that McDonald's and Coca-Cola are its basic diet, and which seeks to export a monochromatic pop sound round the globe that silences the traditional musical voices from a thousand villages.

- The *colonial export of development policies* that destroy rural agriculture, soil rivers and pollute air, uproot village life and encourage urban migration, and has generally increased the gap between the rich and the poor both within and between nations.

- And *a continuing colonization of the mind* by religious fundamentalism and a vicious nationalism that encourages hatred and intolerance of anyone with different ideas or doctrines. We have not, unfortunately, learned how to humanly respond to such intolerance; we know only the language of power that looms as yet another form of neocolonial dominance as witnessed in the Middle East, the Persian Gulf, and the Balkans in the 1990s and in Afghanistan into the twenty-first century.

Finally, Du Bois and Fanon in focusing our attention on the cultural aspects of the question of "race" have brought us to see and appreciate difference. Difference can be delineated in many ways—by gender, sexual orientation, color, social and economic class, levels of educational achievement, political ideology, or religion—and these differences are really at the heart of what we call race and racism today. They are essentially what the contemporary discussion of the "postcolonial" is all about. Wherever there is an Other there will be a concept of race. This point did not escape

Du Bois early on when he wrote in "The Conservation of Races," "what race prejudice really is . . . [is] nothing but the friction between two groups of people" and that this friction is likely to cause what he called "fatal collision[s]."[68] We must also remember that each human being and every human community is some other's Other—I am different from you and in that difference I may be the recipient of your insult or rage. It is a fact of our time that we identify ourselves by these differences and as part of some community. So as we enter the new century our global reality is one of division in our differences. There will not be an occasion for a single and unified message of a "black" race, or any other "race" for that matter, as Du Bois had hoped. There will be, however, many messages coming from smaller communities within larger families—messages of struggle and of hope, messages that must be heard and appreciated; messages that must be tolerant enough to recognize agreement in our differences and that might lead to mutual striving toward some common ends to benefit all—messages that because of their difference will enrich all of our lives. Fanon concludes his address to Negro Writers and Artists in Paris in 1956 with this hopeful sentence: "Universality resides in this decision to recognize and accept the reciprocal relativism of different cultures, once the colonial status is irreversibly excluded."[69] This quote anticipates what was briefly characterized as a "third stage" in the discussion on "race."

In 1953 Du Bois wrote this in a preface to the Jubilee edition of *The Souls of Black Folk:* "Today I see more clearly than yesterday that back of the problem of race and color, lies a greater problem which both obscures and implements it: and that is that so many civilized persons are willing to live in comfort even if the price of this is poverty, ignorance and disease of the majority of their fellowmen; that to maintain this privilege men have waged war . . . and the excuse for war continues largely to be color and race." Color and race do continue to define us and separate us. It is our moral responsibility as human beings to see this more clearly today in order to avoid wars, poverty, and ignorance tomorrow!

A major contribution of African philosophy—and what should be a task taken up by philosophy everywhere—is the delineation of the problem of "race." Cross-cultural philosophy should point a way forward as we see expressed in Fanon and in the message of equality and reconciliation of Nelson Mandela's vision for South Africa. The end we seek is to "penetrate" the meaning of James Baldwin's seven-word sentence: "Negroes want to be treated like men."

4.

African Moral Philosophy I
Community and Justice

What have we done, we, the wretched black men of the earth, for these
Whites to hate us so? What have we done, Brother Depestre, to weigh so
little on their scale?

—René Depestre, "The Bath at Dawn"

In this chapter and the next we identify several moral issues in which, in
Kwasi Wiredu's words, African philosophy is making contributions to
general conceptual understanding. To see how these moral issues are being
articulated and debated in the African context and to place them into the
larger stream of cross-cultural conversation show that *particular* African
concerns speak to *universal* human problems. The moral issues are, first,
the relationship of individual identity and community and emergent views
of justice surrounding liberal individualism and communitarian thinking.
This discussion explores whether there is a different sense in which the
concept of "justice" in the African context is being used, distinguishing
between individual "rights-based" and more communal "compassion-
based" moral thinking and implications of each for rethinking civic order.
The second set of moral issues has to do with the philosophical significance
of suffering and poverty in the African context, and how these two concepts
affect our thinking about justice and human development. It is argued that
these concepts play a more important ethical role in the African context
than in most other parts of the world, especially in the fact of giving voice
to gross *injustices*, and by focusing attention on some of the great problems
of evil embedded in the twentieth century.

Finally, in chapter 5 we continue to explore the meaning of the concept
of "justice" in the African context, but do so with specific reference to the
South African "Truth and Reconciliation Commission (TRC)." Here we
consider whether truth and reconciliation may contribute to an understanding of justice and civic responsibility in the transition from an
immoral apartheid regime to a majority democracy. Criticisms as to
whether "justice" has been served by the TRC process are evaluated.

Although each of these moral issues could be taken up as separate
issues it is argued that in specific African contexts (and these contexts are
relatively widespread) a moderate form of communalism provides a moral

background for why the concepts of identity, suffering, poverty, truth, and reconciliation are each connected with justice, and why they are of particular ethical significance in African philosophy and subsequently of universal importance to non-African moral thought. The discussion among African philosophers on these issues is lively and astute, and it can provide social and political philosophers, those involved in international development ethics debates, and postcolonial critical theorists (both African and non-African), with valuable perspectives on our human being in the world.

Persons, Individualism, and Communalism

Lingering in the background of an understanding of African philosophy (most of African thought for that matter) is a bias often called "unanimism." "Unanimism," says Hountondji, is "the illusion that all men and women in such societies speak with one voice and share the same opinion about all fundamental issues."[1] As we have seen this is inherited from early ethnophilosophical thinking like that of Placide Tempels' view that all Bantu-speaking Africans believe in a unified spiritual life force—an *elan vital*—and because of this have a shared African view of the world. The concept of a "separate being," an individual apart from a bonding force, "is foreign to Bantu thought," says Tempels.[2] "The Bantu speak, act, live as if, for them beings were forces. . . . Force is the nature of being, force is being, being is force."[3] The philosophical foundation for "unanimism" was firmly set by Tempels and recent African philosophical discourse has had to continually engage its assumptions. This engagement has been mostly to "deconstruct" and "liberate" itself from the implications of Tempels' ideas and from various other forms of "unanimism."

Related to this is another popular belief held in a nearly "unanimistic" way, that is, that "Africans" do not think of themselves as "discrete individuals," but rather understand themselves as part of a "community." This is sometimes referred to as African *communalism.* An often quoted line from John Mbiti's widely read book *African Religions and Philosophy* (1969) supporting this view is: "I am because we are: and since we are, therefore I am." It has immediate recognition as a play on and inversion of the well known *"cogito ergo sum"* of Descartes, which identifies the self with the "I am" in isolation from the "we are." It is worth quoting the fuller context of Mbiti's remark.

> [The individual] owes his existence to other people. . . . He is simply part of the whole. . . . Whatever happens to the individual happens to the whole group, and whatever happens to the whole group happens to the individual. The individual can only say: "I am, because we are; and since we are therefore I am." *This is the cardinal point in the understanding of the African view of man.*[4]

This "African view of man" has a very strong hold on how non-Africans conceptualize the African view of the individual. I find it particularly strong among American students—especially among African-Americans who wish to articulate a common heritage in Africa.

A large number of essays were written by professional African philosophers between 1970 and 1990, following Mbiti, trying to show, on the one hand, the nature of African "community" or to demonstrate, on the other hand, that there is a distinctive idea of the "person" or "individual" that has a distinguishable identity in African communities. Most of these essays, particularly the earlier ones, focused on "traditional beliefs" and how concepts of the person were related to their particular traditional society. Generally, African personal identity was seen to be relative to social practices in the specific societies in which people live. And although this shows the plurality of African thinking, some African philosophers were quick to generalize from the individual cases. These essays were often an effort to engage the ethical categories of Western philosophy and demonstrate *either* that something like "individual identity" was a part of an African's self-understanding even if the concept of "community" remains ontologically prior, *or* to show the distinctive character of African "community" against the Western conception of "individuality." Let us look at two recent essays that provide contrasting reflections on this issue of person and identity.

The notion of "personhood" or "being a person" is understood in many African languages and societies as an acquired status that is dependent upon people's relationship to their community. Ifeanyi Menkiti, a Nigerian philosopher, characterized "personhood" as follows:

> The various societies found in traditional Africa *routinely accept this fact* that personhood is the sort of thing which has to be attained, and is attained in direct proportion as one participates in communal life through the discharge of the various obligations defined by one's stations. It is the carrying out of these obligations that transforms one from the it-status of early child-hood, marked by an absence of moral function, into the person-status of later years, marked by a widened maturity of ethical sense—an ethical maturity without which personhood is conceived as eluding one.[5]

Of note here is the dependency of status "as a person" on "one's stations" relative to the community and its social hierarchy. Most roles and obligations are established by tradition and all one needs to do to earn personhood is follow these obligations. Sheer proper ritual participation in one's society gives you "person-status." Somehow gaining "person-status" carries with it "ethical maturity." But Menkiti gives us little clues as to what it means to have ethical maturity, or what functions it may serve in the development of an individual's moral character. In fact, Menkiti concluded that an individual's identity is simply part of "a thoroughly fused collective 'we'."[6]

This socialization view without some account of what characterizes a person's moral life is an unsatisfactory account of what it means to be a person for African philosophers such as Kwasi Wiredu and Kwame Gyekye. Wiredu and Gyekye want to assign specific ethical or moral qualities to what it means to be a person even if these qualities are linked to some form of communalism.

For Wiredu and Gyekye, the acquired status of personhood is understood not as simply a matter of gradual socialization, but as attaining and practicing a particular moral life that contributes to the well-being of one's community. If one can be thought to be "not a person" according to Gyekye it is because of a morally deficient life and not because of a "low station." Gyekye characterizes this as follows:

> The judgment that a human being is "not a person," made on the basis of that individual's consistently morally reprehensible conduct, implies that the pursuit or practice of moral virtue is intrinsic to the conception of a person held in African thought. The position here is, thus, that: for any p, if p is a person, then p ought to display in his conduct the norms and ideals of personhood. For this reason, when a human being fails to conform his behavior to the acceptable moral principles or to exhibit the expected moral virtues in his conduct, he is said to be "*not* a person." The evaluative statement opposite to this is, "he *is* a person" means, " 'he has good character,' 'he is peaceful—not troublesome,' 'he is kind,' 'he has respect for others,' 'he is humble.' " The statement "he is a person," then, is a clearly moral statement. It is a profound appreciation of the high standards of the morality of an individual's conduct that would draw the judgment "he is truly a person".[7]

Children will mature into exercising these moral virtues "in the fullness of time" as they engage and reengage various individual and corporate ethical boundaries in their life—not just because they pass from one status to another. "The upshot," of Gyekye's view, "is that personhood can only be partly never fully, defined by one's membership in the cultural community. The most that can be said, then, is that a person is only partly constituted by the community."[8] This he calls a "moderate communitarianism."

Another important feature of Gyekye's "moderate communitarianism" is his belief that all human beings, though "enmeshed in the web of communal relationships, may find that aspects of those cultural givens are inelegant, undignified, or unenlightened and would thoughtfully want to question and reevaluate them." This implies that each person has the capacity for their own individual judgments—has some autonomy—in spite of the degree to which they may be socialized by their community. He continues:

> The reevaluation may result in the individual's *affirming or striving to amend* or refine existing communal goals, values and practices; but it may or could also result in *the individual's total rejection of* all or some of them. The possibility of reevaluation means, surely, that the individual is not absorbed

by the communal or cultural apparatus but can to some extent wriggle out of it, distance herself from it, and thus be in a position to take a critical look at it; it means, also, that the communal structure cannot foreclose the reality and meaningfulness of *the quality of self-assertiveness* that the individual can demonstrate in her actions.

The capacity for self-assertion that the individual can exercise presupposes, and in fact derives from, the autonomous nature of the person. By autonomy, I do not mean self-completeness but the having of a will, a rational will of one's own, that enables one to determine at least some of one's own goals and to pursue them, and to control one's destiny.[9]

Gyekye's "moderate communitarian" view, without affirming any strong form of individual willfulness, challenges the way we must think about the concept of community in society—African society or any society.

Wiredu's view of the relationship between community and individual persons is even stronger than Gyekye's "moderate communitarianism." He believes that industrialization and urbanization have virtually destroyed the traditional idea of African communalism. He writes:

> The integration of individuality into community in African traditional society is so thoroughgoing that, as is too rarely noted, the very concept of a person has a normative layer of meaning. A person is not just an individual of human parentage, but also one evincing in his or her projects and achievements an adequate sense of social responsibility. . . . One of the greatest problems facing us in Africa is how to reap the benefits of industrialization without incurring the more unlovable of its apparent fallouts, such as the ethic of austere individualism." [10]

Another factor in moderating a "unanimist" view of community and complicating the discussion of personal identity is what is increasingly referred to as "multiculturalism." This is of particular relevance to a number of African societies. The very nature of Africa's history and the postcolonial condition has contributed to its diversity and multiculuralism. W. L. van der Merwe makes this point as follows: "one's identity is a continuous reweaving of various patterns of the cultures one is exposed to."[11] And, of course, Africans have been "exposed" to a multiplicity of cultures—in particular to more highly individualistically oriented cultures—and have had to adjust for their very survival. Economically and politically there are also pressures toward multicultural reconciliation within a society. The colonial waves of Western modernity with its "enlightenment" individualism and more recently the sea of "globalization" through the information technology revolution have severely challenged forms of communalism in African societies and have given new and broad meaning to the term "multicultural." It is true, as van der Merwe says, that "[M]ore and more people participate in and encounter more than one of the various distinguishable diverse ethnic and sociocultural forms of life prevalent in their society." This reality "impels one to enter into dialogue with the traditions of wisdom and thinking of other cultures" and forms of life.[12]

It is important in a cross-cultural as well as within a multicultural context to think about and get clear on the varied implications of such distinctions as community and individual identity. It is too easy to use clichés such as "Western values are driven by individualism" while "African values are driven by communalism." The range on a spectrum from one to the other is both multivaried and complex. To uphold the value of the priority of community does not necessarily deny an individual of her own identity, her potential creative role in a community, nor does it absolve her of personal responsibility for her actions toward the whole community. It is also clear that as multicultural factors increase, new values are placed on older ones—the African concept of "community" must be revalued in light of present realities.

On the other hand, if one asserts the priority of a radical or "austere" individualism, this usually does not imply separation from all law and customs of some ordered society. True, there may be less coinherence and dependency with others, but neither does the individual wish for an anarchistic surrounding—some lawless, each-for-one's-own existence—in society. Self-interest, not to mention "forced-interests," itself implies some cooperative arrangements and some rules for exchange in commerce if not in exchange of other values. A sense of justice and some general well-being seem essential.

Even such radical individualism as one finds in a philosopher like Frederich Nietzsche recognizes that a "sovereign individual" in "transcending" another individual cannot oppress the other, and recognizes in her freedom a moral responsibility to others. Nietzsche's "man of the future" is free to *enter into* relationships out of respect for mutual values held by equally free individuals—values such as trust, the keeping of promises, being accountable for one's own actions, and responsible use (rather than abuse) of freedom. In a Nietzschean society—given that a two-tiered class society is recognized, a "noble" class and the "herd"—those who have the noble sentiment *must not* use their strengths to "lord over" or "oppress" others either within or between classes. In fact, a good "lord" is generous as part of his responsibility. Mutual respect forms the basis for society and one's continued identity depends on the larger community functioning to sustain (and allow) everyone's freedom and well-being. Thus a *community*, however loosely conceived, plays an important and indispensable role.

Now, if I am to understand the values of communalism from a platform where the priority of the individual has been the norm, I must look to see how the well-being of the more communal society is being sustained and what values benefit the whole as well as each individual. How might I come to see these values as being of such a quality in the life of those who hold them that I would commend them to myself and society? To see how it is that the communally-based ideas, institutions, and values are beneficial to others might enable me to see the value of their transferability to my own context and life.

I do not have to look very far to enter the communalism–individualism debate in the Western philosophical context. In what is termed the "communitarian view," Michael Sandel, Alasdair MacIntyre, Charles Taylor, Elizabeth Wolgast, and Stanley Hauerwas all give nearly as strong a view as one finds in many parts of Africa for the priority of the community over the individual's rights. "These communitarians" see each human being as "thickly situated," embedded in a social environment, reacting to and shaping his or her life from strands already present in the community. Sandel says: "We cannot regard ourselves as independent [from society] . . . [we must understand] ourselves as the particular persons we are—as members of this family or community or nation or people, as bearers of this history, as sons and daughters of that revolution, as citizens of this republic." Though my life is subject to revision, it does have "contours"— a defining shape arising from my "projects and commitments" as well as from my "wants and desires."[13] The Western debate was not lost on Gyekye's critique of "communitarianism" and "personhood," when he cites Alasdair MacIntyre, whom he believes to be a more radical communitarian than himself. MacIntyre says:

> For the story of my life is always embedded in the story of those communities from which I derive my identity. I am born with a past; and to try to cut myself off from that past, in the individualistic mode, is to deform my present relationships. The possession of an historical identity and the possession of a social identity coincide. Notice that rebellion against my identity is always one possible mode of expressing it.[14]

Gyekye seems to either misread or misunderstand MacIntyre's last sentence in saying that MacIntyre implies "that the individual *cannot* rebel against her historically grounded identity and social roles."[15] It is precisely one's capacity for rebellion that MacIntyre suggests, and such action becomes a part of the individual's identity. This point aside, MacIntyre's view is stongly communitarian. The communitarian–individual rights debate is one in both the United States and the African context that is lively and from which each side can benefit in both the understanding and development of their respective views.

There is no doubt that the colonial experience in Africa introduced, even if it did not embody, ideas of individualism and egalitarianism from Great Britain and France. It is also true that the banners of liberation from colonial oppression gave rise to new African states that crossed many communal boundaries and espoused universal dignity and individual rights. Sadly, the postcolonial states developed in a different direction and both the values of communalism and individualism suffered. That story is a complex one that we shall speak of in more detail later, but it only partially undermines the general thesis that the values of communalism still retain a significant degree of priority in African life (urban and rural). Values such as generosity, compassion, reciprocity, mutual sympathy, cooperation, solidarity, and social well-being continue to shape the moral practices of Africans and are generally held to be of more importance than the value of individual rights.[16] From such communitarian values should flow both a sense of responsibility of individuals to their community and obligations to one's society, but that has been severely undermined by the course of development of the postcolonial regimes. Gyekye rightly says—and here is where "Western" individualistically oriented thinking can take a lesson—"neglect of, or inadequate attention to, the status of responsibilities and obligations on one hand, and the obsessional emphasis on, and privileging of, rights on the other hand, could lead to the fragmentation of social values and, consequently, of social relationships and integrity of society itself. *Responsibilities*, like rights, must therefore be taken seriously."[17]

The liberal value of "self-respect" is not just a value gained through autonomy or some austere individualism. It may be and usually is in the African context, linked to a number of social identifications: race, gender, age, ethnicity, or religion. K. Anthony Appiah agues that these more communally based forms of identity enhance self-respect and thus support, rather than offend, the liberal principle. Such communal ways of augmenting one's personal identity, being an heir to some traditions, taking pride in ethnic, gender, age, or race solidarity, need not diminish my freedom as a "self"-respecting human being. The *kind* of person an African is is linked not only to the possibilities of individual achievement, but the respect one may carry from his or her village or larger ethnic associations. These values are not instrumentally grounded, but as Appiah argues are symbolically grounded in the tradition of one's communal inheritance.[18] Both one's personal identity and social or collective identity are important. In the African context there is reason to continue to sustain the belief that identity is still significantly formed by values shaped in one's collective associations.

One final note on communitarian values and the values of individual rights. Gyekye states:

> In the communitarian moral universe caring or compassion or generosity, not justice—which is related essentially to a strictly rights-based morality— may be a fundamental moral category. In a moral framework where love, compassion, caring, friendship, and genuine concern for others characterize social relationships, justice—which is about relations of claims and counter-claims—may not be the primary moral virtue.[19]

This remark should cause those who do not embody communitarian values to pause at least. "Justice," he says (and here he has Western theories of justice in mind), "is related essentially to a strictly rights-based morality" and it "is about relations of claims and counter-claims." This is a very thin, though not inaccurate, characterization of what "justice" has come to mean in some Western societies. In American society, for example, there is precious little to commend our understanding of justice as a moral concept; it has fallen to the status of the contention of one "right" or another; litigation resolves disputes and we call that "justice." If we by contrast think of those moral concepts that have been associated with African communal values as well as those from Western communitarian traditions, then perhaps we are given pause to rethink the *thinness* of our "rights-based" values. *Being confronted by the notion of some variation of communal values coming out of African traditional life, and while avoiding the "illusion of unanimism," African philosophers remind us of a new way to rethink the very concepts of justice and responsibility.*

This should not, however, be our only reminder of what has befallen our contemporary idea of justice in the West. In the early 1940s, in the context of the moral bankruptcy that had led the world to war, French moral philosopher Simone Weil had clearly articulated the same view Gyekye expresses fifty years later. Simone Weil had reached across the Mediterranean to African soil in bringing to our attention the compassion-based morality found in the *Egyptian Book of the Dead*; she drew on early pre-Socratic Greek literature to recover a sense of "justice" that included love and compassion (with her brilliant studies of *Antigone* and the *Iliad*); and she reached to what she called "Oriental wisdom"—the *Bhagavad-Gita* and Taoism—to reclaim an earlier sense of morality that was not "rights-based" and that had its roots in much more communitarian-based traditions. Let us briefly sound her "voice" in addressing the "fallen" moral view of justice in her beloved France (and arguably throughout Western culture). Her views may also help us rethink the concept of justice along more community-oriented and compassion-based lines without losing a sense of individual responsibility.[20]

Simone Weil calls our attention to the concept of "rights" in a characteristically unexpected way. She forces us to look again at this clash before our eyes. In the 1930s with facism growing and early in World War II, when so many "rights" were being abused, she writes in her essay "Human Personality": "[to say] 'I have the right ...' or 'you have no right to ...' evoke[s] a latent war and awaken[s] the spirit of contention. To place the notion of rights at the center of social conflicts is to inhibit any possible impulse of charity on both sides."[21] To have bought into rights language is to believe that power can be counterbalanced by power. To say "if we could just achieve equal rights ..." means I must either snatch rights from someone else (one who has a disequal amount) or impose an ideology by force or persuasion to "guarantee" rights in a more or less coercive way (even by civil law). This way of thinking will not easily go away. But in Simone Weil's thinking force cannot be substantially counterbalanced either through force or retribution or through a more equitable distribution of rights. Rather, it is through attention to injustice and coming to a new notion of justice that restores a balance between agrieved parties and that has as its most active ingredient love or charity. We will come back to this point in discussing the significance of the concept of reconciliation given shape through the Truth and Reconciliation Commission's work in South Africa, and how the notion of attention to the *injustices of apartheid* in the form of "gross human rights violations" is part of the very process of arriving at a new notion of "restorative justice" within the South African context. Although "restorative justice" is now being linked to Western "human rights" debates, I believe the TRC's "working sense" of justice is more closely based on a moral sense that is communal and compassion based than on a moral sense that is individual or rights based.[22]

"Rights" tied to a western individual-rights-morality, Simone Weil says, "have no direct connection with love,"[23] and justice in her more spiritual, compassion-based sense of the term has primarily to do with seeing that no harm is done to another human being. And this, of course, is her point: to contrast our current day use of "rights" with what she calls "a new virtue of justice" requiring attention to injustice, renunciation and fellow-love.[24]

We have before us in the powerful essay "Human Personality" two distinct notions: "rights" and "justice." Weil summarizes the difference between them in these ways:

> The notion of rights is linked with the notion of sharing out, of exchange, of measured quantity. It has a commercial flavor, essentially evocative of legal claims and arguments. Rights are always asserted in a tone of contention; and when this tone is adopted, it must rely upon force in the background, or else it will be laughed at.[25]
>
> Justice consists in seeing that no harm is done to men. . . . [it is associated with the cry] "Why am I being hurt?"[26]
>
> The other cry, which we hear so often: "Why has somebody else got more than I have," refers to rights. We must learn to distinguish between the two cries and to do all that is possible, as gently as possible, to hush the second one, with the help of a code of justice, regular tribunals, and the police. Minds capable of solving problems of this kind can be formed in law school.
>
> But the cry "Why am I being hurt?" raises quite different problems, for which the spirit of truth, justice, and love is indispensable.[27]
>
> The spirit of justice and truth is nothing else but a certain kind of attention which is pure love.[28]

Simone Weil goes further in other writings to discuss the placing of justice as compassion and love in the context of community and to show the priority of obligation in the moral life—she calls obligation one of the primary needs of the soul. She says in *The Need for Roots:* "The notion of obligation takes precedence over that of rights, which is subordinate and relative to it."[29] Again, she says that a human soul needs a "disciplined participation in a common task of public value," and it also needs "personal initiative within this participation."[30] Here, again, are Gyekye's two poles of his "moderate communitarianism"—an obligation to the communal well-being and the ability to sustain some creative sense of the self or self-respect in response to the community. Furthermore, Simone Weil says:

> The human soul needs above all to be rooted in several natural environments and to make contact with the universe through them.
>
> Examples of natural human environments are: a man's country, and places where his language is spoken, and places with a culture or a historical past which he shares, and his professional milieu, and his neighborhood.[31]

These "natural human environments" are no less than what we call examples of human community and they fit an African sense of community very well. They are specific contexts in which humans can experience mutual respect, friendship, warmth, shared tasks of value (responsibilities), and some cultural linkage (such as common language, arts, history, and physical work). These environments include those symbolically grounded in tradition and ethnic associations as Appiah noted. These all create environments in which human expectations and aspirations may be fulfilled and in which good and not evil can be realized and flourish in a creative and peaceful way. It is these very natural human environments that were stripped from Africans by their colonial rulers. A recent example was found in nonwhite South Africa where there were forced removals of large communities from land and neighborhoods, the creation of male urban hostels, and the denial of freedom of movement. These, among other things and not unlike facist oppression, made the system of apartheid particularly sinister and unjust.

Finally, Simone Weil was deeply disturbed by colonialism; it was passionately condemned by her. She wrote forcefully about French policy in North Africa and Southeast Asia. The "states" carved out by Europeans were created with little regard to roots and often systematically destroyed or supplanted local traditions. Andrea Nye says, "The loss of human environments that such development brings was for Weil a 'supreme tragedy.' " Nye observes that some traditional environments are particularly fragile for women and colonized cultures where indigenous ways of life were jeopardized. When these environments are destroyed "the only answer is centralization because the 'living intercourse between diverse and mutually independent centers' is impossible. Something infinitely precious and frail is lost, 'the living warmth of a human environment, a medium which bathes and fosters the thoughts and the virtues' (SE 79), the beauties of daily life: 'home, country, traditions, culture' (GG 133) which nourish and warm the spirit."[32]

In addition to those things that are destructive of the natural balances within a country by the creation of artificial states, the legacy of leadership spawned by colonial rule has generally been a disaster—especially in African nation-states. At the heart of a country is the need for legitimacy in those who govern. For Simone Weil legitimacy is claimed by a government and its leaders if it embraces three essential things: "dignity," a "concern for justice," and a concern for "the public good." The central notion in Weil of "concern for justice," is that each person be able to exercise the faculty of consent (or have the capacity to refuse). She writes:

> Justice has as its object the exercise of the faculty of consent on earth. To preserve it religiously wherever it exists, to try to create conditions for it where it is absent, that is to love justice.
>   Consent is made possible by a life containing motives for consenting. Destitution, privations of soul and body, prevent consent from being able to operate in the depths of the heart.[33]

These three things (that dignity, justice, and the public good are being served) are, of course, related to each other, but she says that "as long as the people retain this confidence: that is legitimate government."[34] "Legitimacy," she says, "is not a primitive notion. It is derived from justice. Relative to power, justice requires above all else an equilibrium between power and responsibility."[35] It is this lack of equilibrium between power and responsibility that increasingly feeds injustices in a state. Let us look at a contemporary case in which the equilibrium between power and responsibility had completely broken down.

Witnessing the injustices and unraveling of his own nation-state, Nigeria, Wole Soyinka asked himself "What is a nation?" When can a modern state so artificially created be said to have achieved conditions closer to that of Simone Weil's country? Up to the point of his writing, 1996, he sees so-called Nigerian nation building to be "nothing but a cameo of personalities, a series of transparencies of distortion, each laid over the last" with no "purpose or direction."[36] Nigeria had become what some have called more than one postcolonial African state, a "modern kleptocracy" or a "poli-thug state."[37] Soyinka sees his homeland as "the open sore of the continent." Soyinka argues that no one can find his or her personal identity in any terms that "relate to the existing or historical definition of that space."[38] There is no remaining focus such as language or traditions that mean anything anymore—no one is allowed any meaningful work or associations and once viable neighborhoods (village life) have been systematically destroyed by "the opportunism and adventurism of power." There has been a total breakdown of any interactive structures that might "enhance the daily quality of life," or in Weil's terms, enhance "the living warmth of a human environment." Africans have become victims of their own postcolonial states. Through this example one can also see how the white apartheid regime in South Africa became morally bankrupt. It lost all its legitimacy by its over-exercise of power and its denial of dignity and lack of responsibility to the majority of its nation's people.

This is what Simone Weil called the "uprooting" of the soul. She said regarding a state (especially a state that has lost its legitimacy) that it eats away a country's moral substance; it "lives on it, fattens on it, until the day comes when no more nourishment can be drawn from it, and famine reduces it to a condition of lethargy."[39] It is this scenario of moral malnourishment found too often in Africa and elsewhere that breathes new life into Simone Weil's more conservative instincts about a country and what gives legitimacy to a state. The ends of these conservative instincts are, however, toward a more communal order (very close to a "moderate communitarian" view) in which all humans are given equal regard and any concept of the individual ego is integrally tied to the community through justice, love, and concern for the public good.

A final word on the concepts of community and persons. Returning to the African context, Gyekye believes that the moral virtues of love and compassion "have to be regarded as *intrinsic* to satisfactory moral practice in a communitarian society."[40] Such virtues are often not cultivated in a liberal, individual rights-based society. In the latter there are no obligations to be kind or generous or compassionate—though the liberal ideas of fairness and equality may provide some motivation for generosity and charity. For example, if a friend is being mugged, I may believe it is the right course of action, morally, to intervene and prevent or stop the mugging. But on a "rights-based" liberal view moral ambiguity creeps in. There is no intrinsic "right" that a person be helped, and there is no positive "right" that obligates me to help. Or if I see poverty, I am under no obligation to be generous. Because my notion of a good and any life-plan I may have to realize the good may be different from yours and everyone else's goods and plans, I am in no way compelled to agree with your course of action. I may criticize your good and your plan, but I will be inclined to choose not to interfere so that I do not invite your interference with my good and plan. You can see the easy slide into moral relativism or moral neutrality. Or as Gyekye notes: "The danger or possibility of slipping down the slope of selfishness when one is totally obsessed with the idea of individual rights is . . . quite real."[41] The possibility of moral consensus or a common good diminishes as individualism increases, and the stake I may have in protecting my good from another's goes up as my moral concern decreases. In a "rights-based" society the moral values of love, generosity, and compassion are seldom thought to be "intrinsic." If, in fact, we could assume such values as intrinsic, then the moral practices of the people would, indeed, be different. There would be a greater sense of concern or care for the well-being of one's fellow society members and a greater sense of civic responsibility.

This would be good reason to favor a more communitarian view—perhaps the "moderate communitarian" view we have discussed. Habits die hard, however, and the more "individualistic" we become, the less we feel the pinch of obligations and responsibilities. If we were really *to see* this point, however, it would be an incentive to *work on* letting old habits die. If I were truly a compassionate person I would pay greater attention to those who suffer and are oppressed and less attention to my self-interest.

I would, in a sense, understand what it means to complete oneself morally in the other. My own moral identity as a person would be tied up with my relationship to others.[42] Gyekye echoes the sentiments of Simone Weil when he concludes:

> Most people, I think, will agree that to tend a stranger in sickness is to serve a *human* need and hence should be considered a basic moral responsibility. We would be blunting our moral visions, or demeaning our moral and personal autonomy, if we considered "human needs" to be the needs *only* of people in our own neighborhood or local or proximate community.

And

> Morality requires us to look beyond the interests and needs of our own selves, and that, given the beliefs in our common humanity—with all that this concept implies for the fundamental needs, feelings, and interests of all human beings irrespective of their specific communities—our moral sensitivities should extend to people beyond our immediate communities.[43]

Extending capacities for compassion first requires that attention be given to *injustice*, that we listen, as Simone Weil said, to the cry: "Why am I being hurt?" To those cries we now turn.

Suffering and Injustice

The nature and extent of suffering must never be silenced if the truth is to be known about the African condition. We have, from the beginning, stressed the importance of an aesthetic point of departure for philosophy— the point from which we observe everything around us, year in and year out, in its interconnection with the ordinary practices in human life. It is in this way we see and come to know our world; its truths are embodied in the ways we give voice to, or narrate, what lies around us. If, for example, our surroundings are pervaded by suffering and poverty, the character and spirit of our world—what we come to know—is shaped by these experiences and their connections to larger moral and social practices. Likewise, affluence and greed, or an environment filled with hope and aspirations for a good life, would shape our world differently. Sometimes the combinations of these make our lives extremely complex and tangled. We shall for a moment give some focus to the concepts of suffering and poverty and discuss their importance as ethical concepts and as they relate to justice within the African context.

In observing the kind of world found in many parts of the African subcontinent and in wanting to understand aspects of the truth of the human condition in Africa, one is immediately struck by how much poverty and suffering are pervasive. Since World War II ended, the greatest suffering and conflict in the twentieth century has taken place on the continent of Africa. Consider, for example, Nigeria from its Biafran civil war to the present and the genocide of Rwanda. Mozambique's civil war went on so long that the two sides got weary and simply decided to lay down their arms and stop.[44] There is an intractable conflict in Sudan that Wole Soyinka says "has entailed over three decades of carnage, with the possible consequence of social disintegration of an enduring nature."[45] Liberia, Angola, the Congos, Sierra Leone, and Burundi are in continuing turmoil. All the liberation struggles with colonial powers from Ghana to Namibia and South Africa—from the 1950s to the last decade of the century—left their toll. A continued succession of drought and famine (natural or war caused) has become endemic to many parts of the continent—most notably in Biafra, Ethiopia, Sudan, and Somalia. Along with the drought and famine—and more recent floods in Mozambique and southern Africa (February and March 2000)—there have been and continue to be unprecedented migrations due to armed conflicts sponsored largely by "Western" cold war ideological and economic preoccupations causing the largest refugee populations in the world. Literally tens of millions of land mines lay actively in wait throughout the subcontinent.[46] Social infrastructures are extremely fragile in most nations and resources have been squandered in a manner that leaves the vast majority of the population in an artificially created sustained state of poverty. Just in the past decade the figures emerging on the AIDS crisis in Africa show a catastrophic tragedy.[47] This is all part of the inherited background one discovers in approaching Africa. Rather than turn aside from such features of African life, one task of philosophy should be to find ways to give a voice to suffering in order to discover the truth.

Africa's wounds are deep and its memory is long. What is, above, a litany of recent or present horrors is in some sense an inheritance of colonialism. Wole Soyinka says of this inheritance:

> The crimes that the African continent commits against her kind are of a dimension and, unfortunately, of a nature that appears to constantly provoke memories of the historic wrongs inflicted on that continent by others. There are moments when it almost appears as if there is a diabolical continuity (and inevitability?) to it all—that the conduct of latter-day slaverunners is merely the stubborn precipitate of a yet unexpiated past.[48]

To invoke the possible logic of "inevitability" leads us to think that the suffering is intractable. Furthermore, such a logic renders the voices of suffering silent. And the notion of an "unexpiated past" haunts many African intellectuals and sustains a conversation around issues such as historical justice, guilt and forgiveness, and reparations and reconciliation.

The concepts of "suffering" and "poverty" must be read differently in the continent of Africa than in most other places. The condition of suffering, for example, found in Africa brings forward the common conviction that something is terribly wrong when such levels of harm are done to human beings. All human spiritual striving is thwarted, and sustained harmdoing clouds the capacity for humans to hope for some good. A sense of tragedy and evil grips the most ordinary levels of life. This theme, of course, cuts across cultures and continents; it resonates within the literature of "liberation theology" in Central and South America; it surfaces like a natural spring wherever evil and suffering are a commonplace experience, wherever oppression and economic injustices prevail. Nowhere, however, is this more apparent now than in Africa, and it has been this way for a very long time.

Suffering and the struggle to alleviate and eliminate suffering is, in the African context, a significant moral challenge. One must do more than just describe it. To think about suffering has become a part of thinking about justice and about compassion; it is also at the very foundation of reflections on "remorse," "forgiveness," and "reconciliation" as we shall see shortly in looking at discussions surrounding South Africa's "Truth and Reconciliation Commission." There it is argued that giving voice to suffering is an essential part of the process of healing wounds of the victims of suffering, and of making a more peaceful transition to a just society. Furthermore, thinking about suffering may sustain attempts at giving a meaningful shape to current debates about "restitution" and "reparations." In the literary context, as well as the lived situation, suffering is a condition linked to injustice, but beyond that it carries with it a more comprehensive meaning. As a moral concept how are we to think of this "more"?

One way to think about suffering in Africa would be to refer, again, to how Simone Weil treats this notion. It is customary in political theory to link suffering with oppression, i.e., wherever oppression occurs there is suffering. This linkage, however, did not seem to capture a kind of suffering she experienced among poor factory workers in France during the 1930s, where humiliation of one's humanity seemed endemic, and where she, while engaged in factory work for a year, felt what it might mean to be a slave. Nor did the term "suffering" itself seem to address the level of human despair associated with the deepest forms of it. Thus, in her later writings she replaces the concept of "oppression" with that of "affliction"—there was a sense in which this shifted the meaning of suffering from its use in ideological contexts (Marxist and socialist theory) to a more human, even religious, context. She wrote, "Affliction is an uprooting of life," and it involves a combination of physical pain, spiritual distress, and social degradation—all being more symptomatic of the human despair and emptiness that comes with great suffering and where the cry, "Why am I being hurt?" goes unheard.

Simone Weil's sense of suffering as affliction seems to capture the sustained sense given to suffering in Africa by such writers as Soyinka. In *The Burden of Memory* Soyinka refers to Africa's suffering as "cultural and spiritual violation [that] has left indelible imprints on the collective psyche and sense of identity of the peoples, a process that was ensured through savage repressions of cohering traditions by successive waves of colonizing hoards."[49] This surely suggests a total "uprooting of life" more than does the notion of political oppression. In religious terms, Simone Weil associates suffering as affliction with a notion of spiritual death— what she calls living in the absence of God. "During this absence," she says, "there is nothing to love," and the very capacity to love begins to wither. Without love there can be no justice.[50] Of those who experience such afflic- tion, however, Simone Weil says that against all odds one must go on desiring to love—even hope that some good will comes to the afflicted. In those who are afflicted and who experience the absence of God, there is, she believes, the possibility that one day, paradoxically, by some act of grace, God's presence will become manifest.

Ghanaian philosopher, W. E. Abraham, as early as 1960, suggested that one form of "uprooting of life" that has contributed to suffering in Africa occurs when the communally based infrastructure of village life is radically disrupted and local economies strained. Abraham, from the vantage point of the 1950s, at the beginning of Africa's independence movements, noted that to the extent that obligations are ignored and traditional values and institutions abandoned "society is on the way to atomism."[51] Subsequent urban migration and increased atomization of local communities have clearly altered the landscape of African traditional life and created a new urban poverty. An even more insidious form of uprootedness is "forced removals" of people from their land or homes.

Awareness of the condition of great suffering and the struggle to over- come it for all the reasons given and more have also been characterized by a new theme running through more recent African literature, generating what Kwame Anthony Appiah calls a "second stage" of the African novel. The "first stage" comprised of works such as Achebe's *Things Fall Apart*, Laye's *L'Enfant noir*, Kane's *Ambiguous Adventure*, and Sembene's *God's Bits of Wood* focused on issues such as exile and African "identity" based on nationalism or negritude and anticolonial liberation from the "Western Imperium." Appiah says of these: "The novels of this first stage are thus realist legitimations of nationalism: they authorize a 'return to traditions' while at the same time recognizing the demands of a Weberian rationalized modernity."[52] A second stage in the African novel, particularly Franco- phone novels of the later 1960s and 1970s is motivated by the growing awareness that nationalism was failing and governments had lost their legitimacy and were becoming "kleptocracies." The second stage, says Appiah, is based on an appeal to ethical universals—"it is based, as intel- lectual responses to oppression in Africa largely are based, in an appeal to a certain *simple respect for human suffering*, a fundamental revolt against the endless misery of the last thirty years."[53] There is an emphasis here of both hopelessness and compassion. An emphasis is turned toward *the people* not the nation and to the alleviation of day-to-day suffering. Soli- darity with human suffering becomes a sign of what it means to be African.

The whole sense of what it means to be an African is fragmented and confused in the postcolonial mind; hope is found only in and with the suffering and compassion of all who are victimized. In these later novels there surfaces an embedded sense of both despair and compassion, even if sometimes cynically molded into a novel's characters, rejecting national-istic rhetoric for a basic *humanism*. But even that humanism seems buried. The deep sense of loss, an overwhelming sense of evil cries out to be heard.

In this sense of "suffering as affliction" found in this fiction is another example in which engagement with Africa is a two-way path, in which the quality of the ideas is so compelling as to make non-Africans turn their heads and examine their own lives. Learning to listen to Africa's suffering, then, is the starting point of a meaningful comparative ethics as well as a condition for truth.

Shifting from "fiction" to "actual cases" of African suffering, a case in point is seen in testimonies given before the South African Truth and Reconciliation Commission. Here the voices of victims and perpetrators challenge conceptions of justice and raise questions as to how far surfacing the truth itself can serve justice and reconciliation. We will turn to these issues shortly and see how the *cries of suffering*—called "a signature tune" of the TRC hearings by Antjie Krog—may provide us with an ethical toe-hold for moving toward understanding injustices as a prerequisite for serving the ends of justice.

There is one last point I wish to explore regarding suffering in the African context—a point that underscores the moral significance of this concept at a particular time and place in Africa. I want to suggest that when one is visually confronted with recent atrocities (for example, in Liberia, Sierra Leone, the Congos, Rwanda, Burundi, and the Sudan) on various news media one can be struck by a certain indifference to death; one can have an almost total lack of remorse that should accompany these great sufferings. This may in part be due to the distance and impersonal nature that television in particular induces. However immediate it appears, the suffering is still miles away from the comforts of one's living room; it never really "comes in." This sense of indifference and remorselessness connected to the suffering brings the human spirit as close to a loss of all hope as is possible—close to spiritual death in Simone Weil's terms.

This point has not been lost on some South African writers trying to understand what went morally wrong under apartheid. Philosopher Johan Snyman says that the radical change from "a social system of legally enforced injustice to a political culture founded on universal rights" will take years to fully comprehend.[54] It will be particularly difficult, he says, for "Afrikaans culture" to overcome an "ethos of remorselessness," and "to reinscribe remorse on a landscape, to stop the expansion of a moral and intellectual desert."[55] There remains a huge gap in the perception of what is right and wrong among perpetrators (especially those who applied for amnesty) and those victims who suffered, told their horrific stories, and may find little justice in having done so.

Snyman believes that there is a growing literature, especially within Afrikaans culture, that is struggling "to invent ways to express remorse through a new language [and to] assist a country to heal its scars and to reconcile it with its past and its inhabitants with one another,"[56] and that this literature holds some promise in forging a new moral discourse. In his essay he discusses the work of Antjie Krog, *Country of My Skull,* as an appropriate summary of Afrikaners coming to terms with their suppression of a moral discourse to deal with the injustice of apartheid and the great suffering it caused.

I will not detail Snyman's whole interesting argument and use of Krog, but I will comment on a few of his points linking remorse and suffering. He says that Krog's "book bears witness to voices of and about suffering."[57] In immersing herself in those voices, as the chief broadcast journalist for the daily airing of the Truth and Reconciliation Commission's hearings, she begins to see herself and her past embedded in the lives of the victims' testimony; she searches for ways to say how "utterly sorry" she feels as an Afrikaner; she struggles for a language to say how "deeply ashamed and gripped with remorse" she is. It was the crying during testimony before the Commission that got to Krog. She writes:

> For me, this crying is the beginning of the Truth Commission—the signature tune, the definitive moment, the ultimate sound of what the process is about. She [Nomonde Calata] was wearing this vivid orange-red dress, and she threw herself backwards and that sound ... that sound ... it will haunt me for ever and ever.
> ... So maybe this is what the Commission is all about—finding words for that cry of Nomonde Calata.[58]

Reminiscent of the epigram by René Depestre that opened this chapter, Krog concludes her account of this particular hearing by saying: "When the hearing resumed, Tutu started to sing. *Senzeni na, senzeni na ...* "What have we done? What have we done? Our only sin is the colour of our skin."[59]

Snyman says that "Krog wants to exorcise the memory of the monopolizing of power by the Afrikaner by 'asking for amnesty,' as it were, for Afrikaner culture."[60] Many Afrikaners abhorred her reporting and her open admission of shame and guilt. Many would write her hate mail and remind her how much Boer women and children suffered in British concentration camps during the Anglo-Boer War (1899–1902). Snyman comments:

> With the current centenary commemoration of the Anglo-Boer War [1999] the very topically moral point of such a comparison is sadly missed, namely, that in commemorating the suffering of Afrikaner women and children,

Afrikaners should not only have vowed that such suffering may never happen to them again, *But that they themselves may never become party to the infliction of any such suffering in the future.* Against the bitter irony of a people that want to remember their own suffering and that deny others the recognition of others' suffering, Krog asserts the rights of the marginalised of apartheid to be heard.... They have not been marginalised (only) because of the colour of their skin, but because of their *suffering.*[61]

In an ethos of remorselessness too many may become morally insensitive to suffering when it is not their own. There is not only denial but, as Fanon noted, "bewilderment" and a sense of "sudden incomprehension," as if to say "how ungrateful" rather than to recognize what went wrong and see the nature of the injustice.

In the end there seems to be no adequate language to capture the meaning of the suffering; it is the cries themselves that tell the truth. South African theologian Fanie Du Toit comments on Krog's struggle for a new moral discourse that would restore remorse. Du Toit writes:

When reflecting further on this absolutely unrepresentable and indeed holy character of the presence and testimonies of the victims at the hearings, it becomes clear that they *became the incarnations of the absolute horror of violence in a way that disrupts the comfort and security of any dialogue about the horrors of the past.* The truth of the South African past fits into no neatly constructed 'meta-narrative' or systematised texts, but is found rather in the upsetting cries of the suffering, that threatens to rupture or terminate all such dialogue.... So it is that the stories of South African citizens that have filled and saturated the air in South Africa over the past two years prompt one to a wordless silence. Such has been the raw indicted pain, the indescribable dignity and the unconditional forgiveness of these victims emerging to tell their lonely tales of suffering, that any texts following these stories will be haunted by the silence they invoke.[62]

Citizens in South Africa heard on radio and national television, day in and day out for almost two years, the cries of those who suffered affliction. Of course not all citizens reacted to what they heard in the same way. There was considerable indifference, even "opposition to the TRC process in the white community in general and the Afrikaner community in particular."[63] These cries were, nevertheless, heard in ways that they have not been heard in the Congo and Sudan, in Angola and Rwanda, even though the histories of all these countries share some common background—a history forged in a similar colonial framework. Outside of South Africa, however, African societies are generally less racially diverse. With respect to dealing with their human rights violations there has been little or no public confession and corporate expressions of guilt or complicity and fewer formal processes to expose or give voice to the severe nature of the violence. These are very important differences. Du Toit, perhaps too optimistically, sums this up as follows:

[I]n the South African case, graciously and unexpectedly, the truth borne by the suffering did not silence discourse permanently. Rather, like a symphony of frogs after heavy storms, these tales of suffering have released a myriad of new voices and ideas, prompting dialogue to renew and reinvigorate itself. *Just as we thought we have lost the ability to write at all, just as we were about to become mute, the unrepresentable truth of victims gracefully reinvigorated our discourse.*"[64]

One can only hope that such "new voices" continue to be released and that the conversation is sustained. There is a paradox here—in the face of near spiritual death, some new spiritual life may be being born. It is as if a new substantial ethical debate is reborn, given new life. One condition for unveiling the truth of a country's past is that suffering be given a voice. In South Africa this became suddenly apparent. The truths told "should become," in the words of Willie Esterhuyse, "a trigger for transformation."[65]

This point was never lost on the Commission's hearings themselves as story after story was pursued and the victims' and nation's grieving continued. The purpose of the hearings with their heartrending stories grew increasingly more clear in the commission's life. In its preliminary Report given to the government in October 1998, the stories of suffering were linked with the task of reconciliation in the following way.

> Each story of suffering provided a penetrating window into the past, thereby contributing to a more complete picture of gross violations of human rights in South Africa. The nation must use these stories to sharpen its moral conscience and to ensure that, never again, will it gradually atrophy to the point where personal responsibility is abdicated.[66]

So what makes "suffering" a distinctively moral concept in the African context? It is not only that it is pervasive, but that it has been allowed to exist unheard, voiceless, and has evoked little remorse or guilt from those who abused power and inflicted the harm. It seems clear that justice, if it is to be conceived as a matter beyond just an individual's "rights," requires a public forum to hear the voices of *injustice*, and in this corporate voice of suffering there may be a condition for truth. It is just such a forum that the "Truth and Reconciliation Commission" sought to provide and that may be a model for other countries to follow. We will say more about this in our next chapter, but first let us turn to the links between suffering in Africa and its pervasive poverty.

Poverty and Human Development

Poverty is perhaps less heinous than the remorseless suffering as affliction experienced across much of Africa, but poverty is no less important as an issue for philosophical reflection. Bessie Head wrote in the 1960s, "Poverty has a home in Africa—like a second skin. It may be the only place on earth where it is worn with an unconscious dignity."[67] The truth of this remark has been borne out since then even as the scale of poverty has vastly increased during the past three decades. It is easy to romanticize such a statement and lose sight of the immense suffering and indignity that accompanies all forms of poverty. Because of the "unconscious dignity" worn by so many poor in Africa—especially the rural poor—and the "mythology" surrounding the concept of African "communalism," outside observers often overlook the depth and breadth of the poverty altogether. John Iliffe, in his impressive history, *The African Poor*, found one obstacle to people's awareness of the extent of poverty to be

> the widespread belief that until recently there were no poor in Africa, because economic differentiation was slight, resources freely available, and the "extended family" [communalism] supported its less fortunate members. Only with the coming of colonial rule, market economies, and urbanization, so it is often claimed, did things begin to fall apart. This "myth of Merrie Africa" was widely held during the colonial period. "The rules and regulations of every African Community leave no ground for idle women, prostitutes or vagabonds, and create no possibility for the existence of waifs and strays", a Lagos newspaper explained in 1913. "No Barnado's Homes, no Refuge for the Destitute grace the cities; because the conditions producing them are absent."[68]

This myth has been perpetuated as recently as 1972, notes Iliffe, where we find in a report of the United Nations Regional Advisor on Social Welfare Policy and Training, Economic Commission for Africa:

> In rural Africa, the extended family and the clan assume the responsibility for all services for their members, whether social or economic. People live in closely organized groups and willingly accept communal obligations for mutual support. Individuals satisfy their need for social and economic security merely by being attached to one of these groups. The sick, the aged and children are all cared for by the extended family. In this type of community nobody can be labeled as poor because the group usually shares what they have. There is no competition, no insecurity, no big ambitions, no unemployment and thus people are mentally healthy. Deviation or abnormal behaviour is almost absent.[69]

This is all very hard to swallow, and I dare to say this illusion has continued in the minds of many non-Africans, as well as some Africans, well beyond 1972.

All this being said, Iliffe continues: "Although much nonsense has been written about African families as universal providers of limitless generosity, it is nevertheless true that families were and are the main sources of support for the African poor, as much for the young unemployed of modern cities as for the orphans of the past."[70] He notes that in several

African languages the common word for "poor" implies lack of kin and friends, and a household lacking an able-bodied male to work has been a source of poverty "throughout Africa's recoverable history." Pointing to the plurality of kinds of family or communal structures in Africa, Iliffe concludes:

> *Equally important, however, is the fact that Africans lived in different kinds of families*, from the Yoruba compound with scores of related residents to the elementary households of Buganda. Each kind of family had its particular points of weakness and excluded its particular categories of unsupported poor—orphans in one case, barren women in another, childless elders in a third. Moreover, family structure was not an immutable ethnic characteristic but could change to meet changing needs. The intimate connection between poverty and family structure has been neglected by historians of Europe and may be Africa's chief contribution to the comparative history of the poor.[71]

The fact of "different kinds of families" is crucial. Just as he notes there is not one kind of family, so there is not one Africa to deal with on the issue of poverty. No "unanimistic" conclusions can be drawn from one region to another.

Iliffe ends as he begins his book with these thoughts. With the exception of a brief period of prosperity in the 1960s, poverty has increased sharply in the past three decades due to mass famine, prolonged violence, and economic mismanagement. In the late 1970s Africa had more poverty than Latin America and its relative position to both Latin America and Asia has deteriorated since then. *The inequality between rich and poor in Africa also showed the greatest rise in differential of any continent on the globe.*[72] In spite of this, Iliffe echoes Bessie Head's opening sentiment when he says the mostly rural poor seem to have "lost little of their resilience and capacity for survival."[73] Seeing this, Iliffe said that one of the motivating reasons for writing his book was his "belief that Africa's splendour lies in its suffering. The heroism of African history is to be found not in the deeds of kings but in the struggles of ordinary people against the forces of nature and the cruelty of men."[74]

There is poverty virtually everywhere, but the connections of poverty to both family and to the political, economic, and environmental factors of a region make its nature complex and important for any meaningful philosophical discussion of ethics. On this complexity, moral philosophers such as Amartya Sen and Martha Nussbaum have written a great deal and have shaped a new ethical landscape related to issues of third-world development and justice.[75] I will conclude this section with a discussion of some of the important ideas given us by Sen for measuring poverty with respect to justice and equality. Sen's work in economics and philosophy has made him a major voice in postcolonial studies.

The strands of suffering and poverty are so interwoven as to be inseparable in Africa. Philosophers would be remiss not to detail the role of these two concepts in any ethical discussion of concepts such as justice and equality. This is done with great skill by Sen in his *Inequality Reexamined,* in which he challenges John Rawls' notion of "justice as fairness." Sen's counterproposal as we will see is much more appropriate for considering justice and equality in a cross-cultural and multicultural perspective. In any systematic account of harmdoing and evil, the specific histories of poverty in different cultures and the kinds of poverty should be introduced. One must ask: Is the poverty a consequence of famine, of inaccessibility to food, of larger systemic problems or unemployment, of lack of health care, or of communal "shunning" or "taboos" linked to family structures? Awareness of these heighten one's grasp of the meaning of other ethical concepts currently of universal philosophical interest such as "care," "compassion," and other "relational" ethical concepts found, for example, at the center of recent communitarian and feminist ethical theory debates.

I said earlier that suffering is a significant moral concept, not just a descriptive one. This is true also of poverty. When thinking about justice and equality, for example, in the African context, "suffering" and "poverty" become, in Amartya Sen's theoretical scheme, "focal variables— the variable(s) on which the analysis focuses, in comparing different people." With the use of "focal variables" the judgment and measurement of inequality or injustice are seen as "thoroughly dependent on the choice of the variable," e.g., income, happiness, wealth, kinds of resources, needs, etc.[76] One of the benefits of Sen's "focal variables" is that they point out the differences and diversities between peoples and situations. He says "that 'poverty' is a major evaluative concern in most societies, and how we identify poverty is a matter of some practical moment in the contexts" compared.[77] For example, what is often measured as "absolute poverty" according to "income level" may not be a good measure of one's happiness or one's capacity to maintain a level of dignity in one society compared to another. If one compares poverty as measured by an income "poverty line" or access to "commodities," for example, as is done in the United States,[78] with poverty in Africa by the same standard, you simply would multiply your poverty statistics in Africa and do little to understand poverty and its relationship to the kind of suffering experienced in Africa. Nor would you have given consideration to different ways in which moral character is formed, its relationship to community and family structures, or to such notions as *ubuntu,* which in some contexts may be significant for our understanding.[79]

If, however, explicit consideration is given to the relative levels of poverty with respect to kinds of suffering and deprivations in different spaces and how that may limit "the capacity to lead secure and worthwhile lives," then the variable of poverty allows a different reading of the space and people. This would have important effects on choosing development strategies and how best programs of wealth distribution or capital investment should take place. Health care delivery systems, for example, may have more to do with the limiting of poverty and giving people a capacity to lead a secure and worthwhile life than one's level of income. Here we find poverty closely linked with issues of development and the distribution of food and availability of basic services. To see the linkage between poverty and development strategies is, in itself, an important ethical issue that is receiving much current attention.[80]

With respect to what are called "capability factors," the understanding of poverty may vary considerably. For example, the "poverty line" measure in the United States relates in part with a family's capability to purchase certain consumer goods. In an African context having similar consumer goods may be irrelevant to one's happiness and well-being. More important factors would be adequate nourishment and health care, the capability to lead a life without shame, and some social freedoms, i.e., to move about without coercion. This, of course, may change as overall consumptive patterns or standards of living change in the society. But the "dignity" associated with "poverty" in Africa asks little of consumptive powers. Rather, a human being expects *to be capable* of certain small pleasures or freedoms above adequate nourishment, shelter, and health care. Sen defines poverty as "the lack of freedom to have or to do basic things that you value."[81] "Well-being" itself may be understood differently. So the questions: Whose well-being? Which capabilities? are crucial in evaluating and understanding the moral relevance of poverty. In considering who is poor and why, Sen would have us ask not what minimal goods or what income level a person may have, *but what capabilities they have to do certain things that show their overall well-being.* Crocker says of Sen's view: "Capabilities add something intrinsically and not merely instrumentally valuable to a human life, namely positive freedom in the sense of available and worthwhile options."[82]

Understanding the differences in a concept's meaning and use is crucial and seeing connections between "focal variables" and the community's overall functioning and well-being is essential to clear ethical thinking. Sen concludes, "the ordering of poverty and the identification of the poor may be very different if it is done entirely in terms of the size of income (as is the standard practice in most countries) compared with what it would be if the focus is on *capability failure.* ... By focusing poverty study specifically on incomes as such, crucial aspects of deprivation may be entirely lost."[83]

Sen and Nussbaum have clearly brought a new moral language into development theory. They have given a human face to economic theory. To measure poverty by considering a person's ability to function as a human being and to consider a community's overall well-being by factors other than income level or a "commodities approach" gives voice to the poor in ways that "normal" Western economic and development strategies had not done. Here is a case in which ethical, philosophical reflection has changed the direction of a discipline and in which the patterns of wealth redistribution may be genuinely affected. The very criteria used by IMF and World Bank for loans and numerous wealthy nations in their foreign aid schemes, for example, have changed substantially. Sen and others have helped give voice to the poor for greater self-determination in ways that earlier Marxist ideological language was often unable to do. In the African context family structure, local traditions, and "basic needs" and their effect on human *capabilities* are looked at differently; they become factors in development and redistribution of wealth equations in ways that have been previously ignored. This is philosophy at work in a very concrete way; it is philosophy being "used for a particular purpose," as Wittgenstein encouraged.

Let us return, finally, to Bessie Head's notion of wearing poverty "with an unconscious dignity." *Such dignity is a feature of moral character achieved by one's particular capability to contribute to the well-being of the community and not a feature of the poverty itself.* And this is seen as particularly important in the continued condition of scarcity of goods and resources when each person must help the other to survive and sustain a meaningful life. Here, of course, communal values may play a major role, but the dignity is carried by an individual person and this is not simply a product of the whole. Here is where discussions of virtue ethics, ethics viewed as relational (as in feminist ethics), and communitarian ethics converge in the African discussions with Western philosophical discussions; where it is viewed as important not only to identify oneself in terms of one's community alone, but to form one's own individual moral character by acting toward one's fellow human beings with compassion and care as was discussed previously. There is little doubt that an understanding of the African concepts of suffering and poverty could enrich that discussion and that both concepts are essential to meaningful cross-cultural discussion of equality and justice.

5.

African Moral Philosophy II
Truth and Reconciliation

Southern Africa isn't like the rest of Africa and is never going to be. Here we are going to have to make an extreme effort to find a deep faith to help us to live together.

—Bessie Head, *A Woman Alone*, 31

Not all storytelling heals.

—*Truth and Reconciliation Commission Report*, Vol. 5/9, Section 6

The South African "Truth and Reconciliation Commission" (TRC) is an example of what Bessie Head had referred to thirty years earlier as "an extreme effort to find a deep faith to help [Southern Africans] live together." One finds in the Commission's unfolding process a unique convergence of several important moral and political concepts. Looking at these concepts brings out the liveliness of this important philosophical discussion in Africa. One also sees through the work of the Commission its relevance to the larger discussion of "justice" related issues throughout the globe.

To highlight these larger issues we will, in this chapter, organize the discussion around several interrelated topics:[1] First we will look at the legacy of communalism in South African society, then turn to what Elizabeth Wolgast, following Wittgenstein, calls "the grammar of justice" within the South African context. This "grammar" requires that we assess the relative value of truth and reconciliation to justice and also evaluate the meaning of the notion of "restorative justice" within the TRC process. We will then sort out some important critical issues that have generated much controversy among philosophers and other critics in their continuing assessment of the TRC process, particularly whether "justice" was forgotten in the process and whether reparations and restitution to victims of apartheid will be realized. Finally we will ask what the overall value of the TRC process may be in the South African context and as a model for moral and political transformation beyond the region. In this chapter, and especially in the last section, we will see how the concepts of community, suffering, and poverty discussed in chapter 4 are essential to our discussion of truth, reconciliation, and justice within the African context and for cross-cultural understanding.

Linking Communalism, *Ubuntu*, and Restorative Justice

In May 1976, the Anglican Dean of Johannesburg, Desmond Tutu, wrote an open letter to Prime Minster John Vorster. Among several specific grievances his general appeal was from one reasonable Christian to another. Tutu says to Vorster, "We Blacks are exceedingly patient and peace-loving. We are aware that politics is the art of the possible."[2] Possible, that is, if there is a mutual willingness to talk to one another. Tutu writes as one who knows "what it has meant in frustration and hurt, in agony and humiliation, to be a subject people."[3] He asks Vorster how long he thinks a people can "bear such blatant injustice and suffering." Aware that "a people made desperate by despair, injustice and oppression will use desperate means," says Tutu, "I am frightened, dreadfully frightened, that we may soon reach a point of no return, when events will generate a momentum of their own...." This momentum, he fears, is moving in a direction of a "bloody dénouement." In spite of this Tutu can say: "I am deeply committed to real reconciliation with justice for all, and to peaceful change to a more just and open South African society in which the wonderful riches and wealth of our country will be shared more equitably."[4] Tutu later said that Vorster had "treated [his] letter with disdain."[5] But we must ask: From where does such a sentiment as Tutu expresses come? Equitably sharing the riches of the country in the midst of "real reconciliation with justice for all"? How, after decades of affliction under the apartheid regime and centuries of white oppression, is reconciliation with justice to be achieved?

Twelve years earlier Nelson Mandela, while defending himself at the "Rivonia" trial in 1964 (which sent him to Robben Island for life imprisonment), said:

> I have fought against white domination and I have fought against black domination. I have cherished the ideal of a democratic and free society in which all persons live together in harmony and with equal opportunities. It is an ideal which I hope to live for and to achieve. But if needs be, it is an ideal for which I am prepared to die.[6]

Later reflecting on his twenty-seven years in prison, Mandela distills this message: "I knew as well as I knew anything that the oppressor must be liberated just as surely as the oppressed. A man who takes away another man's freedom is a prisoner of hatred, he is locked behind the bars of prejudice and narrow-mindedness.... The oppressed and the oppressor alike are robbed of their humanity."[7] Where does the idea that the oppressed must seek to liberate the oppressor come from?

The direction toward "bloody dénouement" of which Tutu spoke in 1976 shifted in an unexpected way a decade later. By the mid-1980s secret talks began toward working out some negotiated settlement between the black majority party (the African National Congress) and the government of the white National Party (the architects, builders, and keepers of apartheid) whose system was morally bankrupt. With the release of Nelson Mandela from prison by President F. W. de Klerk in February 1990, the negotiation direction settled into an inevitable course toward "majority rule." The unfolding of this extraordinary story from the early 1980s to Mandela's inauguration as the first black President of South African on 10 May 1994 is brilliantly documented and narrated by two journalists (Alastair Sparks and Patti Waldmeir) and by the two principal leaders themselves (Mandela and de Klerk).[8]

Wole Soyinka has also given us insight into what he calls "the muse of forgiveness" and "the muse of reconciliation" in Senghor's attitude toward the French after the independence of Senegal. Soyinka traces with some astonishment how some Africans seem to be able to forgive and reconcile enmity after so much suffering and injustice.[9] Thirteen years earlier, in his Nobel lecture (1986), Soyinka had noted that "[t]here is a deep lesson for the world in the black races' capacity to forgive, one which, I often think, has much to do with ethical precepts which spring from their world view and authentic religions, none of which is ever totally eradicated by the accretions of foreign faiths and their implicit ethnocentrism."[10]

Given that this "miracle" of South Africa did happen, what seems almost beyond the miraculous is the fact that leaders like Mandela and his African National Congress did not seek retribution against whites during negotiations with the National Party and the writing of the Interim Constitution. Rather, they sought as had others like Senghor, and continue to seek, *reconciliation* among all South Africans: black and white. This idea, in fact, is deliberately inscribed into the Interim Constitution: "There is a need for understanding but not for vengeance, a need for reparations but not for retaliation, a need for ubuntu but not for victimisation."[11] This pattern is perhaps most surprising because it is spoken of as a "natural" moral way of being while to Western ears this may seem so "unnatural." How is this possible? What are these "ethical precepts," in Soyinka's words, that "spring from [the African's] world view and authentic religions?" To try and answer this question, I will pick up a thread from our discussion of communitarian ethics first "spun" by Gyekye.

In our last chapter, while developing his central thesis for a "moderate communitarianism," Gyekye said, "in the communitarian moral universe caring or compassion or generosity, not justice [in a rights-based sense] . . . may be a fundamental moral category." We then went on to talk about "compassion" and "caring" in relation to a more communitarian sense of justice, but said little about "generosity" or what Gyekye refers to as "supererogatory acts." These moral categories were, according to Gyekye, *intrinsic* to a communitarian ethic and would, in practice, lead persons to give greater attention to other persons and less attention to one's self.

I believe Gyekye's larger discussion of "communitarianism and supererogationism" has some bearing on our understanding of forgiveness, reconciliation, and justice in some African contexts. Gyekeye writes: "a supererogatory act (*super* in Latin means 'above') is generally defined as an act that is beyond the call of duty, that is, over and above what a moral agent is required to do."[12] He engages several Western philosophers who discuss the role of "supererogatory acts" in moral theory and whether such acts should be understood as either intrinsic or necessary. John Rawls, for example, believes that although such acts may be good, they are neither intrinsic nor part of one's obligation in being moral, largely because they involve incalculatable risks. Those like Rawls who deny the intrinsic qualities of supererogatory acts believe, says Gyekeye,

> that moral conduct is essentially to be confined to acts that human beings can or want conveniently to perform and that will promote their own individual ends . . . they think that *some* form of self-sacrifice cannot be required of any and every moral agent. But the question is: which form of self-sacrifice can or should be required of the moral agent, and how do we determine that?[13]

Gyekye, on the other hand, believes "generosity" and other supererogatory acts *should be* required of the moral agent. He says:

> The scope of our moral responsibilities should not be circumscribed. The moral life, which essentially involves paying regard to the needs, interests, and well-being of *others*, already implies self-sacrifice and loss, that is, loss of something—one's time, money, strength, and so on. There is, in my view, no need, therefore, to place limits on the form of the self-sacrifice and, hence, the extent of our moral responsibilities.[14]

Such generosity promotes the welfare of others, and for Gyekye, it "should be considered a basic moral responsibility," and is so considered in many African societies.

I think there should be little doubt that part of the success of South Africa is the consistency with which the opposition leaders—Mandela, Tutu, Mbeki, Kader Asmal, Joe Slovo (the leader of the South African Communist Party) and others[15]—believed that morality required supererogatory acts. A peaceful transition to majority democracy required a way of acting that implied both self-sacrifice and regard for the well-being of others. There must be inclusion without retribution, and equality for *all* people in spite of the sins of apartheid in the *new* South Africa—"the oppressor," says Mandela, "must be liberated just as surely as the oppressed."

Thinkers such as Gyekye, Mandela, Soyinka, and Tutu believe that such acts are natural extensions of a way of life that is characteristic of, if not intrinsic to, an African identity. Acting for the benefit of all relates in part to the development of moral character tied to communitarian-based thinking. In Tutu's case it is also tied to his Christian theological convictions. For Mandela the idea, having been planted in his Xhosa-Thembu upbringing, came to full flower ironically and paradoxically as a consequence of long years of reflection while in confinement as well as through his daily encounters, like so many others, with the affliction of his people. The notion of another's needs was always part of Mandela's thinking; he always looked beyond his own self-interest toward his fellow South Africans. This is not to say that Mandela was not engaged in "politics" and that this entails mixed motivation. I think, however, there is little doubt that Mandela's "politics" were moderated by his "ethics," and that the well-being of *all* South Africans was always part of his political vision. This is confirmed by Alex Boraine when he says of Mandela: "From the day of his release to the present time, he has focused on the need to come to terms with the past, but always with a readiness to forgive and to move on.... He stretched out a hand of reconciliation and friendship."[16]

This point is often illustrated by referring to the concept of *ubuntu*. Boraine credits South Africa's ability to come to terms with its past in the way it did to "the holding in balance of the political realities ... and an ancient philosophy which seeks unity and reconciliation rather than revenge and punishment."[17] The word *ubuntu*—an Nguni word—is a kind of "shorthand" for this "ancient Philosophy." As noted above, it was used deliberately in the Interim Constitution. Boraine goes on to say:

> In reflecting the *ubuntu* philosophy, the Truth and Reconciliation Commission pointed to the need for more community-orientated jurisprudence that acknowledges the reality that individuals are part of a much larger social context.[18]

The concept of *ubuntu* is tied to one's personal identity as we saw earlier and is intrinsic to this "community-orientated" outlook. Desmond Tutu in an interview remarked, "In our understanding, when someone doesn't forgive, we say that person does not have *ubuntu*. That is to say he is not really human."[19] Not to have *ubuntu*—love, forgiveness, generosity— according to both Gyekye and Tutu (and Kwasi Wiredu as well), then, is viewed as a moral deficiency. This is true, in part, because of the context of community in South Africa and the qualities of moral character that flow from this more communitarian way of being.

Of course not all Africans share this moral outlook of black South Africans, nor believe that ethics requires such "supererogatory acts." Tutu remarks: "It doesn't always happen, of course. Where was *ubuntu* in the Belgian Congo in the early 1960s? Why did the Rwandans forget *ubuntu* in 1994 and instead destroy one another in the most awful genocide ... ? I don't really know except to say that honouring *ubuntu* is clearly not a mechanical, automatic and inevitable process and that we in South Africa have been blessed...."[20] The philosophical debate is far from one sided on this issue, and the question of how to bring about reconciliation between parties who had been at war is not an easy one to answer.[21]

There are also those who believe that *ubuntu*, even *or especially* in the South African context, suffers from the "illusion of unanimism"—that "the notion of *ubuntu* may be as much a current invention as a recovery of past practices."[22] The ebullient Archbishop, however, can discuss aspects of *ubuntu* in the specific ways he sees it connected with justice. In a live television interview, faced with this question: "Where is the justice in the Truth and Reconciliation Committee's proceedings?" Tutu replied that there are different *kinds* of justice. "Retributive justice," he said, "is largely Western. The African understanding is far more restorative—not so much to punish as to redress or restore a balance that has been knocked askew. The justice we hope for is restorative of the dignity of the people."[23]

Although Archbishop Tutu's "thumb print" and his understanding of *ubuntu* inform the concept of restorative justice, the *Report* of the Commission has its own voice and expresses this concept well. It notes first that "individual and shared moral responsibility cannot be adequately addressed by legislation or this commission," but "*what is required is a moral and spiritual renaissance capable of transforming moral indifference, denial, paralysing guilt and unacknowledged shame, into personal and social responsibility.*"[24]

It is in a correlation between *ubuntu*, rooted in whatever forms of "communalism" may survive in South Africa (moderate or otherwise), and the kind of justice referred to as "restorative justice," that we find the foundation stones for the Truth and Reconciliation Commission[25] and a possibility for a moral and spiritual renaissance. In Tutu's own words:

> I contend that there is another kind of justice, restorative justice, which was characteristic of traditional African jurisprudence. Here the central concern is not retribution or punishment but, in the spirit of *ubuntu*, the healing of breaches, the redressing of imbalances, the restoration of broken relationships. This kind of justice seeks to rehabilitate both the victim and the perpetrator, who should be given the opportunity to be reintegrated into the community he or she has injured by his or her offense.[26]

Setting aside whether *ubuntu* is an underlying *elan vital* in "traditional African jurisprudence," it is clear that justice can be conceived in several significantly different ways and one's conception will result in different social consequences. What the TRC has called "restorative justice" does embrace broad goals of "restoring trust" between alienated parties,[27] and is more likely to enhance goodwill in approaching issues in the rebuilding of a civil society than is "retributive justice." John Braithwaite says: "Restorative justice is about restoring victims, restoring offenders and restoring communities."[28] There seems to be a different grammar to the very concept of "justice" emerging here. Johnny De Lange, commenting on the emergence of the commission's mission, writes: "There ha[d] to be justice, but justice in its broadest sense—a collective justice, social justice, a restorative justice that seeks to address and deliver to [all the people]— that is aimed at nation-building and reconciliation."[29] Let us look more closely at the grammar of "restorative justice."

Understanding the Grammar of Justice after Apartheid

An important universal moral question in philosophy is "How does one get to the truth of and deal with human harmdoing and injustice?" In South Africa this question has the particular form: "How does one get to the truth of and deal with the aftermath of apartheid's evil?" This question was directly confronted by the people of South Africa when it proposed a commission on truth and reconciliation in June 1994 as one of the new government's first orders of business.[30] To get to the truth of apartheid's evil and restore dignity to apartheid's victims was what the South African TRC wanted to do. The process of this Commission over about a six-year period ignited a lively discussion on the very meaning of justice. It has contributed to the broader discussion of how societies in transition to democracy should deal with past atrocities. Its chief tool in achieving this end turned out to be the power of the language of its ordinary (and extra-ordinary) people—the language of truth-telling. In the words of the Deputy Chairperson of the TRC, Alex Boraine,

> Truth-telling is a critical part of [civic] transformation which challenges myths, half-truths, denials, and lies. It was when listening to ordinary people relating their experience under apartheid that one was able to understand the magnitude and horror of the system which damaged and destroyed so many over so long a period.[31]

This can be illustrated by a brief look at the very successful play about the TRC, *Ubu and the Truth Commission*. The play's director, William Kentridge, comments that the commission's victim hearings as they unfolded live in the cities and rural areas around South Africa provided him and the playwright, Jane Taylor, with a "Found Text." Kentridge says:

> None of us had the courage or skill to write our own text. We then thought of working with a Found Text: this in the hope of finding in the words that people use to describe extreme situations, a bed rock connection between human experience and the language we use to talk about it.[32]

Their "Found Text" was the actual testimony of the victims and perpetrators of apartheid's crimes. "Ubu stands for an aspect, a tendency, an excuse," writes Ms. Taylor. He captures the "voices ... we have heard in the hearings." She continues:

> Over the past eighteen months of listening to the disjuncture between the testimony of those looking for amnesty and those seeking reparation, it has been chilling to note the frequency with which an act of astonishing cruelty has been undertaken, as it were, negligently, with no sense of the impact of such action on other human lives; when confronted with the families of victims or survivors, those perpetrators who seem to have some capacity for remorse, appear to be shocked at observing, as if from the outside, the effect of their behaviour. Others simply show no response at all, so profound is the denial, or the failure of moral imagination.[33]

The painter Cezanne once wrote to Emile Bernard: "I owe you the truth in painting and I will tell it to you."[34] Art often has this capacity of truth-telling, of releasing us from certain forms of blindness, of revealing aspects of our world that we might miss were it not for the angle of vision provided by the art. *Ubu* combines art with real life, lifting up the ironies in harm-doing and pointing to the disjunctures in language itself. Astonishing cruelty and heart-rending pathos are "worded" side by side. The logics of denial and mourning somehow coexist in a way that reveals the truth. The TRC hearings present us with a theatrical picture—a form of "civic theatre" Kentridge calls it.

In his Director's Note, Kentridge writes

> Its hearings are open to the public, as well as being televised and broadcast on the radio. Many of the hearings are presided over by Archbishop Tutu in full purple magnificence. The hearings move from town to town setting up in a church hall, a school auditorium. In each setting the same set is erected. A table for the witnesses (always at least as high as that of the commissioners so the witnesses never have to look up to the commissioners). Two or three glass booths for the translators. A large banner hangs on the wall behind the commissioners, TRUTH THROUGH RECONCILIATION. One by one witnesses come and have their half hour to tell their story, pause, weep, be comforted by professional comforters who sit at the table with them. The stories are harrowing, spellbinding. The audience sit at the edge of their seats listening to every word. This is exemplary civic theatre, a public hearing of private griefs which are absorbed into the body politic as a part of a deeper understanding of how the society arrived at its present position.[35]

So we have this theatrical picture rooted in truth-telling—a desire to have the truth reveal or "unconceal" itself in the telling. We could understand this process as a living moral tale; in the best of worlds the TRC process can be understood as an historic philosophical dialogue, shaping a new discourse upon which South Africa may build a new civil society.

How did this process of truth-telling with its new grammar of "restorative justice" emerge, and what did it, in fact, achieve in terms of truth, justice, and reconciliation? One thing that the notion of "restorative justice" does is to evoke the importance of transition from a culture of violence—with its gross human rights violations, forced removals, and denial of human dignity—to a culture of human rights with greater dignity for all. The concept of restorative justice blunts a certain "legalism" found in retributive justice systems and that threaten to reduce the concept of justice to one of contentiousness between aggrieved parties. *Justice is not simply found in the rule of law but in human practices that create a civil society, where all people have equal claim to human dignity and accept responsibility for the well-being of all its citizens.*

It is this sense of justice that needed to be *restored* in South Africa, and for which the TRC was essentially designed. Martha Minow characterizes the overall design of the TRC as follows: "On behalf of bystanders and perpetrators, as well as victims, it seeks to establish a base line of right and wrong, to humanize the perpetrators and to obtain and disclose previously hidden information about what happened, who gave orders, where missing persons ended up."[36] If such a baseline is clearly established and the truth is revealed, then national healing and reconciliation might have a place to begin.

To have a "baseline of right and wrong" and establish a meaningful sense of justice requires some common moral discourse. Under the apartheid regime moral discourse had been skewed and repressed by the perpetrators of apartheid and it had been too long silenced by fear and rage in black souls by apartheid's oppression.[37] Something like the experience of the TRC was necessary to forge a new moral discourse and some meaningful sense of justice. As South African philosopher Johan Snyman said, there was a need "to reinscribe remorse on a landscape" and restore the people's moral voice. Or as Antjie Krog wrote, we must find "words for that cry of Nomonde Calata," and make public the wounds of a society that had lost its moral way.

To understand the grammar of restorative justice one needs first to reveal the truth of apartheid's *injustices*—to confront those, especially among the white community, who had become morally bankrupt. This is what is meant by "truth" in the "truth commission." It could be said that the TRC process offered the South African public what Simone Weil once called "that interval of hesitation, wherein lies all our consideration for our brothers in humanity."[38] Such intervals create reflective space, however painful for some and irritating to others, in which new questions could be asked and new risks taken by both victims and perpetrators of violence. *Attention* needed to be given to the decades of harm done to nonwhites by the former white-ruled regime in order for *a new sense of justice* to be restored.

This aspect of looking at injustice draws attention to those circumstances in life that give us pause to question whether there is any meaning to our use of the term "justice." Elizabeth Wolgast writes: "To call something unjust is to take it out of the realm of disinterested reportage ... saying that something is a wrong or injustice *marks it* for moral indignation and moral concern."[39] Wolgast also says: "In the face of wrong, justice is demanded and cried out for, and with passion and intensity. 'We must have justice!' and 'Justice must be done!' are its expressions, and they characteristically have imperative force as well as urgency."[40]

The very urgency of the cries of victims heard day in and day out for eighteen months helped fasten attention on injustice. The new majority dispensation has the formidable task of restoring a sense of justice that had "been knocked askew," but first the truth of the past had to be unveiled. Part of the Commission's mandate was to recommend reparations for victims and grant amnesty to some perpetrators. The latter was a qualified amnesty provision, that is, amnesty for full disclosure and truth of violations committed. This route was chosen rather than one through a "Nuremberg-type" tribunal (a retributive or punitive justice model) or to grant blanket amnesty or give impunity for those who committed past atrocities. Such restorative justice opens up the possibility of thinking about a kind of justice that is *compassion based, embracing human self-esteem, benevolence or generosity and mercy; and a justice grounded in a shared obligation to the well-being of one's fellow human beings.*

What is "new" about the notion of restorative justice in South African society is found as much in its departure from patterns of retributive justice that dominate Western legal jurisprudence as in its own inventiveness. There are precedents to thinking about the concept of justice in this more "moral and spiritual" way. We discussed this briefly with regard to "communitarian" thinking, to "supererogatory acts" and the way of justice as compassion found in Simone Weil. Although the Commission stresses truth for reconciliation and its very name excludes the term or word "justice," its intention clearly points toward a new kind of "justice." The TRC believed that its process of listening to the cries of the victims of apartheid's injustices is indispensable for truth, justice, and reconciliation.

What can be argued, and what is being underscored here, is that *embedded in the TRC process and their Report is the making of a new "moral and spiritual" discourse and a call for a kind of justice called restorative justice. Restorative justice is intended to be the glue between "truth" and "reconciliation," and which encourages both moral and social responsibility and such virtues as compassion, mercy, and forgiveness, all for the purpose of helping to forge a new more just South Africa.*

Let us look more closely at the virtue of mercy as a feature of the grammar of justice found in the concept of "restorative" justice. Mercy seems a more appropriate way of describing the manner in which amnesty has been given under the TRC mandate than the "blanket amnesties" granted in some of the recent Latin American transitions from military dictatorships to democracies.[41] In his essay, "Mercy Within Legal Justice," Andrew Brien puts his finger on a feature often missing in discussions of theories of justice, especially justice of a retributive or punitive kind—that is the role of "mercy" in justice. He argues that if one wants to advocate a legal system "that aims for moral outcomes" and that supports "the general aim of promoting human flourishing, community, harmony, reconciliation, and individual and societal well being," then it must have room within its legal system for virtues such as friendship, compassion, sympathy, and mercy (especially mercy).[42] How does Brien's notion of mercy fit in with the TRC process?

Given the particular circumstances of South African history and the nature of its new Constitution, it is just those virtues that should be a part of its legal system. Through the victims' hearings the new government in power in South Africa exposed the injustices of the past in the form of gross human rights violations and also faced up to the issue of amnesty for the perpetrators of the injustices. One of the ironies and the strengths of the amnesty hearings lay in the effects of the perpetrators' testimony on their own lives and the nation's conscience. William Kentridge, again discussing his production of the play *Ubu and the Truth Commission,* which ran in Cape Town near the end of the commission's hearings, asks: "What was the perpetrator's inducement to testify?" And answers:

> A full confession can bring amnesty and immunity from prosecution or civil procedures for the crimes committed. Therein lies the central irony of the Commission. As people give more and more evidence of the things they have done they get closer and closer to amnesty and it gets more and more intolerable that these people should be given amnesty.[43]

They had to ask would amnesty be within the interest of justice? If one's sense of justice is restorative the answer to the question is Yes!—that is, if you have (or want) a legal system "that aims for moral outcomes" and "societal well-being," then part of that system must have room for forgiveness, pardon, compassion, and mercy—though pardons would not come without much reflection and attention to individual cases. In the new South Africa one clear *moral outcome* desired by the new dispensation *is reconciliation.*[44] Therefore the legal system—to promote reconciliation within justice—ought to include mercy. This was shown in its exchange of amnesty for truth (full disclosure of past crimes). This is, in part, what is meant by "restorative justice." This is like a wholesale challenge to most modern conceptions of "justice."

The term "mercy" is particularly appropriate to understanding restorative justice because of the reversal of positions of power in the political transition in South Africa, where the preceding white minority regime had little sense of mercy.[45] "Mercy," says Brien, "provides sight to the moral agent; it enables her to perceive, be sensitive to, and understand the world, and to evaluate the salient moral properties of the people with whom she has contact. This virtue enables an actor to use power wisely."[46] The TRC process seemed to proceed with something like this kind of wisdom, sensing the need to understand the pain of victims and perceive the need that truth must be revealed so as not to bury the past without regret. One could say that as its hearings unfolded it brought a new moral sight to people's eyes that enabled them to evaluate human beings in new ways, and to be reminded that power must always be used wisely and with compassion and mercy.

Classically, mercy "means restraining the mind from vengeance when it has the power to take it, or the leniency of a superior towards an inferior in fixing punishment."[47] The new majority government certainly had the power to seek vengeance. Remarkably, it did not! Rather it showed mercy without losing sight of punishment. On the issue of "fixing punishment," restorative justice does not shy away from the importance of some kinds of punishment to achieve justice. We will look at kinds of punishment in the following section. South Africa's new leadership had sufficient "moral sight" to enable them to see and hear the cries of the afflicted—both victims and perpetrators. The Commission was clear on its desire to encourage the nation to retain its newly found "moral sight." The Commission *Report* says: "Each story of suffering provided a penetrating window into the past, thereby contributing to a more complete picture of gross violations of human rights in South Africa. The nation must use these stories to sharpen its moral conscience and to ensure that, never again, will it gradually atrophy to the point where personal responsibility is abdicated."[48]

Brien calls mercy a "gentle virtue" that "promotes a humanizing and civilizing effect in the world in which the inhabitants are almost continually surrounded by violence and gratuitous displays of power and domination . . . [and] this virtue brings into the world those sorts of actions that break the cycle of revenge and retribution into which actors and even whole communities can so easily fall. It promotes harmony in the community, reconciliation, and flourishing."[49] Nussbaum, too, speaks of mercy as "a gentle art of particular perception, a temper of mind that refuses to demand retribution without understanding the whole story. . . ."[50] The TRC was clearly concerned with "the whole story," but it was under severe time and legal constraints. Even with those constraints it went a long way to that end. What the testimonies (from both victims and perpetrators) did, combined with the public nature of the process, was to provide an "imaginative exercise" that could penetrate "the life of another," and perhaps aid in the "struggles of other concrete lives."[51] In this way the TRC process reached beyond its own boundaries, hoping to "break the cycle of revenge and retribution." This is at the heart of the TRC's idea of "restorative justice" and what it hoped to achieve. To what extent it may have achieved some of these ends remains to be seen. There are more than enough skeptics in South Africa who believe the TRC's work and goals too difficult or too unrealistic to sustain and achieve.

As important as love, compassion, or mercy may be in sustaining justice in a society, equally important in "restorative justice" is the restoration of dignity denied by offering victims the chance to regain their self-esteem. Jonathan Allen refers to this as a kind of "justice as recognition," which is embodied in and emerges from the TRC process. This is, Allen says,

> a form of recognition that acknowledges the historical fact of exclusion from legal recognition and seeks to reverse the imposition of passive status by encouraging victims to act in public by telling their stories. This would be an inappropriate concern in a law court, but it is important as a kind of public ritual of recognition of the moral agency of those previously excluded—a public marker of these citizens' rightful passage into equal consideration and respect. It is recognition as acknowledgment and admission. And it is related to justice in an additional way because it acknowledges the injustice of the exclusion that made the specific abuses possible.[52]

If, indeed, some new sense of justice is restored, then the possibility of "reconciliation" is enhanced, and if reconciliation is enhanced then the possibility for sustained love, compassion, or mercy within justice is also enhanced. So, in effect, the notion of "justice" was not left out of the equation of the TRC as many have argued. Rather justice comes in through a radical rethinking of the grammar of justice itself and through the process of human compassion and restoration that is understood to be as important as, and should become a part of, the rule of law in a time of difficult transition.

"Not All Storytelling Heals": Criticisms of the TRC Process[53]

There are a number of criticisms of the TRC process that need to be addressed. The first is that the TRC process was too narrowly defined, and that if it served any kind of justice it served only a small fraction of the victims of apartheid. Mahmood Mamdani called this "a diminished truth that wrote the vast majority of apartheid's victims out of its version of history."[54] By focusing only on "gross human rights violations"— receiving over 21,000 statements from people claiming to be victims of such gross violations—it overlooked the victims of apartheid's worst evils. The greater human rights violations, many believed, were done to those forced to "wither away in the cul de sacs of enforced poverty" by the "forced labour tenancy, forced removals, the establishment of bantustans and token local authorities, migrant labour, segregated towns and cities and the hostel system."[55] These latter victims, estimated at some 3.5 million, Mamdani says "comprise faceless communities, not individual activists" whose "communities were shattered" and "livelihoods destroyed."[56]

At the heart of this criticism is that real *social* justice was not served by the Commission and thus an important opportunity was missed. Mamdani's criticism is extended by Sampie Terreblanche who forcefully argues that the Commission missed an opportunity to deal *with systemic economic injustice* by not having more clearly condemned the business community of South Africa that had been complicit with both colonialism and the apartheid regime for the entire century.[57] Terreblanche argued before the Commission, saying the following: "I am in agreement with Mamdani that social justice demands that those who have been the beneficiaries of the power structures of white political supremacy and racial capitalism have a responsibility to make quite a substantial sacrifice towards those who have been the victims of these power structures."[58] In the business communities Institutional Hearings before the Commission they argued "a twisted version of the truth" according to Terreblanche— they claimed that they were "the victims of apartheid" rather than beneficiaries, that their businesses suffered under apartheid, especially after 1972. Although this point was questioned by the Commission and some of their activities were condemned, the Commission did not go far enough in its criticism and in making a specific recommendation that might have pressured the business community to make real sacrifices and hold them more accountable for their past sins.[59] Terreblanche believes that "the Commission would have done well to concentrate more explicitly on the reasons for the abject poverty and the extravagant wealth" in South African society.[60] This would have exposed the consequences of racial capitalism more clearly. All this implies for Terreblanche, as it did for Mamdani, that the Commission's mandate was much too narrow to achieve the desired goals of justice and reconciliation for the majority of the people of South Africa.

One of the side effects of Mamdani's and Terreblanche's criticism is the problem of "scapegoating." By focusing on individual gross human rights violations, it is the "De Kocks" and "Benziens" (two of the worst perpetrators of violence to blacks) and actions out of Vlakplaas death farms that were revealed in the hearings that are being forced to take the blame. This lets the "politicians" and other "institutions" off the hook. By this scapegoating one easily loses sight of the 3.5 million victims of the larger social evils of apartheid and in the end does not hold the real powers who sustained apartheid accountable. It is true that the top political leaders of the past regime escaped even the punishment of going through the amnesty process. They are, however, still open to both civil or criminal prosecution under South African law.

These are important and difficult criticisms and are only partially mitigated by certain positive, and sometimes unexpected, "spin off" effects of the TRC process. For example, Judge Richard J. Goldstone wrote of the TRC:

> Few South Africans have been untouched by it. All sectors of its society have been forced to look at their own participation in apartheid—the business community, the legal, medical, and university communities. A substantial number of white South Africans, all of whom willingly or unwillingly benefited from this evil system, have experienced regret or shame or embarrassment.[61]

In the same context, Goldstone said that the Commission's hearings "stopped denials of the many serious human rights violations committed by the apartheid forces." To have stopped denials brought considerable shame to many of the apartheid regime, both to those perpetrators who filed for amnesty as well as to many professional communities that benefited from apartheid. Although these revelations of truth may have prevented legal prosecution of perpetrators, they also revealed injustices and were a form of public shaming that is itself "a form of punishment" and serve a kind of justice.

It should be noted that what is called "restorative justice" is not without forms of punishment or retributive aspects. They may be "softer" forms of punishment, but they can be clearly and effectively built into a legal and judicial system "that aims for moral outcomes." Even though Simone Weil's views on justice were compassion-based, she had strong ideas on punishment with moral ends clearly in sight. For her, the key within a legal system was to train those within the judicial system to have sufficient moral sight to enable them to see and hear the cries of the afflicted. Punishment must be meted out in a framework of moral and spiritual rehabilitation related to one's social obligations. Only then would justice be served.[62]

To have stopped denials also forced a significant proportion of the white community "to look at their own participation in apartheid." If those who have financial power would see their responsibility (even if awakened by guilt or shame) to shape economic development toward impacting the lives of the majority of dispossessed South Africans this could go far toward reconciliation and a restored sense of justice. The Commission, however, left such service "voluntary" and, as such, past beneficiaries of apartheid will, no doubt, require continued nudging and persuasion, if not legislation, if any serious restitution is forthcoming.

The question here is not whether anyone should be punished or whether justice can be served without some form of punishment. Rather, we must rethink what the ends of punishment are and whether they served just by making sure that "punishment fit the crime." In South Africa's case, one could argue that the punishment resulting from the public shame, loss of one's job, or the loss of self-esteem connected with alienation from one's family and community is sufficiently harsh. Alex Boraine asks us to remember the context of the social transition and the crucial balance achieved between political realities and amnesia. The qualified amnesty did not leave punishment out of the equation of justice.

There were challenges in court to the amnesty provision of the TRC by those who wanted a jury to decide the matter of punishment for criminal acts and gross human rights violations. The South African Constitutional Court denied a major challenge. Boraine notes: "Those who believe it is the duty of the state to punish those responsible for gross violations of human rights will argue against [the court's action] for years to come."[63] There have been high profile trials related to apartheid crimes in South African courts both before and after the commission. Some of those who were denied amnesty are sure to face criminal prosecution in the future. Boraine comments again:

> The time is long overdue that we acknowledge that the initial impulse to punish perpetrators of gross human rights violations is not enough. These acts of violence do not take place in isolation. They often have deep historical roots, sometimes accompanied by long-held grievances. They are frequently informed by deep divisions between rich and poor. If we are going to deal only with the perpetrators without seeking to restore the community in which these violations have taken place, all we will do is to make certain that the cycle of violence continues.[64]

Short of actual legislation, what is crucial in moving toward reconciliation and a new civil democratic society now that the TRC's evolving process enters new phases is to work toward the reconstruction of what Simone Weil called "natural human environments." This involves greater trust and cooperation in the workplace, in schools, on sports fields, and in neighborhoods where humans can experience mutual respect, friendship, warmth, shared tasks of value (responsibilities), and some cultural linkages where *mutual respect for differences* may be seen to enrich each other's life. Government, the business community, NGOs, and religious institutions should work hand-in-hand to this end.

Another point of criticism of the TRC process is the overidealization of the moral concept of "reconciliation" itself. Many say "reconciliation" must be problematized as well. "It doesn't always happen," says Tutu. The hard cases are the everyday ones. A dramatic example of one who highly problematizes the very notions of guilt, forgiveness, and reconciliation is found in the 1999 Booker Prize winning novel *Disgrace* by J. M. Coetzee. Lucy, the tragic heroine of the novel, wrestles with the issues of retribution, forgiveness and reconciliation in the "new" South Africa. A single white woman raped by some local black men on her farm struggles with guilt for having been white and thus somehow complicit with the minority regime. With all the implications of power reversals, how is guilt to be overcome? After fifty years of apartheid oppression, how is retribution to be avoided by those oppressed? Is forgiveness possible and a life of inverse subjugation thinkable? Is the effect of "airing" sins of the past and forging a new public discourse enough to sustain peace and justice? These questions and more are quietly and hauntingly woven into the fabric of this novel. The problematizing of these moral concepts brings out the dilemmas that are found in them more realistically than evoking terms such as *"ubuntu"*; they require answers of a more subtle ethical nature.

There is a less idealistic way to conceive of the notion of reconciliation that fits what was intended in the TRC process and that makes it appropriately "African"—that is, it fits into patterns of rural democracy linked to the village palaver that exists in many parts of Africa and that will be discussed in chapter 6. Kwasi Wiredu articulates this more realist political view of reconciliation based on a rural consensus model of democracy. He writes:

> Reconciliation is, in fact, a form of consensus. It is a restoration of goodwill through a reappraisal of the importance and significance of the initial bones of contention. It does not necessarily involve a complete identity of moral or cognitive opinions. It suffices that all parties are able to feel that adequate account has been taken of their points of view in any proposed scheme of future action or coexistence. Similarly, consensus does not in general entail total agreement.[65]

This view of reconciliation as a form of consensus allows for a more pragmatic, though no less plausible, account of how the South African political transition happened. It was politically negotiated until some consensus was arrived at on the shape of majority government. This consensus did not entail total agreement, but minority interests (in this case the white minority that once had all the power) needed to be taken seriously and they ultimately had to consent to make it work. As Wiredu noted, this process did not "involve a complete identity of moral or cognitive opinions," but only that "all parties" felt as if their interests were heard and somehow integrated into the future shape of the society. This happened in a remarkable way through years of tough negotiations that had to end with something close to consensus in order for some reasonable trust to survive. More than seven years on now, in the South African case, considerable trust seems to be holding. Some would argue that this trust would have held because of this consensus reconciliation without the necessity of any kind of truth commission.

Another way of problematizing these ethical precepts has been to take issue with the juridical manner in which South Africa chose to deal with its past in setting up its Commission. There is a chorus of internal criticism, but it also can be heard from outside South Africa. For example, Wole Soyinka strongly disagrees with South Africa's way of conceding to the enemy. This he sees symbolized in the TRC. His arguments and concerns are worth looking at in some detail—they represent another side to this recent and significant philosophical debate on forgiveness and reconciliation among Africans. He raises the question also on the minds of many South African's themselves: Is justice being served? Soyinka asks this question in the larger historical context of reparations for centuries of oppression of Africans—from the slave trade to apartheid.

Soyinka has been involved in what he calls "a millennial reckoning"—a pan-African discussion on reparations in compensation for the African slave trade in particular and more generally 500 years of African "enslavement." The reparations would be paid by countries involved in the slave trade and those responsible for both political and economic colonialism. Soyinka sees the necessity of "truth" before "reconciliation," but believes there must be an intervening stage as well. "Truth alone," he says, "is never enough to guarantee reconciliation."[66] Elementary justice requires some sort of mitigation of the guilty—some punishment or retribution before reconciliation, and Soyinka believes an appropriate punishment and mitigation of guilt in our time would be reparations: "a healing millennial trilogy: Truth, Reparations, and Reconciliation."[67]

Many, says Soyinka, "appear to be caught up in a *fin de millénaire* fever of atonement," and he cites a number of recent examples, such as the redress by the Spanish Government of "the 1492 edict of Ferdinand and Isabella that evicted Jews from Spain." Even though this redress was long in coming, he notes that the first slaves had been exported from the West African coast fifty years before the edict. Soyinka addresses the Western white economic power communities and asks:

Which of these memories, then, least deserves the peace of amnesia? How come that a five-centuries-old "crime against humanity" committed against the Jewish race has not been relegated to the archives of lapsed injustices? Is it nothing but idle compulsion that drives humanity to exhume and atone for past crimes against its kind? And is the African world then, yet again, of another kind, one that is beneath the justice of atonement and restitution? Justice must be made manifest either for all, or not at all.[68]

Soyinka has three main suggestions for reparations. First "for us, in these dire times, reparations, like charity should begin at home, and the wealth of the Mobutus, the Babangidas, the Abachas, but also the de Beers, Shell Surrogates Incorporated, [Anglo-American Corporation], etc. of the continent should be utilized as down payment, as evidence of internal moral cleansing, that would make any claims for worldwide reparations irreproachable."[69] This suggestion echoes Terreblanche's suggestion for South Africa. Second, reparations should

> involve the acceptance by Western nations of a moral obligation to repatriate the post-colonial loot salted away in their vaults, in real estate, business holdings, and cover ventures by those African leaders who have chosen to follow the European precedent in the expropriation of a continent. The plunder could never have been possible, would never have reached such mammoth proportions, without the collaboration of those same commercial centers of Europe and, lately, the wealthier Arab nations.[70]

Soyinka would include in this "repatriation," the "expropriated" African art now to be found in the great museums and private collections of the West. Finally, his third suggestion is the forgiveness of debts by creditors to African states. There are other sources calling for this third move, and it is gaining some momentum—even yielding some modest results for Africa. Several wealthy nations as well as some major Church organizations are calling for a "year of Jubilee" in connection with the larger "Jubilee 2000 Campaign" in which all debt would be forgiven to the poorest of the "third world" countries.

Soyinka is aware of his critics and sees the most difficult obstacle to reparations to be the corrupt condition of Africa's state leaders and governments themselves. He says: "We remind ourselves yet again that the internal slavery currently inflicted on a continent's surviving millions by their own kind renders moot the entire notion of reparations."[71] Who, save a few states and leaders like Mandela and South Africa, have the moral legitimacy to carry a case to a universal court with any conviction? "The righteous armor of demand for ancient wrongs is thus sadly dented. The ignominious role of ancient rulers, continuing into the present, serves to remind us of their complicity in the cause for which reparations are sought."[72]

Truth in this issue is the unveiling of wrongs and the "Truth and Reconciliation Commission" started their search for the truth, hoping that opening the wounds would be promoting reconciliation. Soyinka thinks otherwise and brings us to reflect on our amnesia. What he calls the "muse of forgiveness" too often sheds "the burden of memory" too quickly. Perhaps the truth has not illuminated the darkness of Africa's past sufficiently to remind the world of the racism and suffering that the slave trade, colonialism, and racial capitalism brought to the continent. Although Soyinka believed that the strategy of the "negritude" movement in challenging colonialism was wrong ideologically, he has a deep appreciation for the "negritude" poets and their passion with such laments as that of René Depestre: "What have we done, we, the wretched black men of the earth, for these whites to hate us so? What have we done . . . to weigh so little on their scale?"[73] Soyinka is somewhat mystified, after their articulate and enraged literary assault on their colonial oppressors, how Africans still seem to have an infinite capacity for forgiveness and reconciliation. One response to Soyinka that has been argued in chapter 4, and that he is aware of himself, is that it is in the conditioning of centuries of suffering and poverty and whatever remains of the heritage of a more communitarian moral framework in which part of the answer to Soyinka's puzzlement lay.

Seeing the situation of suffering, poverty, and reconciliation "as it is" in specific contexts in Africa is no easy matter for non-Africans. And to reconfigure the grammar of "justice" is even harder. We must always try and situate each concept in the lived reality that is particular to its circumstances in Africa, recognizing that those circumstances are not ours. To see each reality "as it is," however, does reveal limitations in our own manner of seeing and being, and may (or may not) awaken in us the challenge that can be found in the humanity and dignity of many Africans. Referring back to our opening chapter, and its opening epigram, it is never a matter of settling for "the charm" of one point of view over another. *There is no "charm" in affliction or poverty anywhere, and the highly "self"-conscious nature of Western liberal individualism with its penchant for atomizing human wants and needs makes the admission of guilt or even the understanding of concepts such as reconciliation or ubuntu or mercy or forgiveness only remote possibilities. Facing up to the challenge of the TRC process in all its moral and philosophical complexity is what makes it so important to non-Africans.*

Justice and Political Transformation

Finally we shall briefly note a few of the values that have emerged from the example of the TRC process and our revision of the grammar of justice that may aid in the task of political transformation and that makes understanding this process so important for cross-cultural philosophy.

Wilhelm Verwoerd articulates two clear achievements of the TRC. First he says: "the relationship between amnesty, justice and the TRC can be seen as one of 'partial justice' rather than 'no justice'. Instead of regarding amnesty and the TRC process simply as a 'sacrifice' of individual justice, we may describe the TRC process as a 'principled compromise' which sacrifices some, but retains other, key elements of justice."[74] We have sufficiently supported this point and gone even further in looking at features of the grammar of "restorative justice" and in responding to some criticisms of the TRC process.

Second Verwoerd says: "From the perspective of 'restorative justice', the TRC is not a 'second-best option' but a contribution to a different, more complete kind of justice."[75] On this point we have linked the concept of restorative justice with its larger communitarian context and with such notions as forgiveness, self-esteem, compassion and mercy. We have also seen how the TRC's notion of justice is illuminated by comparing it with the more communitarian, "compassion-based" justice found in Simone Weil and others whereby justice requires compassion and mercy and a sense of obligation to the overall well-being of one's community.

It may not be self-evident to everyone that a community, compassion-based justice system is better than an individual, rights-based justice system, nor that restorative justice is of greater value than retributive justice. But if one wants a system of justice that "aims for moral outcomes," or as Seneca suggests a legal system that "cultivates humanity" and moves away from cruelty or retributive anger,[76] then there is every reason to include mercy and move toward a compassion-based, restorative justice system. There is surely a case to be made for the greater value in "restoring" a community, compassion-based justice when a society has been fractured and great harm done to its people, and when there is some evidence that traditions in the local society suggest communal-based democratic structures even if they have been badly bruised or fragmented. In such cases there is more likely to be a prospect for civic cohesion and greater openness to reconciliation. In the South African situation—and indeed in most human societies—it seems both plausible and preferable to opt for a "restorative" rather than a "retributive" kind of justice. This was "the best option" given the political realities of South Africa's peaceful, negotiated transition and the open and transparent process of its Truth and Reconciliation Commission. Likewise, other democratic societies—especially those societies that are multicultural in nature—could benefit from a compassion-based, restorative justice system. In societies in which differences must be respected and in which there is a continual need for reconciliation, a compassion-based system of justice would best serve the end of greater justice, in its broadest sense, for all.

It does not seem too difficult to see the relationship of justice to truth and reconciliation once the concept of justice is "restored" to the wider grammar that it deserves. The manner in which truth and reconciliation were both conceived and revealed in the TRC process brought out its connection with this wider conception of justice by focusing on human injustices and listening to the cries of the afflicted. *This public process fore-*

*closed the culture of deception that apartheid had perpetuated, and intro-
duced a culture of truth-telling and a desire that all members of society
would accept responsibility for building a peaceful and democratic
future.*[77]

Although it is true that "not all storytelling heals," the TRC, as was
noted in chapter 4, gave credence to the value of the stories told. "Each
story provided a window into the past, thereby contributing to a more
complete picture of gross violation of human rights in South Africa . . .
[and] sharpened the moral conscience" of the nation. Furthermore, the
stories help us remember. "We must remember because remembering is a
moral duty," said Paul Ricouer. "We owe a *debt* to the victims. And the
tiniest way of paying our debt is to tell and retell what happened [to
them]. . . . We learn from a Jewish story-teller like [Elie] Wiesel that the
horrible—the inverted image of the admirable—needs to be rescued still
more from forgetfulness by the means of memory and narration."
Wilhelm Verwoerd concludes from this that "the moral duty to remember
the victims and to rescue the horrible from forgetfulness should be the
primary lenses through which we should read this complex process [of the
TRC]."[78]

In addition to providing us with "a more complete picture"—the revelation of truth—and sharpening a nation's "moral conscience," the storytelling during the TRC process provided civic life with the possibility of a
new moral discourse. A conversation has begun "between strangers," noted
Fanie Du Toit, and "some of the radically different discourses in South
Africa public life did indeed start a dialogue with one another in a peace-
able way during the proceedings of the TRC, and they continue. In this way
despite the pain of meeting the stranger, a certain hope was created in many
citizens in South Africa. . . ."[79]

All of this being said, the TRC process is not sufficient to bring about
reconciliation or social transformation in South African society. Nor was
that its intention. Charles Villa-Vicencio, the former Director of Research
for the TRC, says clearly that "the Commission from the outset defined
itself as *simply contributing towards* the laying of a foundation on which
national unity and reconciliation *could* be built."[80] It existed to "promote"
national unity and reconciliation and must be joined by government,
NGOs, and the private sector to move toward greater unity and reconciliation and a new sense of civic responsibility. President Thabo Mbeki has
always said that there can be no reconciliation until major transformation
to majority governance and greater economic and social equity are
achieved. He wrote: "[T]rue reconciliation can only take place if we succeed
in our objective of social transformation. Reconciliation and transformation should be viewed as an interdependent part of one unique process of
building a new society."[81] Conversations that have begun between
strangers must be sustained and a mechanism to enable and encourage
people to continue telling their stories must be created; "the yawning gap

between rich and poor in South Africa simply must be bridged," and democratic institutions must be strengthened.[82]

Priscilla Hayner, in her *Unspeakable Truths,* discusses over twenty Truth Commissions that have taken place since the mid-1980s. Each had (and continues to have) the tasks of establishing the truth about past "gross human rights violations" in a country and strengthening democratic institutions. Those that have been relatively successful in promoting some form of reparations and reconciliation and perhaps less successful in bringing perpetrators of crimes to accountability are Chile, Argentina, El Salvador, Guatemala, and South Africa. Their individual successes and limitations continue to be the subject of intense debate in human rights and philosophical circles around the globe. Because South Africa's TRC was the most public and publicized and involved a large number of its citizens it has received the most attention. The moral issues these commssions have raised around amnesty, justice, reconciliation, and the rebuilding of civic peace and order have revitalized cross-cultural philosophy in the past decade. Hayner's book not only lays out the landscape of these commissions, it raises important philosophical questions that must be confronted on every continent.

The importance of gaining a perspective and coming to understand such moral concepts as suffering, poverty, reconciliation, and justice in various African contexts cannot be overemphasized, especially for non-Africans who wish to understand the African condition. These concepts among others provide us with a way of reading the postcolonial African situation. To have suffered such affliction as apartheid requires that one "read" the human condition in South Africa and elsewhere on the subcontinent of Africa "through the wound," in the words of theologian Walter Brueggemann.[83] Such a reading of history "through the wound" requires that we listen to the cries of injustice and "find words for that cry of Nomonde Calata" and so many others. Brueggemann believes that all the social history of the twentieth century must be "read through the wound." It is such a reading that gave rise to liberation theology in Latin America, to the African-American civil rights movement, and to the women's suffrage and liberation movements. When this is done a new recognition of the marginalization of people is seen, injustices are given voice, and new hopes arise. That the cries and voices of the suffering and some perpetrators were *actually,* and publicly, heard and recorded is not only central to *truth,* but also to the concept of "restorative justice" and reconciliation as conceived by the Truth and Reconciliation Commission.

A fundamental and persistent problem in our understanding the affliction of African people, or their sense of reconciliation in the face of that affliction, is our own lack of experience in being afflicted. In our more affluent non-African settings we lack the experience of being touched by suffering or poverty, of being a slave, or of reading the human condition "through the wound." This hinders the prospect of a two-way conversation. We can listen to Soyinka, to Krog and Tutu, to Sen and Edward Said, to Fanon and to the stories of the wounded, and perhaps feel our discomfort in hearing them, but may still not be moved to understand. These voices are drawn forward to engage us in the conversation. Because of our bereft capacity to understand directly, we must seek some *imaginative transfers* in experience. Here is where the "narrative" aspects come into play with philosophical reflection, where personal stories, literature, and art may enable us to see and hear another's world, where another's life may enter our own.

6.

Narrative in African Philosophy
Orality and Icons

[S]tories are at the heart of what explorers and novelists say about strange regions of the world; they also become the method colonized people use to assert their own identity and the existence of their own history.... The power to narrate, or to block other narratives from forming and emerging is very important to culture and imperialism....

—Edward Said[1]

Just as we said that Africa's interface with European modernity is itself a philosophical text to be read, critically appraised, and understood—as part of "postcolonial African philosophy"—so, too, African literature is a central part of that text. We share in forming and expressing our particular life-worlds through our narratives, as Said says. It is through such narratives that we see both the uses and abuses of power and human identity. Out of the liberation struggles come the poetry, the stories, the telling of Africa's suffering and indignity. From the cries of injustice, the memory and narration, come a new and broader sense of justice and the hope of the transformation of communal values to engage modernity. This "telling" from these "texts" is part of the narrative enterprise that is the "memoir" and "diary" for philosophy. Philosophy takes account of the contexts in which the conversations of human life take place. It is this aspect of philosophy that is expressive of varied ways in which human life is articulated— the values, ideologies, and truths of individuals and communities. It is the narrative aspect of philosophy that ties it to a culture and gives it its existential texture. It is also the narrative aspect of philosophy that preserves it from abstraction.

Among the central kinds of narrative texts in Africa and of particular importance to philosophy are those to be found in its oral traditions and in its recent literature and art. Furthermore the development of civil society in particular African nations needs to be tied as much to patterns found in local council structures and the rational dialogues of village palavers as to either one party or multiparty democracies or to Western social engineers. To call forward traditions of orality alongside art and literature and explore how these contribute to an African philosophy may be anathema to some like Hountondji, but I believe they are essential to grasping the present African reality, especially if the grasp is from outside the African context.

As was stated in our first chapter, it is the "narratives," both oral and written, that enable us to *see and hear* the realities that are African. These narratives are an aesthetic entryway into African experiences "as they are." It is the varieties of narrative forms that enable non-Africans to encounter "an aspect of" a particular African experience. Through such narratives I am, as Wittgenstein noted, presented with "a definite sense" of what a particular African self-expression is and, furthermore "I [can] perceive it." Such narratives are "instrumental inflections" for seeing the truth. They, in the words of Annie Gagiano, "project . . . the anguish of the actual in a way that the theoretical discussions of the same issues cannot achieve, making possible a kind of understanding not . . . accessible by other means—something *akin* to a 'participatory' understanding. . . ."[2] By seeing specific African realities through the eyes of its own many voices, understanding them will be more than just hearing my own voice; I will be able to participate in them and respond to them.

This is all related to what it means to approach the nature of our understanding from *an aesthetic point of view*. The very order of being in the world is like an intricate weave of perception and response, of reacting and embracing the world we see, and familiarizing ourselves with (or reading) the grammatical background found in the particular experiences of our life. The point of departure of an African's *seeing* of her world may be different from my own, but as it is narrated it is the point of access that I have for understanding it. It is through our aesthetic consciousness that we see the reflexivity of our human being and the dialogical nature of our knowing and understanding of the world, however "strange" it may appear to us. In this chapter we will encounter a multiplicity of kinds of narratives from oral to written to iconic forms. In exploring each kind and their relationships to one another we may catch a glimpse of Africa unfolding before our eyes over the past centuries, and in so "glimpsing" and "responding" our knowledge and understanding will be formed and enhanced.

The Philosophical Significance of Oral Narratives

Philosophy invites dialogue in order to draw us toward understanding one another; dialogue encourages both attention to, then active participation in, the particulars of the world in which we find ourselves. Africa's reality has its own particulars that command attention to grasp its complexity. We could say that Africa's narratives (whether written or oral) are like its private diary open to public scrutiny, inviting us to enter into conversation with them and to react toward them. Africa's oral narratives actively and critically involve their participants in a dialogue in which many questions are posed but for which not all the answers are directly supplied.[3] To listen to these narratives even if once or more removed from them shows the critical level of their operation and reveals their significance for philosophy. We have already hinted that this dialogical process is suggestive of a Socratic dialogue. This, of course, should come as no surprise. Socrates, in fact, provides us with *an oral "master class"* in what philosophy is—an example of a philosophical text *par excellence*—and thus gives us an important example for comparison with other kinds of oral narrative situations.

We do have some of Socrates' "master classes" recorded by Plato in the only manner possible—as conversation or written dialogue—to capture its immediacy and existential engagement for those who may wish to "listen in" a generation or more later. Africa's "fictitious literature" functions in much the same way—it engages the reader, enabling her to "listen in" and respond in a critical-dialogical manner. So too do the oral narratives of Africa's *philosophical sages*—those who Odera Oruka said were "thinkers," not just storytellers. We will now look at the philosophical nature and significance of some of these forms of narrative: the oral tradition in its sage and community palaver contexts, in contemporary fiction writing, and in art and other iconic forms. The intention here is to extend what is discussed in African philosophy as "the oral tradition in philosophy" to what I more broadly call *narrative* in African philosophy and the place of our aesthetic consciousness in understanding those narratives.[4]

As we saw at the end of chapter 2, Socrates as philosophical sage sought to elicit and challenge alternative views on issues of moral and civic importance. Though we certainly must accept the notion that without Plato, Socrates would be at best a faint memory, we can also construct from the early Platonic dialogues a picture of Socrates' philosophy that has some autonomy from Plato's philosophy. Even though we are indebted to Plato's transcriptions, the Socratic philosophy is philosophy in *an oral mode* and is not strictly dependent upon Plato's criticisms. Initially, Plato sought to render Socrates' thought in its oral mode by reconstructing it in dialogue form—a distinctive tribute to Socrates' particular form of oral reflection. In the Socratic dialogues, Socrates' philosophy has its own internal narrative life. Socrates, *as oral philosopher*, makes his way into subsequent philosophical history independent of Plato as his critic and he gives shape to a distinctive philosophical style. Socrates was not only engaged in doing philosophy with his fellow citizens in the streets of Athens, but the very form of *elenchus* caught in his dialogues and the literary form of dialogue itself shaped the thought of scores of philosophers who followed him in a distinctly Socratic mode. Even though we have a *written* literature from these followers, they were engaged in the active search for truth and trying to justify and ground the concepts of justice, virtue, piety, beauty, knowledge, and truth, in a manner reminiscent of the *oracular* lifelong quest of Socrates in the *agora* of Athens and thus hoping to draw the reader into the dialogue.

What is specifically philosophical in the situations that give rise to Socratic discourse? The situations that forced dialogue for Socrates were what I would call narrative situations common to ordinary life. Euthyphro sought to justify his court actions against his father's alleged crime, and subsequently got caught up by Socrates in his lack of clarity in the use of religious law over philosophical reflection in deciding what was the just course of action. Gorgias strained to provide some substantive foundation for his rhetorical exercises and discovered that rhetoric itself may be empty of content and may be of little concern to determining what is a "good" course of moral action, and Polus, Gorgias' student, when confronted with the prospects of suffering, would choose evil over good to preserve his pleasures and avoid suffering. Protagoras and Callicles wrested power for themselves on the grounds that self-interest took precedence over concern for one's society. These views and others were challenged by Socrates, drawing the reader into the dialogue. He wanted to get to the root of, or at least render problematic, why one might choose evil rather than good, or self-interest over the interest of the whole of the community, and to see if justice is truly served by such choices. The ordinary struggles of human life are played out in these narrative situations—popular views are expressed, disputes are put forward, and human concerns are voiced. A narrative situation, if it is to be of some philosophical interest, will generate discussion leading toward alternative views, resolutions to the disputes, or just solutions to expressed human concerns. As noted earlier, each new situation that forces such dialogue in a critical fashion is the narrative "stuff" of philosophy.

Rational Dialogue, Democracy, and the Village Palaver

If we search for what kinds of narrative situations force critical dialogue in the African context we need not look far. We have the numerous examples of philosophical sages given us by Odera Oruka and others. But perhaps as unique in rural African society, and certainly more widespread than the voice of a philosophical sage, is the village palaver. The village palaver forms a foundation stone of African civil society and is a very interesting form of local democracy. The very nature of village life yields many such critical dialogues. A property dispute is brought before the elders and debated— why? So justice can be served. When concern for illness or a community crisis arises, we might ask why a diviner, prophetess, or healer is called or a council is convened? To determine the cause of the illness or the reason for the crisis is not merely to commiserate or "spirit" them away. It is not too much of a stretch to see the public hearings and testimony of victims in local communities made possible by the South African TRC as a kind of palaver. Whole communities gathered at the hearings in support of one of their own members who had been a victim. If not quite a palaver, the TRC testimonies and stories were certainly a narration of a nation mourning, inflecting its pain and suffering. It was a bit of philosophical orature, shaping and reshaping the ethical landscape of remorse, reconciliation, mercy, and justice. The village palaver or council model in many parts of Africa is a model of free discourse for the purpose of making good judgments and for doing justice for individuals and the community. These narrative situations force dialogue and give rise to human reflection, and they are far from uncritical. Each dialogical situation has earmarks of the Socratic enterprise; each is formative of the values characteristic of that community; each reflects the existential texture of human life; each dialectically serves to move a community from injustice to justice, from wrong to right, from brokenness to wholeness, from ignorance to truth. As each community revaluates its life in terms of new external factors, it can critically evolve its traditions to meet modernity.

There is an Akan proverb that Gyekye cites: "Wisdom is not in the head of one person." It is certainly not clear that when one speaks of "democratic" roots being found in village governance and symbolized by the village palaver, that this closely resembles what is called liberal democratic institutions in the West. It is, however, not a long stretch to discuss the nearness and overlapping values of each. These connections Gyekye discusses in his chapter 4, "Traditional Political Ideas, Values, and Practices," including critics within the African context. His evidence points to "democratic features of the indigenous system of government," and suggests an ethos for the development of a more modern democratic form of governance. What is meant by "democratic features" here? Gyekye says simply: a democracy is government of, by, and for the people, and in Africa that means involvement of and by all the people in the decision-making processes concerning their general welfare.

A feature of this involvement is the extent to which the people participate at the level of village life through palavers or as represented in village councils. Gyekye cites Ndabaningi Sithole as saying: "Those who have lived in Africa know that the African people are democratic to a point of inaction. Things are never settled until everyone has had something to say. [The traditional African] council allows the free expression of all shades of opinions."[5] This simplified response does not necessarily make the practice of such a palaver either "democratic" or "philosophical." It does, however, suggest that beyond "a point of inaction" some due process may be taking place and extensive consideration is given to the important issues concerning village life—issues such as fairness, equality, kinds of punishment, general welfare, and the just resolution of disputes. These are, of course, the very issues of concern in all the recent studies of justice in Western philosophy, i.e., by Rawls, Nozick, Dworkin, Sandel, and others. To say this does not make the village process philosophical, but if one were to look at the individual issues taken up by a village council or sifted through a village palaver, those issues could be used by philosophers in ways that would lead to the gradual development of better governance. Let us look at a few examples to see how this may be the case.

Kwasi Wiredu in his essay "Democracy and Consensus" has some critical insight into how traditional political patterns may be instructive in thinking about general reform of governance in parts of Africa. He says, for example, that the Ashanti traditional system of governance was a "consensual democracy," and that this is different from the "majoritarian democracy" imposed upon them and others by Western colonial pressures. The latter encourages democracy under a multiparty structure and has, not surprisingly, led to "frustrations and disaffections," leaving minority parties "outside the corridors of power." This has only exacerbated ethnic rivalries, as "parties" in the "multiparty" system have tended to fall along ethnic lines to serve local interests. The elected, majority party, however, makes all the rules to serve its interests. Wiredu sees this as "the most persistent cause of political instability in Africa."[6] A similar and expanded version of this thesis is developed by political theorist Mahmood Mamdani in *Citizen and Subject*. What Mamdani calls the "decentralized despotism" imposed by late colonial rule in Africa was a primary cause of ethnic rivalry in contemporary social and political life. The legacy of decentralized despotism, furthermore, is not a natural evolution of "traditional" governance patterns in Africa but is a construct of colonialism in order to control the "native problem." Mamdani, like Wiredu, sees this as responsible for much of the political instability in Africa.

A consensual democracy, according to Wiredu, is a much more representative form of government that necessarily must keep the interests of all the members of the society in mind. He says that the consensual model was a premeditated form of governance, and is actually widespread in traditional African society. He provides this example to illustrate one of its best features:

> [It] is given expression in an art motif depicting a crocodile with one stomach and two heads locked in struggle over food. If they could but see that the food was, in any case, destined for the same stomach, the irrationality of the conflict would be manifest to them. But is there a chance of it? The Ashanti answer is "Yes, human beings have the ability eventually to cut through their differences to the rock bottom identity of interests." And, on this view, the means to that objective is simply rational discussion. Of the capabilities of this means the Ashantis are explicit. "There is," they say, "no problem of human relations that cannot be resolved by dialogue."... So much did the Ashantis (and the Akans in general) prize rational discussion as an avenue to consensus among adults that the capacity for elegant and persuasive discourse was made one of the most crucial qualifications for high office.[7]

Furthermore, Wiredu says, "On the Ashanti view, substantive representation is a matter of a fundamental human right."[8] And he concludes this point by saying:

> The Ashanti system was a consensual democracy. It was a democracy because government was by the consent, and subject to the control of the people as

expressed through their representatives. It was consensual because, as a rule, that consent was negotiated on the principle of consensus. (By contrast, the majoritarian system might be said to be, in principle, based on "consent" without consensus.)

    ... For all concerned, the system was set up for participation in power, not its appropriation, and the underlying philosophy was one of cooperation, not confrontation.[9]

Another example of consensual governance is given by Mahmood Mamdani from a very different region and people from the Ashanti. Citing documents from a Transkei-based community organization in South Africa, these show the difference between a "traditional chiefship in the preconquest period with the one under colonial rule."

> The traditional chief functioned in "an advisory and consultative context, unlike the bureaucratic model imposed under colonialism." The administrative power of such a chief consisted mainly in "the right to allocate land," but it was a right exercised through a double consultation: "with his (sometimes her) counselors, but primarily in consultation with the wider community," for the chief was "the custodian" of the land, not its proprietor. And custody "could only be exercised through a consensus of the community as a whole." The ultimate popular sanction against a despotic chief was desertion: "You tried to increase your following, rather than encouraging desertion to a neighboring chief, or to a rival relative." Colonial conquest built on the administrative powers of the chief, introducing "a highly bureaucratic command-and-control system." Under apartheid, "the administrative powers of the chief were systematically strengthened" but were made accountable to "a new consensus" one that "emphasized the state as the determiner of the consensus."[10]

Mamdani makes a very strong case for how the colonials worked hard, using long years of experience in India and in colonies further to the north in Africa, to undermine the governance structures of the traditional preconquest periods. They did so in order to assert both local and national despotic control over the rural native peoples.[11]

    The point here, and in Botswana among Tswana and in the Kingdom of Swaziland societies as well, is that through councils and a variety of peer structures there were numerous checks and balances to a chief's garnering too much power and authority. Such public consensual forms of deliberation and governance were systematically dismantled by colonial administrations—"public assembly was turned into a forum where decisions were announced but not debated."[12] The colonial state reconstituted some "local structures" and "chiefs' authority" but retained a "veto" over all chiefly decisions. Mamdani concludes, "From African tradition, colonial powers salvaged a widespread and time-honored practice, one of a decentralized exercise of power, but freed that power of restraint, of peers or people. Thus they laid the basis for a decentralized despotism."[13]

    Let us look at a different and equally specific example of this form of oral narrative that also expresses its inherent philosophical and democratic characteristics. It is no secret that any written form, including the written dialogue, fails to capture a spirited, critical discussion among human beings. There is something linear about any written form that has difficulty capturing the layered planes and nuanced features of speech. Here the model of *a community palaver* in many traditional central African villages is instructive.

Ernest Wamba-dia-Wamba, with whom I have had several extended conversations on this issue, has observed that "the palaver is an appropriate community method and practice to resolve contradictions among the people and to strengthen organic mutual links of solidarity among all the members of the community."[14] The palaver is a means of "free" or "liberated" speaking by community members, but it is not uncritical or unreflective. If, for example, the equilibrium of a community is threatened, its causes may be identified and dealt with by calling a palaver. This becomes a forum for self-questioning of and by all the community members and it is rule governed "in a manner sanctioned by the ancestors."[15] Furthermore, there are usually leaders, the *Nzonzi*, who are known specialists or who emerge on the spot, as "masters of the clarification of speech." They function as competent handlers of

> dialectics; they are therefore dialecticians. . . . They are very able detectors of the divisive "bad word"—and stimulators of the palaver; they help assure that it does not degenerate into violent antagonism. They know how to make severe criticisms without offending or silencing the one criticized. . . .[16]

Wamba-dia-Wamba goes on to note that a good *Nzonzi*

> must know how *to listen* attentively and tirelessly; *to pick up* the essence of each word spoken; *to observe* every look, every gesture, every silence; *to grasp* their respective significance . . . and to elaborate . . . arguments to counter . . . unjust positions and/or to re-affirm or reinforce correct positions.[17]

In a word, *Nzonzi* are like Socratic midwives, guiding the palaver to just and wise conclusions.[18] The palaver clearly reflects *a philosophical situation*—it reflects a real critical effort on the part of its participants to resolve its common dilemmas.[19] Furthermore, like the Ashanti, consensual model of community governance, the village palaver in central Africa is an exceptionally democratic form of local governance. In the palaver can be found a rich source for philosophical reflection in the African context that critics of orality, like Hountondji, underplay and at times scorn even though they lay claim to a form of philosophical reflection of a Socratic nature. These are more than just "philosophical fragments from our oral tradition." They are the self-expressed forms of life of Africans; they are embedded forms of rational discourse that democratically order their lives.

It is from such local, human narrative situations as these examples illustrate that the narrative aspects of philosophy arise. If, as Hountondji says, philosophy "writes its memoirs" and "keeps a diary," then such a memoir or diary must include the sharpest oral "ruminations" about human life. A memoir or diary is a narrative, and a philosophical memoir or diary does not change its narrative character; rather, it reflectively streamlines the life story to a more self-critical and pragmatic form. There are differences between the narratives of a palavering community, the narratives of literature (epic, fiction, drama), and what Hountondji calls "critical" philosophy, but their differences are not simply those between *art* and *science* as he suggested. The multiple narrative aspects of philosophy often reflect the manner in which both art *and* science are woven into the fabric of life. In coming to terms with what something *is* and how it presents itself *for* understanding, philosophy cannot make a sharp distinction between "artistic" and "scientific" literature. This is clearly and dramatically illustrated through a wide range of ritual actions in the African context.

Although it is certainly true, as Fanon said about thirty years ago, that "African culture will take concrete shape around the struggle of its people," that struggle is also expressed by and lived through the manifold forms of their local democratic traditions. It could be said that such traditions are expressive of the people in similar ways to their "songs, poems and folklore." These are part of the memoir that is Africa's philosophy; they are part of the conversation, both oral and written, that Africans must keep going in a creative fashion and to which non-Africans must attentively listen.

I want now to turn to the uses of African literature, especially fiction writing, as a crucial narrative component of African philosophy.

Finding Pictures and Fictitious Narratives "Surprising"

Wittgenstein writes in the *Philosophical Investigations* (a book normally understood as dealing exclusively with the philosophy of language and the philosophy of psychology):

> Don't take it as a matter of course, but as a remarkable fact, that pictures and fictitious narratives give us pleasure, occupy our minds.
>
> ("Don't take it as matter of course" means: find it surprising, as you do some things which disturb you. Then the puzzling aspect of the latter will disappear, by your accepting this fact as you do the other). [Wittgenstein, PI, 524]

Once again Wittgenstein causes us to turn our heads and take note of something we might easily not have seen. "Find it surprising," he says, those "fictitious narratives that give you pleasure"—don't take them as a "matter of course." They are not. They are expressive of a culture's contemporary reality—of particular African realities in our case. The narratives tell us what is its suffering, its colonial and postcolonial alienation, its democratic struggles. Africa's reality in its many and diverse local circumstances should be taken as "a remarkable fact," challenging our prefigured biases and asking us to "occupy our minds" with its particulars of life as well as our own, because the two are irrevocably intertwined with one another.

What Wittgenstein is saying is that philosophy's *prose* is often unequal to the task of showing us what a thing *is*, and we must approach it from another angle, from the perspective of a parable or poem, a proverb or story—from the perspective of a "picture." The philosophical prose of much analytic and technical reflections, with its restrictive empirical norms, has lost the capacity to find the world surprising. In reaction, Wittgenstein insisted we take pictures and fictitious narratives seriously. He believed such pictures and narratives important to philosophy; indeed, philosophy should serve the same end as the pictures and narratives. Wittgenstein also compares, on the one hand, "propositions" [that well understood term that was paradigmatic to "meaning and truth-claims" among logical empiricists] and *how* they "picture states of affairs," *with*, on the other hand, "what a painting or relief [sculpture] or film does." The most "a proposition can do," he says, "is what a painting or relief or film does"—they *show* us something of our world (PI, 520).[20] "Propositions" and "pictures," then, are not so different in their application. "So why should not paintings and film be a part of our philosophy?" we might ask. In the two entries preceding his remark "find it surprising," of PI, 524, Wittgenstein says:

> If we compare a proposition to a picture, we must think whether we are comparing it to a portrait (a historical representation) or to a genre-picture. And both comparisons have point.
>
> When I look at a genre-picture, it "tells" me something, even though I don't believe (imagine) for a moment that the people I see in it really exist, or that there have really been people in that situation. But suppose I ask: "*What* does it tell me, then?" (PI, 522)
>
> I should like to say "What the picture tells me is itself." That is, its telling me something consists in its own structure, in *its* own lines and colours. (What would it mean to say "What this musical theme tells me is itself"?) (PI, 523)

What a picture tells us "consists in its own structure, in *its* own lines and colours." The same is true with a musical theme, or a ritual drama, or a novel, or a film, or an oral narrative—all tell us something about an aspect of the world in a manner that attempts to preserve its surprise. And the better the "iconic" form is executed, the greater will be its "surprise" or its "pleasure" or its "disturbance," and the more it will continue to "occupy our minds" (PI, 524). This is true of any culture's best iconic forms.

Furthermore, I can read the pictures or fictitious narratives from the place where I am and connect them up with their own context as well as my own. There is a far smaller epistemological gap in such iconic representations and ordinary human responses than is often suggested by relativists.

The Bushman or San rock engravings and paintings (dating back, in some cases, thousands of years, found in northwestern Namibia and elsewhere in Botswana and South Africa) are neither mysterious nor indecipherable in their own expression ("*their* own lines and colours"). They continue to "surprise" and "occupy our minds" in exciting and natural ways whether observed by oneself or a local herdsman.

Many narrative situations in African fiction can also "occupy our minds" in surprising ways; they mark important moments in the life of its people. Wole Soyinka sees in the contemporary African novel the human struggles that so deeply wound and constrain the current African reality; the novel can be a creative instrument for expressing the anger, the suffering, and the hope that is part of the African experience. Both the liberation struggle and the self-expression of the deepest values of its people are found in what Soyinka calls the culture's "iconic tradition."

An iconic tradition is more than a collection of artifacts, stories, symbols, and formalized ritual; it is a primary and reflective mode of human expression and, as such, is philosophical in nature—"compare a proposition to a picture," both have their point. Contemporary African fiction, ritual drama, music, and visual arts are not a spontaneous eruption of raw emotion. They express a highly structured and reflective life-view. They are, in Soyinka's words, "material evidence of the integration and cohesiveness of a culture *in situ* . . . they are celebrative instruments of an integrative world."[21] This, too, is the way Malcolm Ruel saw the Kuria ritual practices to function—as celebrative instruments of their ordered life.

Part of the narrative consciousness of a culture is its *aesthetic consciousness*, and the aesthetic consciousness of a culture is expressed through its iconic traditions. An aesthetic consciousness is itself a reflective consciousness—one step removed from the immediacy of sensible experience. An aesthetic consciousness orders sensible experience to express human hope and wholeness. When a work of art is produced from the aesthetic consciousness and displays only the fractured, disorienting, and suffering nature of human life, it is making a judgment on the culture that is itself fractured and hurting, pointing to the incompleteness of human life. Such a work presupposes a sense of what wholeness is and what the beautiful could be. Soyinka remarks that "the true icons of a people are themselves the repository of a worldly wise human history."[22] They have a sagacity that transcends time and cultures.

Soyinka gives special focus to the moral and metaphysical concerns of African people as expressed through their "fictitious narratives." He says—and this I believe a very important remark—that *an African philosophy, in its narrative aspect, should "translate the inherent or stated viable values of a social situation into a contemporary or future outlook."*[23] The "inherent or stated viable values" are those embedded in one's particular narrative situation, and the continuous translation of these values is, for Soyinka, a revolutionary activity. This translation is what he calls the "revaluation" of traditional values, and this revaluation requires the selective lifting up of the deeper [viable] traditional values of a community and recasting them to meet today's realities. There is more than a hint here of Nietzsche's notion of the "transvaluation of values" central to his *The Genealogy of Morality* and *Beyond Good and Evil* to be found in Soyinka's formulation here. This is a crucial element in linking local "fictitious narratives" with philosophical reflection.

One of the finer philosophical features of African "fictitious narratives" is shown in how African writers transform the orality of their cultures into a literary self-expression of the truths of ordinary human life. A people's earlier consciousness may resurface in a fragmented and fractured way both orally and in writing as a challenge to the alienation of their present reality. As this happens it creates the possibility of a disjunctive "leap" toward some "future outlook." There is no continuous, linear "stream" of consciousness that has moved Africa toward its postcolonial situation. Its iconic forms, fictitious narrative or "pictures," have been part of its "lurching" toward its future.

This is how I believe Soyinka's translation of the "inherent [traditional] values" function; they are selectively "revalued" to meet today's reality. "Tradition" is understood as embedded in the oral narratives that "catch-up" selective aspects of the "collective consciousness" of ordinary living: The orality of a sage retelling his community's stories and myths; the orality of communal governance in a village palaver; the orality of a Samburu *moran* (warrior) or Kuria warrior-youth competitively reciting (and dancing) a praise song, boasting of his virtues and courageous acts; an elder's self-praise at a beer party;[24] or a young Maasai woman's sung lament over losing a child. These are all transformed into a modern literary or iconic idiom by African writers and artists—consider the central role of the "Praise-Singer" in Soyinka's "Death and the King's Horseman," pricking the conscience of Elesin and reminding him of his moral and metaphysical duties. These transformations from indigenous oral resources to literary texts, for example, are not only central to literary critical theory,[25] but are important to our philosophical reflections on recent expression of African identity and the manner in which Africans form their responses to the postcolonial context. African writers and their texts (whether in indigenous or Europhone languages) speak with a special authority and are among the best resources available to non-Africans about the lived realities of Africans.[26]

These transformations are possible because of the aesthetic consciousness of writers. Their sensibilities are attuned to their particular world; they see and translate their world into words—they are the modern "smithies," word-smiths of their culture. The written texts imaginatively and metaphorically carry over the perceived connections of the narrative contexts in which the orature takes place. We have here examples of Wittgenstein's *"übersichtliche Darstellung,"* as discussed earlier, where what is in the narrative field of the person's experience is made transparent by being portrayed in a certain light so that its parts come together in a perspicuous way in the author's words.

We could also see this as a form of *translation* as discussed in chapter 1— the kind whereby the native writer views the world on the level of her own aesthetic experience, as "eye witness" within her culture, then transforms what is seen and heard into a literary form. This, too, involves the writer's aesthetic consciousness and imagination—a reflective consciousness one step removed from the immediacy of the sensible experience, ordering it and rendering it into words and pictures.

It is here that the concept of "narrative"—expressed in all kind of iconic forms—becomes important in our (a non-African's) understanding of "African" philosophy. The point of departure of an African's *seeing* of her world may be different in many ways from my own. Both the inherited background (the social history surrounding the slave trade and manifest forms of colonialism, present suffering, and poverty) and the postcolonial reality that shapes Africa's current social and moral environment must be made accessible to me if I am to claim an understanding of it. There must be ways in which I can listen to and hear the many voices of Africa and connect them up with my own understanding. As Edward Said wrote: "[S]tories are at the heart of what explorers and novelists say about strange regions of the world; they also become the method colonized people use to assert their own identity and the existence of their own history. . . . "[27] We share in forming and expressing our particular life-worlds through our narratives—that is common to our humanity. It is through such narratives that we see both uses and abuses of power and human expression.

Let us look at several specific examples in greater detail to see how this transformation from orality to "fictitious" literature has been made. Soyinka discussed Camara Laye's way of doing this in Laye's *The Radiance of the King* (1956). Laye, himself, said he was concerned with eliciting certain values from traditional society. "He was, he felt," says Soyinka, "initiating a process of revaluation which was itself revolutionary in the anti-colonial situation."[28] What Laye is doing is educating Western readers to the complexities of African life. Clarence (the white antihero of the novel) has revealed to him the complex art of drumming and this undermines both his arrogance and confidence. He is brought to see his own blindness to what is essential and subversive to even a menial "drummer-boy."[29] What was revealed was a subversive art, like the spirituals sung by African slaves in the American south. There is no reason why the same principle cannot be equally true in the "postcolonial situation." Soyinka's concept of revaluation of the *viable* values of traditional life—or just ordinary life—is developed in a manner that avoids the dangers of nostalgia for the return to "roots" and the various pitfalls of the theory of negritude or black consciousness. Heeding Fanon's warning, it must be continuously asked: How can one "enter into the African system of values" without being either too nostalgic or too adulatory? Soyinka's own plays and stories clearly show us how African fiction and ritual drama can provide a clear entry into deeper metaphysical and moral values that enable us to see possibilities for the revaluation of values in the contemporary contexts of our lives. His very notion of "revaluation" must first problematize the original values being examined.

We can see further how this mode of the revaluation of values takes place in Ousmane Sembene's novel, *God's Bits of Wood* (1970). Sembene moves beyond mere story telling to record "human strengths and weaknesses, heroism and communal solidarity. . . ."[30] He forces upon his readers a vision of "a new society in the process of coming to birth."[31] He does this by having Bakayako, a labor organizer on a colonial owned railway line, help his people find themselves by becoming aware of "the *missing* practices of his people,"[32] and restoring those practices that were found viable to the new situation.

In this revaluation, Bakayako represents a contemporary voice—an authentic African self-expression and has quite the reverse effect of the ethnophilosophical description of traditional values. Soyinka writes:

> Bakayako is portrayed as understanding and controlling the future (or at least the path towards it); he supersedes all existing moral authority and forges, through his inflexible will, the unique community of the Railway Line into a force that robs the other deity, the Colonial Super-reality, of its power.[33]

Sembene sees, as do many other African fiction writers, the necessity of liberating oneself from the values of others—namely, "the destructive alien intrusion" of Euroculture.[34] When this is done, however, some new values must be ready to fill the void. It is here that the "missing" practices of the people come into play—the consensus practices, the democratic processes of the village palaver—and, when revalued, constitute a new outlook "whose reference points are taken from within the culture itself."[35] This Soyinka calls a "positive apprehension" of a particular African situation—perhaps even a culture—and he tries to identify some of the values he sees as viable for revaluation just as we saw him and others in South Africa do with the concepts of forgiveness, mercy, reconciliation, and justice.

One of the consequences of "problematizing" precolonial or traditional values is that it forces harder reflection on what is said to be of value in them. What are taken as values in contemporary life are forged, not from "whole cloth," but woven from fragmentary strands of the memory of past values and the practical necessities of present life. The "fictitious narratives" are not without real value in recovering some of those fragmentary strands and they also try to reinsinuate such values as may be viable into the modern situation. What *cannot* be assumed is that there is a universal body of moral practices—a precolonial ethics—that will provide a model for today. What Soyinka means, and I think can only mean, by "revaluation" of traditional values, or Nietzsche by the "transvaluation of values," is the necessity of a more radical critique of values from all the material at hand (traditional, pragmatic, modern, postmodern) that will give coherence and meaning to life in one's present situation. That is what, in fact, is meant by a "genealogy of morality."

What makes traditional values problematic is not *just* that without written codes their transference to the present is unreliable. It is also that the process of colonization radically changed the social governance arrangements and ordinary life in African communities so much that what may have been thought to be "traditional" is no longer recognizable. For example, Ifi Amadiume, in trying to grasp the colonial impact on gender relations in the African experience, says we must look at the systems of power and ideology in gender relations and not just whether a society was a matriarchy or a patriarchy. The space of women may be more autonomous than recognized within a patriarchially structured system, and that there may be more equilibrium and tension in traditional life between genders than is suspected. She and Mahmood Mamdani believe "this autonomous space was uniformly destroyed by colonial rule. And in this sense the 'world historical defeat' of the female gender was experienced in Africa not as much with the onset of state organization as with the consolidation of the colonial state."[36]

A good illustration of this point of Amadiume is found in Chinua Achebe's *Things Fall Apart* in which we learn something important about "autonomous female organization" coexisting in a patriarchic system. Okonkwo, the tragic hero of the book, seems blind, even hostile, to the importance of women. Having been exiled to his Mother's clan homeland (Mbanta) for inadvertently transgressing a religious practice in his own clan home (Umuofia), he makes some new discoveries. The sagacious Mbanta elder, Uchendu, instructs his nephew Okonkwo as to why we say *Nneka.* Uchendu says:

> Why is Okonkwo with us today? This is not his clan. We are only his mother's kinsmen.... Can you tell me, Okonkwo, why it is that one of the commonest names we give our children is *Nneka*, or "Mother is Supreme"? We all know that a man is the head of the family and his wives do his bidding. A child belongs to its father and his family and not to its mother and her family. A man belongs to his fatherland and not to his motherland. And yet we say Nneka—"Mother is Supreme." Why is that?[37]

Okonkwo does not know the answer to the question. Uchendu instructs him by saying that the reason that they name so many children "Nneka" is to remind themselves of the importance of sympathy, suffering, love, and protection—values associated with mothers. There are other things that women do that lift up these values in their practices as well—all to the end of preserving the autonomous space and the importance of women within their society.

Ato Quayson in his recent book, *Postcolonialism*, helps us extend the philosophical possibilities for literature by showing how certain novels reveal "the intersection between the aesthetic and the political" and how this may "be fruitful for a *liberatory politics*."[38] The aim of this intersection of the aesthetic and the political is to show how the novel's "vision" (its way of seeing the world) can itself be transformative of a world gone awry. Quayson says that the novel becomes a possible "passageway beyond the 'nervous conditions' engendered by the incoherences of the African postcolony." He asks "in what ways literature is able to refract social reality while at the same time rendering such social reality unsatisfactory *and* encouraging us to find ways of transcending it."[39] This, too, is part of Soyinka's "self-apprehension" and "revaluation," to see one's local reality in its broken or alienated state and then devise ways to overcome it. For Quayson and Soyinka this requires that the novel first "dislocate" us from the "familiar" and then in unexpected (nonformulaic) ways "relocate" us in a newly, yet unimagined environment.[40] Here the local philosophy (ethical and political) becomes particularized. In this sense the narrative mode makes philosophical reflection concrete.

Returning to Sembene's *God's Bits of Wood*, we find first that the "hero" is somewhat mysterious—usually in the background—almost faceless, though not voiceless. This stands in contrast to Achebe's Okonkwo who is a "traditional" hero, a strong male presence and voice wanting to lead his people in open struggle with (revolt against) the new colonial intervention. Bakayako in *God's Bits of Wood* is more subversive. He "defamiliarizes existing categories" and what you see in Sembene's novel is the women coming forward to lead. Certain traditional categories are decomposed while at the same time new constructions reach beyond them. This is to "revision" the Africa postcolony and inject a new particularized liberating power. Soyinka might say that the strength of women was there all along but what was viable, but not often visible, gets revalued and made visible. In this way the aesthetic—in the form of a novel such as *God's Bits of Wood*—makes an ethical intervention (Quayson calls this an "ethical inflection") and introduces new moral possibilities for society; it diverts "attention from the incoherence and corruption of the state" and destablizes in the mind of the reader the political codes of the postcolonial state that is despotically ordered by male power. We are thus enabled to see an aspect of the African world differently.

Quayson, in concluding his account of how the aesthetic intersects politics, cites Ben Okri in an interview. Okri says:

> I've come to realize you can't write about Nigeria truthfully without a sense of violence. To be serene is to lie.... In an atmosphere of chaos art *has* to disturb something.... Now think of the fact that for anything new, for something good to come about for it to reach a level of art, you have to liberate it from old kinds of perception, which is a kind of destruction. An old way of seeing things has to be destroyed for the new one to be born.[41]

To give birth to something new, as philosophy should be trying to do with its critical conversations, aesthetic interventions are essential. They can operate at many levels, notes Quayson, not solely "at the level of the representational regimes, whether realist, magical-realist or otherwise, but at all the intersecting levels of language, characterization, generic conventions, moral frameworks and codes of spatiality and temporality. With these we may see the political and yet reach beyond its lulling seductions into another and hopefully more revolutionary under-standing."[42]

Still thinking of the relationship of "traditional" values "revalued," and of how "fictitious narratives" critically bring this to our attention, but turning away from the intersection of aesthetics *with politics*, let us look at another kind of literary example. This example returns us to our first concern of how it is that a "fictitious narrative" critically serves to bring significant philosophical issues to the surface and *the issue here focuses attention on the nature of the aesthetic consciousness itself in the African context.* Early in his novel *Ambiguous Adventure*, Cheikh Hamidou Kane has the sagacious Chief of the Diallobé people say and ask: "If I told them to go to the new school ... they would go *en masse*. They would learn all the ways of joining wood to wood which we do not know. But, learning, they would also forget. Would what they would learn be worth as much as what they would forget? I should like to ask you: can one learn *this* without forgetting *that*, and is what one learns worth what one forgets?"[43] *This* is the new way of the colonizer and *that* is the Diallobé's traditional way. In this question we have, as Wittgenstein said "A whole cloud of philosophy condensed into a drop of grammar."

It may be too late to assess the relative worth of *this* to *that*. What Africa mostly has now is *this*, and with it must move forward in its post-colonial reality. The Chief, of course, afraid of forgetting too much of who they are, has the prospect of a colonial education for the young of the village weighing heavily on his mind. He must take the matter to all his people for council. "The time has come," he says, "for our country to reach a decision. The chief of the Diallobé [in true traditional 'democratic' fashion] has said to us, 'I am the hand which acts. It is you, people of the Diallobé, who are the body and the brain. Speak, and I shall act.' What shall we say?"[44] They decide, with the persuasive voice of the Chief's older sister, the Most Royal Lady, to send their children to the new school, and their nephew Samba Diallo—in whose hands they believe the future of their people rests—learns *this* all too well and becomes alienated from *that*. Samba Diallo ends up a philosophy student at the Sorbonne and through an agonizing personal trial comes to realize that "he cannot go home again." He says one evening to African friends in Paris:

> It still seems to me that in coming here I have lost a privileged mode of acquaintance. In former times the world was like my father's dwelling: everything took me into the very essence of itself, as if nothing could exist

except through me. The world was not silent and neuter. It was alive. It was aggressive. It spread out. No scholar ever had such knowledge of anything as I had, then, of being.

After a short silence he added:

Here, now, the world is silent, and there is no longer any resonance from myself. I am like a broken balafong, like a musical instrument that has gone dead. I have the impression that nothing touches me any more.[45]

One could, I believe, make an interesting case for how Kane's narrative of the young Samba Diallo's visionary perceptions of how "everything took [him] into the very essence of itself," is very close to Martin Heidegger's characterizations of Truth as the "unconcealment" of Being or its "presencing." Samba Diallo's "knowledge," before his self-alienation, comes close to a "presencing" of or an "attunement" with his beloved land.[46] Samba Diallo's way of seeing the world affirms, too, the aesthetic consciousness as we have seen Wittgenstein characterize this. Samba Diallo's original way of seeing was like Wittgenstein's notion of "perception" and "natural reaction" and our presentness to one another—Samba Diallo's very being was like the intimacy of "going up to someone," or entering "my father's dwelling." It is here that he sees things "as they are," and in turn enables us [the reader] to see things "as they are."

Another point of philosophical interest in this "fictitious [though truth-revealing] narrative" can be found in Samba Diallo's ethical sensibilities and his sense of justice. These are closer to an ethics of caring and compassion than to a "rights-based" ethic. This moral tension creates an abyss for Samba Diallo that he can neither cross nor reconcile. If he did his dignity would be lost. He says: "I see very well what distinguishes us from them. Our first move is not to conquer, as they do, but to love. We also have our vigor, which takes us at once straight to the intimate heart of a thing. Our knowledge of it is so intense that its fullness intoxicates us. Then we have a sensation of victory. But where is that victory? The object is intact, the man is not stronger."[47] The West consumes the present and all that is in its path with "no break in its advance;" there is no room to love, only to conquer. Their victory either destroys or ignores all that Africa is, while Samba Diallo's "victory" leaves all its objects "intact." He cannot in the end answer the question that the Most Royal Lady put to him as he left for "the foreign school": "Go find out, among them, how one can conquer without being in the right."[48] It is as if an answer to this question could not register in the soul of the Diallobé.

There are many beautiful antiphonal moments in this "fictitious narrative" between the values of *this* and *that* which I will not recite here. What this profoundly philosophical piece of narrative, and the others we have briefly looked at, is telling us "consists in its own structure," as Wittgenstein said. It is in "its own lines and colors" that we find its interventions and "inflections" for liberation or for revelation of a piece of, or aspect of, African reality and for providing glimpses of a way forward in the post-colony.

Author Bessie Head calls herself a "dreamer and storyteller." She says of those who dream and tell stories that they "have seen life" at eye level and are "drunk with the magical enchantment of human relationships," and she notes that one "always welcome[s] the storyteller." And what do such dreamers and storytellers provide for us? "Each human society," she says, "is a narrow world, trapped to death in paltry evils and jealousies, and for people to know that there are thoughts and generosities wider and freer than their own can only be an enrichment to their lives."[49]

Storytellers, with their pictures and fictitious narratives [both oral and written], enrich our lives beyond our own narrow world. Thus I can see something of Southern Africa through the stories of Bessie Head, and she something of my familiar narrow world in the Southern United States, with its "paltry evils and jealousies," through stories of Flannery O'Connor or William Faulkner. Through these stories we can enrich each other's lives.

Head's stories tell of human innocence and the individual desires of women and men to neutralize evil and to love beyond and grow beyond their traditional village customs of arranged marriages, clan struggles, and communal taboos [see her stories "The Lovers," "Village People," and "Property"[50]]. She writes of the dignity found in poverty and humility—African virtues born of circumstances, and virtues, as we have noted, that free a human being for forgiveness and hope. The hope that grows out of this poverty may even bring about a revaluation of some economic practices.

The poverty of which Head speaks is partly imposed by colonial invaders. She writes: "thieves had stolen the land and were so anxious to cover up all traces of the theft that correspondingly, all traces of the true history have been obliterated. We, as black people, could make no appraisal of our own worth; we did not know who or what we were, apart from objects of abuse and exploitation."[51] Her works are portraits of the recovery of human worth. Annie Gagiano says of Head's novel *A Bewitched Crossroad—An African Saga*, that it can be read as a major act of reclamation. "It is a text which works throughout by recognizing all those rights and dignities which were denied by the colonial sneer and the settler's brutal greed."[52] Head was determined not to glamorize the black African, but rather "to insist on the deep human worth of the actual people and the need to portray their lives accurately."[53] Head wrote of the need to "[reclaim] that humility that has been trampled on and abused."[54] In *A Bewitched Crossroad*, and other works, power was recast in forms of compassion and dignity; her characters used power to humanize society.

This "unconscious dignity" among Africans is linked to their desire to avoid evil, whether by "spells" or "medicines," or by the avoidance of violence, or by accommodation to circumstances. Bessie Head's story "The

Power Struggle," about the avoidance of evil and the maintenance of dignity, begins:

> The universe had a more beautiful dream. It was not the law of the jungle or the survival of the fittest but a dream that had often been the priority of Saints—the power to make evil irrelevant. All the people of Southern Africa had lived out this dream before the dawn of the colonial era. Time and again it sheds its beam of light on their affairs although the same patterns of horror would arise like dark engulfing waves.[55]

The picture/story then painted/told of two brothers, Davhana and Baeli, and their rival struggle for power is a story of good and evil. The way this story is presented has an interesting parallel to Kierkegaard's account of the parable of Jesus at the house of Simon the Pharisee [Luke 7: 36–50] when an unnamed woman bursts in and weeps and anoints Jesus' feet with oil. Kierkegaard notes that the woman says nothing, that "she is what she does not say . . . she *is* a characterization, like a picture: she has . . . forgotten herself, she, the lost one, who is now lost in her Savior, lost in him as she rests at his feet—like a picture."[56]

Davhana, the symbol of the good, is also "like a picture" lost in life, forced to choose goodness over evil, peace over violence, life over power. It is his silent dignity that helps him avoid intrigue, and his actions to avoid evil are *his* "characterization." We *see* Davhana, like a picture, and react to what we see. He frees himself from burdens of power, like a child, to maintain a sense of innocence. It is such pictures that give us pleasure and cast a "beam of light" on goodness rather than evil, thus keeping a dream alive. In our reaction to such stories we have "made room for" aspects of Africa's vision; we have allowed Africa to come to us. In doing this we receive something from them to enrich our understanding and our lives. In this way the narrative in African philosophy instructs not only our understanding of Africa, but our own self-understanding.

Gagiano says of African fiction texts that many are "interactive with actual societies and circumstances;" they on the one hand, "eminat[e] from [their respective] societies," and on the other hand, "comment analytically on those societies."[57] As such they unveil truths of several African realities and are thus useful philosophical reflections on Africa itself. She sees many of the authors from whom we have drawn our illustrations providing "an inestimable spiritual as well as intellectual resource." By "spiritual" she means: "a) being inspirational; suggestive; encouraging; b) being concerned with the profoundest human needs—e.g., for justice; for acceptance; and for a recognition of one's identity and worth."[58] There is no mistaking the philosophical significance of this literature, critically addressing and rearticulating those issues central to the philosophical conversation taking place in Africa.

The temptation to generalize about "world-views"—African or Western or Oriental—recurs and is strong, and must be resisted. Better that we sit and wait for the storytellers to remind us of our "narrow worlds" *and* of "thoughts and generosities wider and freer than our own." Such wider and freer "worlds" we can see only if we are attentive and "full of innocence," and are not "trapped to death" by the paltry games of our adult, self-centered lives. Is not this a "universal" idea, born of being human, and not a local or exclusive "rationality"? Are not the notions of love and dignity, poverty and power common to humanity and expressed by "dreamers and storytellers" everywhere? Should we not find our whole world "surprising," even those things we claim to know by reason of "scientific certainty"?

Iconic Forms and the Aesthetic Consciousness Revisited

Let us ask again: "So why should paintings, sculpture, and film [music and dance] not be a part of our philosophy?" We have seen how "fictitious narratives" express aspects of African reality; now we will take a few examples from other iconic forms—specifically from music and sculpture. This will further our argument that critical aspects of literary (oral and written) and artistic genre are of significance for reading and understanding African philosophy. As with literature, iconic forms "occupy our minds" in "surprising" ways; they are a primary and reflective mode of human expression and, as such, may be foundational for philosophy. Again, this is not to say that all iconic forms have philosophical import, but insofar as they are "celebrative instruments" that give rise to critical judgments they do have such import. A substantial amount of African iconic forms are reflexive in this way, that is, they are expressive of and connect with our aesthetic consciousness; they give rise to new questions, interests, and ways of seeing, knowing, and acting in the world. In this sense they *are* philosophical.

There is *a critical reciprocity* in some iconic forms that open both the other's world and one's own. The world is, by and large, "before our eyes and ears" to see and to hear, to touch and feel, and thus potentially within our sensible grasp if we learn to approach it properly. John Chernoff says the following of his odyssey to West Africa to learn and understand drumming, and then interpret what he learned about African music to a "Western" audience. "Such an interpretation is an attempt to render the reality of a foreign culture in the world of our own understanding without absorbing or reducing the distinctiveness of that culture. Simply speaking, we describe and make sense of something different from us."[59] On the point of how a non-African should properly approach understanding African music, he writes:

> A Westerner who wishes to understand African music must begin with a recognition of his own fundamental attitudes about music so that he may adjust to a fundamentally different conception. [And then,] to understand

the artistry and purpose of the African musical event, it is necessary for him to sidestep his normal listening tendencies, slow down his aesthetic response, and glide past this initial judgment. The reason why it is a mistake "to listen" to African music is that African music is not set apart from its social and cultural context.[60]

Just "to listen" is not enough without understanding that African music mediates the life of its community.

Music and dance as they are conjoined throughout Africa, for example, are a literal "instrumental inflection" of the immediacy of human life. African music, says Andrew Tracey, is "designed directly to translate African thought into action and sound, . . . African music seems to express in a precise way some basic truths about what Africans consider important in life."[61] Among central truths "translated" in African music are "community" and moral "character." Chernoff says, "in the African context performance in music and dance respond ultimately to a single aesthetic concern, the realization of community," and also that "music making in Africa is above all an occasion for the demonstration of character."[62] And commenting on music and other iconic forms' larger philosophical meaning, Chernoff writes, "Africans use music and the other arts to articulate and objectify their philosophical and moral systems, systems which they do not abstract but which they build into the music-making itself."[63]

The idea of its philosophical meaning being built into the music making itself is important. This stresses the activity of music making—the fact that it arises from the forms of life being given expression and is critically refined in the process of performance through careful listening and responding on the part of the participants. In the midst of the ceremonial procession led by Elesin in "Death and the King's Horseman"—his entourage moving toward his intended death—Soyinka writes the following: "Elesin executes a brief, half-taunting dance. The drummer moves in and draws a rhythm out of his step. . . . He performs like a born raconteur, infecting his retinue with his humour and energy."[64] The two telling notions here that underscore the reflexive character of the dance/ceremony is the drummer "draw[ing] a rhythm out of [Elesin's] steps," and Elesin "infecting his retinue with his humour and energy" lending to the overall festivity of the event.

Drumming, as a primary instrumental form of African music, associated with dance and masquerading, translates in a visual and auditory manner particular living forms of a given community and involves all participants in the event physically and spiritually.[65] In so doing the music evokes our aesthetic consciousness, eliciting a kind of reflexive response that may then move us. It moves us, first to an understanding of the music's performative or ceremonial context and meaning, and then challenges our self-understanding. Through African music, says Chernoff, we "stretch and adjust" our capacity to understand.[66] Iconic forms, like literary forms, make possible "a kind of understanding ... *akin* to 'participatory' under-standing." Music and accompanying dance are perhaps the most complex and difficult of iconic forms in African life for non-Africans to understand. They are *an event in life*, and as such understanding them demands a certain involvement and intimacy—a participatory sensing, to modify Gagiano's remark about literature.

Given the acute "sensibility" factor, that one responds either in or to performance, that is, to the participatory nature of music making itself, implies a continuously critical act. Africans measure performance by their own critical standards of order and cooperation. There is always develop-ment to instruct and improve among performers (musicians, dancers, engaged bystanders) while participating, and thereby all are contributing to the success of the occasion. Chernoff writes:

> A good rhythm, if it is to enhance itself, should both fill a gap in the other rhythms and create an emptiness that may be similarly filled. One note placed at the right point in the music will prove the strength of the drummer more than the execution of a technically difficult phrase. The good drummer has the strength to listen to all the ongoing rhythms and still find a place to add his own beat, balancing his accents on the edge of disorder and confusion, rendering a complementary wholeness out of the separate and conflicting parts.[67]

This is not a matter of technique or technical skill as one familiar with Western music might think, it is a critical reflexive process, learned in *the conversation of performers* that is the music making. The drummer, for example, may draw a rhythm out of the dancer's steps and in so doing consciously contribute to the end of character making and community building. Tracey says of Chernoff's point: "it implies more than a musical relationship between players; it has to imply also a network of interper-sonal respect, a fine appreciation of others.... African music demonstrates a dynamic balance between the individual and the group, between depen-dance and independance ... it embodies human relationships as they ought to be."[68]

Returning to Soyinka's "translation of viable values into a contempo-rary outlook" (or revaluation of values) and Nietzsche's "transvaluation of values," it is clear that iconic forms function in a similar way to "fictitious narratives" in "telling" or "showing" aspects of African reality. African musical traditions have passed on from one generation to another the values of community and character. Music, poetry, and song have also acted as subversive forms to heighten a consciousness of resistance and revolt as we saw in discussing African liberation movements and the poetry of the negritude movement. In recent development in the musical traditions of South Africa we see what is called the "music *Indaba*" in response to apartheid and as expressive of the new South Africa.[69] The fusion of musical styles and traditions has been used to recover and reassert lost values. This fusion, says Ingrid Byerly, "can borrow from the past to actualize the present . . . it can utilize the past to reveal the present while creating a future."[70] In a similar vein, Chernoff says: "African musicians create in a balance through which they draw upon the depth of a tradition while they revitalize it and adapt it to new situations."[71] African musical traditions are rarely static, but always in the process of revaluation and development. The values in these traditions are transmitted only through the sensible means of performance and response, aesthetically involving its participants in the process. This "perceptively" transfers its most viable values through its particular sensible medium. The values present in the performance become for the viewer and hearer (African or non-African spectators) what can be grasped from an aesthetic point of view. The aesthetic consciousness is active here, both among the performers and between performance and spectators.

It is important in thinking about African iconic forms for philosophy not to impose a Western definition of "art" upon them, but to see them *in situ* and have our understanding of them shaped by their own context and self-expression. A good example of how *not* to understand African iconic forms—sculpture, for example—is to view it in a museum exhibit that has been selected and curated by "Western" art standards. K. A. Appiah provides us with a wonderful illustration in his account of an African Art exhibition in New York in 1987.

Among several co-curators selecting works for the exhibition "Perspectives: Angles on African Art" with curator Susan Vogel was Lela Kouakou, Baule artist and diviner, from Ivory Coast. Vogel qualifies the selection process in the following way: "In the case of the Baule artist [the only native African artist co-curator], a man familiar only with the art of his own people, only Baule objects were placed in the pool of photographs." At this point, notes Appiah, we are directed to a footnote to Vogel's essay, which reads:

> Showing him the same assortment of photos the others saw would have been interesting, but confusing in terms of the reactions we sought here. Field aesthetic studies, my own and others, have shown that African informants will criticize sculptures from other ethnic groups in terms of their own traditional criteria, often assuming that such works are simply inept carvings of their own aesthetic tradition.

Appiah continues [with a not-so-veiled sarcasm],

> Let me pause to quote further, this time from the words of David Rockefeller [another co-curator], who would surely never "criticize sculptures from other ethnic groups in terms of [his] own traditional criteria," discussing what the catalogue calls a "Fante female figure": "I [Rockefeller] own somewhat similar things to this and I have always liked them. This is a rather

more sophisticated version than the ones that I've seen, and I thought it was quite beautiful . . . the total composition has a very contemporary, very Western look to it. It's the kind of thing that goes very well with contemporary Western things. It would look good in a modern apartment or house."

Later Appiah concludes:

This Baule diviner, this authentically African villager, the message is, does not know what *we*, authentic postmodernists, now know: that the first and last mistake is to judge the Other on one's own terms. And so, in the name of this, the relativist insight, we impose our judgment that Lela Kouakou may not judge sculpture from beyond the Baule culture zone because he will—like all the African "informants" we have met in the field—read them as if they were meant to meet those Baule standards.[72]

So much for "perspectives" and "angles" on African art; we seem to be given only one angle. This exclusive Western "rational" point of view of Vogel's (not to mention the "ethnic criteria" of Rockefeller) is just nonsense. What makes Rockefeller's "culture zone" or "angle"—"the kind of thing that goes very well with contemporary Western things"—any more worthy than Baule's judgment? What warrants refusing Lela Kouakou a voice if your aim is to provide us with "perspectives"?

What is expressed in the art of a culture, in its iconic tradition, is not accidental. Nor is it simply the spontaneous expression of emotions and feelings; it is, rather, the conscious creation of considered and often wise reflections of a people on its age, and as such deserves to be taken seriously as part of the narrative portrait of the people's most important concerns. The "picture" or other iconic forms offers critical perspectives on our human being; they enable us, from an aesthetic point of view, "to get down upon the flat level of experience and interpolate [human experience] piecemeal between distinct portions of [our] nature," as William James once said.[73]

In African "iconic" traditions there are equally telling visual and aural arts where, as Wittgenstein said, "what the picture tells me is itself," and what these pictures tell us are *what that life-view is*. Now consider a different reading of a work from this same New York City African Art exhibition—a reading by an African-American and an African. One of its pieces illustrates the accommodative and integrative way in which African culture expresses itself and how it continues to "surprise."

African-American writer James Baldwin was one of the invited co-curators for the 1987 New York City exhibition. He selected a piece that alone was not "in the mold of the Africa of [an earlier] exhibition [entitled] Primitivism."[74] It was a piece labeled *Yoruba Man with a Bicycle*. Appiah notes what Baldwin said about it:

This is something. This has got to be contemporary. He's really going to town. It's very jaunty, very authoritative. His errand might prove to be impossible. He is challenging something—or something has challenged him. He's grounded in immediate reality by the bicycle. . . . He's apparently a very proud and silent man. He's dressed sort of polyglot. Nothing looks like it fits him too well.[75]

We have, above, commented on the attitudes toward this exhibition by co-curator David Rockefeller and also about the director, Susan Vogel's comments barring another co-curator, an African artist, Lela Kouakou, from selecting entries from outside of his own traditional area in Ivory Coast—he was not allowed to make a judgment on *Yoruba Man with a Bicycle*. What I want to emphasize here is the liberating effect that this one piece, which seemed to break the mold, had on Appiah (an African)—as it did on Baldwin, an African-American—and the surprising effect it would probably have on most viewers, African or non-African, who are attentive to it. Appiah's comments speak for themselves:

> I am grateful to James Baldwin for his introduction to the *Yoruba Man with a Bicycle*—a figure who is, as Baldwin so rightly saw, polyglot, speaking Yoruba and English, probably some Hausa and a little French for his trips to Cotonou or Cameroon; someone whose "clothes do not fit him too well." He and the other men and women among whom he mostly lives suggest to me that the place to look for hope is not just to the postcolonial novel—which has struggled to achieve the insights of a Ouologuem or Mudimbe—but to the all-consuming vision of this less-anxious creativity. It matters little who it was made *for*; what we should learn from it is the imagination that produced it. The *Man with a Bicycle* is produced by someone who does not care that the bicycle is the white man's invention—it is not there to be Other to the Yoruba Self; it is there because someone cared for its solidity; it is there because it will take us further than our feet will take us; it is there because machines are now as African as novelists—and as fabricated as the kingdom of Nakem.[76]

Baldwin's remark on this sculpture and Appiah's appraisal need little further comment. They show something profoundly true about the contemporary African self-image; they reflect "the imagination that produced it" and capture the "surprise" in the not-so-surprising fact of how much alike all human beings are and how our mutual understanding is never far away.

Yoruba Man with a Bicycle and African drumming both reflect a self-image of Africa *that is itself*; they reflect a self-image that is "surprising" and "truth-telling," and that evokes a sense of "innocence" in all viewers and hearers. They are pieces of the postcolonial African reality that speak of character and community in highly creative, artistic, and philosophical ways.

7.

Some Concluding Remarks

A recent graduate of my college spent the same time period in South Africa that I did (January to July 2000). We did not know the other was there. A difference in our experience was that I lived in a mostly white (Afrikaner) suburb of Cape Town while she lived in an all black (mostly Xhosa) township of Cape Town. We were only thirty minutes from each other, but in fact, two cultures apart. Both "aliens in a strange land"[1] trying to understand ourselves in response to our different worlds; both having to learn anew how to "go up to someone." Karen expressed her experience as follows:

> From my perspective, both before my time abroad and at present, there is no way—as someone far removed from that place—I can significantly do-good in South Africa. However, I can let others on the inside teach me and learn a lot about myself and my culture in the process. And perhaps that is where my hope for human progress and human understanding resides—no longer as an outsider but as a participant in a social, dialogic process.[2]

This expresses simply the cross-cultural thesis of this book. I have, however, given the reader a variety of African voices to learn from and respond to. I have organized these voices in order to narrate the debates going on among African thinkers around classical and contemporary issues in African philosophy. In this way perhaps the reader will become "a participant in the dialogic process."

We began by noting Peter Winch's concern that one must learn to see and "make room for" the other's concepts and categories as they *are* before one can make them one's own. Understanding African philosophy in this conversational mode points to its dynamic nature and underscores the reciprocity and balance of individual identity and community, of personal struggle and hope drawn from shared traditions. This is an underlying feature of all of contemporary African life. Understanding African forms of life requires non-Africans to listen to and see the many ways in which Africans express themselves, then to respond by finding in their own selves "landmarks" for self-understanding. This is the beginning of the conversation. By seeing Africa through the eyes of its multiple ways of "picturing" itself and hearing its own many voices, understanding will be more than just hearing one's own voice.

Our approach from *an aesthetic point of view* has been tied to the very nature of our understanding itself. The order of being in the world is like an intricate weave of perception and response, of reacting and embracing the world we see, and familiarizing ourselves with (or reading) the grammatical background found in the particular experiences of our life. This is, in itself, a philosophical conception of the world. How we go about the very activity of *understanding* has been at work throughout this book. It shows the reflexivity of our human being and the dialogical nature of our knowing and understanding of the world however "strange" it may appear to us.

Martin Heidegger once wrote: "Art is truth setting itself to work," and that the truth of art is a "presencing"—"the work as work, in its presencing, is a setting forth, a making."[3] Earlier we said of Samba Diallo's "world" that it had a "resonance"—like a "musical instrument"—between himself and his being-in-the-world. He had "a privileged mode of aquaintance" with it and set forth its truth. One could understand in Samba Diallo what Wittgenstein meant when he said "meaning is like going up to someone." The "world" or "worlds" out of which African life finds expression—in all its narrative forms—provide a surrounding from which the truths of Africa's reality is made present. Africa has its own particular modes of "presencing" itself, and this is part of its particularity that non-Africans must come to understand. The "world" or "worlds" out of which Africa's various "pictures" come are not to be thought of as a hegemonic Africa. The subcontinent and its cultures are too diverse to err in that direction. There are, however, many family resemblances among particular worlds. These resemblances are of significance for philosophy, for the very act of knowing and understanding another's world.

When non-Africans enter into the space of Africans they must be wary of becoming "like a broken balafong, like a musical instrument that has gone dead." We must, rather, allow Africa to "touch us," to enliven our imagination and our aesthetic sensibilities to its life. This can be done by giving proper attention to the many modes of Africa's self-expression. It is *the special task* of cross-cultural philosophy to equip a reader to be so attentive—to help a reader find Africa "surprising." It is *the ordinary task* of anyone who wants to approach Africa to do so with an open mind, a readiness for self-criticism, and a willingness for honest dialogue.

It certainly is true that under the pressures of "modernity" and "globalization," African economies and social structures—its ordinary life—are rapidly changing. The very fabric of African communal life in the post-colonial context is under great strain, and in many areas has all but disappeared. The *"illusion* of unanimism" with regard to the concept of community, for example, must be recognized. This, however, does not mean that the values that were once more integrally embedded in African communal life cannot be revalued in the continuous reconstitution of contemporary civic life. Nor does it imply that such values pushed forward in the "negritude movement," embedded in African "fictitious narratives," built into the structure of African music and iconic forms, and orally sustained in many rural patterns of governance do not have their philosophical significance. There is in each of these narratively expressive patterns the possibility of political, moral, and metaphysical renewal that may enrich human life. Each has its effect on our aesthetic consciousness and draws our responsiveness; each connects us with the familiar and grounds our humanness. These are not "passing" values (fashions of time and place); they are seeds that can take root (however barren the soil may be) wherever human beings seek to live creatively and at peace with one another.

notes

Preface

1. There were exceptions in terms of literary sources. I have mentioned Egyptian and Ethiopian texts (see especially Claude Sumner, ed. *Classical Ethiopian Philosophy*, 1994). Attention may also be drawn to Arabic influences on the many early texts (fifteenth and sixteenth centuries) found in Timbuktu and other Islam-influenced empires in West Africa. Although numerous early African scripts survive, few were put to philosophical-reflective uses. Attention should also be drawn to the important historical works of Cheikh Anta Diop, especially his *Precolonial Black Africa: A Comparative Study of the Political and Social Systems of Europe and Black Africa from Antiquity to the Formation of Modern States,* trans. Harold Salemson (Trenton, NJ: African World Press, 1987), and *The African Origins of Civilization: Myth or Reality,* trans. Mercer Cook (Westport, CT: Lawrence Hill, 1974).

2. Again, there are a few exceptions to be noted. Most important is the dialogue generated by eighteenth-century philosopher Anton-Wilhelm Amo with German philosophers. Amo was born in Axim, on the Gold Coast (now Ghana) in about 1703. He studied in Germany and taught at the universities of Halle, Wittenburg, and Jena between 1730 and 1740 before returning to his home in Ghana. Amo wrote a thesis of political and cultural value entitled "The Rights of Africans in Europe." See the essay by Paulin Hountondji, "An African Philosopher in Germany in the Eighteenth Century: Anton-Wilhelm Amo," in *African Philosophy: Myth and Reality*, 2nd. edition (Bloomington and Indianapolis, 1996), pp. 111–130.

Chapter 1: Understanding Another Culture

1. Ludwig Wittgenstein, "Remarks on Frazer's *Golden Bough,*" *The Human World*, no. 3, May 1971, trans. A. C. Miles and Rush Rhees, with an "Introductory Note" by Rush Rhees, p. 36. This English translation is also published with the German text by The Brynmill Press, 1979, without Rhees' long, but helpful Introduction. (Although most of the manuscript of Wittgenstein's remarks on Frazer dates from 1931, it was not published until 1967 and first appeared in English translation in 1971.) It is certainly one of the more interesting and imaginative discussions of issues in the philosophy of religion in Western literature since William James' *Varieties of Religious Experience* (1902).

   Citations to this work, to Wittgenstein's *Philosophical Investigations*, ed. G. E. M. Anscombe and R. Rhees, trans. Anscombe (Oxford: Basil Blackwell, 1953), and *Philosophical Occasions*

(1912–1951), ed. James Klagge and Alfred Nordmann (Indianapolis: Hackett Publishing Co., 1993), will be noted in the text as (RF, page) (PI, numbered remark or page), or (PO, page).

2. Peter Winch, "Understanding a Primitive Society," *American Philosophical Quarterly*, I, 1964. This is reprinted in Brian Wilson, ed., *Rationality* (New York: Harper Torchbooks, 1970). References to this essay will be cited from Wilson.

   Of special note is the response Winch drew from Alasdair MacIntyre. In fact, this debate was initially referred to as "the Winch–MacIntyre debate." Cf. MacIntyre, "Is Understanding Religion Compatible with Believing?" in Wilson. Seeds for Winch's procedure and this debate had been planted in Winch's celebrated book *The Idea of the Social Sciences and its Relation to Philosophy* (London: Routledge & Kegan Paul, 1958).

3. Three edited collections of essays trace and summarize this debate: Brian Wilson, *Rationality* (1970); Robin Horton and Ruth Finnegan, *Modes of Thought: Essays on Thinking in Western and Non-Western Societies (*London: Faber and Faber, 1973); and Martin Hollis and Steven Lukes, *Rationality and Relativism* (Oxford: Basil Blackwell, 1982). A critically illuminating essay on this entire debate, and one that offers some interesting conclusions, is Stanley J. Tambiah, "Rationality, Relativism, the Translation and Commensurability of Cultures," in Tambiah, *Magic, Science, Religion, and the Scope of Rationality* (Cambridge: Cambridge University Press, 1990), pp. 111–139. Robin Horton and his widely published essays did a great deal for raising the profile of a distinctively "African" philosophy among non-African readers.

4. Among the more important early essays by African philosophers to specifically respond to this "Western" debate were Robin Horton in the edited *Modes of Thought* (1973); Paulin Hountondji, *Sur la philosophie Africaine* (Paris: Maspero, 1976); Barry Hallen, "A Philosopher's Approach to Traditional Culture," *Theoria to Theory* 9, 1975, and Hallen, "Robin Horton on Critical Philosophy and Traditional Thought," *Second Order* 1, 1977; Kwasi Wiredu, "How not to Compare African Thought with Western Thought," in *African Philosophy: An Introduction*, ed. Richard Wright (Washington, DC: University Press of America, 1979); Kwasi Wiredu, *Philosophy and An African Culture* (Cambridge: Cambridge University Press, 1980); Henry Odera Oruka, "Four Trends in African Philosophy," in *Philosophy in the Present Situation of Africa*, ed. Diemer Alwin (Weisbaden, Germany: Franz Steiner Erlagh GmBH, 1981); and P. O. Bodunrin, "The Question of African Philosophy," *Philosophy* 56, 1981.

5. Winch, "Can We Understand Ourselves?," *Philosophical Investigations* 20 (3), July 1997, 198.

6. Winch, "Can We Understand Ourselves?," p. 197, my emphasis.

7. Winch, "Can We Understand Ourselves?," p. 203.

8. Winch, "Can We Understand Ourselves?," p. 193.

9. Clifford Geertz, "Found in Translation: On the Social History of the Moral Imagination," *The Georgia Review* 31, Winter 1977, 799.

10. See Paulin J. Hountondji, *African Philosophy: Myth and Reality*. In this second edition Hountondji replies to his critics on this point and clarifies his earlier position, now claiming: "Much controversy would

have been spared if I had written more cautiously. By 'African philosophy' I mean the set of philosophical texts produced (whether orally or in writing) by Africans" (p. xii).

11. Winch, "Understanding a Primitive Society," in Wilson, p. 102.

12. Anthony Giddens, *Sociology: A Brief but Critical Introduction* (New York: Macmillan Education, 1982), p. 20.

13. W. L. van der Merwe, "African Philosophy and Multiculturalism," *South African Journal of Philosophy*, 16(3), 1997, 76.

14. Winch, "Can We Understand Ourselves?" p. 197.

15. I started this process in my "Narrative in African Philosophy," *Philosophy* 64, 1989, 363–379, where I reviewed the current debate among African philosophers over whether philosophy must begin only with written, "scientific" texts of a culture as Paulin Hountondji argued, or whether philosophy may also arise from within oral, literary, and iconic forms as H. Odera Oruka and Wole Soyinka would claim. In this study I extend and develop the latter claim.

16. Wittgenstein, *Culture and Value*, ms 128 46: ca. 1944.

17. Stanley Cavell, *This New Yet Unaproachable America: Lectures on Emerson after Wittgenstein* (Alburquerque, NM: The Living Batch Press, 1989), p. 60. Cavell's reading of Wittgenstein on language is developed most fully in his "Excursus on Wittgenstein's Vision of Language," in *The Claim of Reason* (Oxford: Oxford University Press, 1979). Our view of Wittgenstein's procedure as "an aesthetic one" connects with Cavell's reading of Wittgenstein although it was developed independently. Cavell's reference to *Emile* is, of course, to Jean Jacques Rousseau's classic.

18. Winch, "Critical Notice" on Norman Malcolm, *Wittgensteinian Themes, Essays 1978–1989. Philosophical Investigations* 20(1) January 1997, 60.

19. Winch, "Critical Notice," p. 62.

20. For a full discussion of the nature of Frazer's explanations and their difficulties see Rush Rhees' "Introductory Note" to *Wittgenstein's Remarks on Frazer*. Also see Richard H. Bell, "Understanding the Fire-Festivals: Wittgenstein and Theories in Religion," *Religious Studies* 14, 1978, 113–124; Jonathan Z. Smith, "When the Bough Breaks," *History of Religions* XII, May 1973, 342–371; and Frank Cioffi, "Wittgenstein and the Fire Festivals," in Cioffi, *Wittgenstein on Freud and Frazer* (Cambridge: Cambridge University Press, 1998), pp. 80–106.

21. The German of this last sentence is: "Wir können uns nicht in sie finden." Although Ms. Anscombe's phrase "find our feet" is a good one here, more literally the German means "We cannot find ourselves in them," which has a closer resonance with the point we are making. Fergus Kerr drew my attention to this point.

22. Even though Soyinka wrote this play while in exile in Cambridge, England some four years after Wittgenstein's "Remarks on Frazer" had appeared in English, it is unlikely that he would have been acquainted with this piece. Soyinka, however, knew first hand how the world stood for the Yoruba vis-à-vis its former British colonizers.

23. Wole Soyinka, "Death and the King's Horseman," in *Contemporary African Plays*, ed. Martin Banham and Jane Plastow (London: Metheun Publishing Limited, 1999), p. 367.

24. Soyinka, "Death and the King's Horseman," p. 366.
25. See the dialogue in the play, pp. 355–358.
26. As a non-African trying to understand aspects of African cultures, in addition to attending closely to recent philosophical literature from Africa, especially those that will be noted throughout this study, I draw upon African fiction, poetry, and other "iconic" forms, twenty-five years of teaching African philosophy and religions, as well as four extended research periods in East Africa (Kenya and Tanzania) and Southern Africa (Namibia and South Africa) that have contributed some first-hand observations.
27. See Malcolm Ruel, "Icons, Indexical Symbols and Metaphorical Action: An Analysis of Two East African Rites," *The Journal of Religion in Africa* June 1987 98–112. Also collected in Malcolm Ruel, *Belief, Ritual and the Securing of Life: Reflexive Essays on a Bantu Religion* (Leiden: E. J. Brill, 1997), pp. 60–75.
28. W. L. van der Merwe, "African Philosophy and Multiculturalism," p. 77.
29. Ruel, "Icons, Indexical Symbols and Metaphorical Action," p. 107.
30. "Life-view," as here used, is similar to that used by Søren Kierkegaard in *On Authority and Revelation*, trans. Walter Lowrie (New York: Harper & Row, Publishers, 1966), p. 8. See also pp. 163–165 and 171–173. Kierkegaard was trying to understand why magister Adler who had a strange revelatory experience would express it as he did. Kierkegaard thought Adler lacked an appropriate "life-view" to capture the revelation he had—there was no living conceptual framework for his new experience to find an expressive home.
31. The argument in these last few paragraphs was first made in my essay "Wittgenstein and the Fire-Festivals," in *Wittgenstein and Kierkegaard*, ed. R. H. Bell and R. E. Hustwit (Wooster: The College of Wooster, 1979), pp. 85–106 (including "response" by David Burrell), and further developed in R. H. Bell, "Wittgenstein's Anthropology: Self-understanding and Understanding Other Cultures," *Philosophical Investigations* 7(4), October 1984, 295–312.
32. This last public hearing in mid-1997 brought to an end a unique experiment in South African history. The full transcript of this "Shepherd's Tale" is recorded in Antjie Krog, *Country of My Skull* (London: Jonathan Cape, 1998), followed by Krog's interpretation of it. See pp. 210–220.
33. Antjie Krog, *Country of My Skull*, p. 218. Krog also makes an interesting remark about the interpreter of Lekotse's "tale," Lebohang Matibela, and the kind of "translating" that she has to undertake to convey Lekotse's story. See p. 220. In a larger sense one could say that the white South African Security Police had no conception of what it meant to "go up to another human being."
34. Krog, *Country of My Skull*, p. 219.
35. This remark is from Wittgenstein's *Remarks on the Philosophy of Psychology*, Vol. I, trans. G. E. M. Anscombe (Oxford: Basil Blackwell, 1980), p. 961. Stephen Mulhall expands on the use of this notion from Wittgenstein in his *On Being in the World: Wittgenstein and Heidegger On Seeing Aspects* (London: Routledge, 1990), p. 188f.
36. Wittgenstein, *Philosophical Grammar*, ed. Rush Rhees, trans. A. J. P. Kenny (Oxford: Blackwell, 1974), p. 153.

37. See similar point in Fergus Kerr in his "Metaphysics and Magic: Wittgenstein's Kink," in *Post-secular Philosophy*, ed. Phillip Blond (London and New York: Routledge, 1998), pp. 244–247. Also see Richard H. Bell, "Religion and Wittgenstein's Legacy: Beyond Fideism and Language Games," in *Philosophy and the Grammar of Religious Belief*, ed. Timothy Tessin and Mario von der Ruhr (London: St. Martins Press, 1995), especially pp. 227–230.
38. Wittgenstein, *Philosophical Grammar*, p. 153.
39. I am indebted to Ato Quayson for suggesting the term "instrumental inflection" as one way in which philosophical status may be given to literature, or a way in which literature may serve as a reflection of the truth.
40. Annie Gagiano, *Achebe, Head, Marechera: On Power and Change in Africa* (Boulder, CO: Lynne Rienner Publishers, 2000), p. 35f.
41. Gagiano, *Achebe, Head, Marechera*, p. 37.
42. A good example of this kind of translating is found in Clifford Geertz' essay, "Found in Translation," pp. 788–794, where he begins with a long "eye witness" account "from a nineteenth-century Western writer on what is probably Bali's most famous, or notorious, custom"—a ritual sacrifice (called *suttee*) of young concubines at the funeral of the Rajah whom they had served. Geertz goes on to illustrate the whole range of problems inherent in all three kinds of "translations" in his essay and reminds us, elsewhere, that "cultural analysis is intrinsically incomplete. . . . And, worse than that, the more deeply it goes the less complete it is." [Geertz, *The Interpretation of Cultures* (New York: Basic Books, 1973), p. 29f.] He continually reminds us, as does Wittgenstein, of the multitextured nature of our language and how it manifoldly expresses a culture. His essay, "Found in Translation," is an important watershed in linking philosophy with cultural anthropology and literary criticism. I have discussed links between Geertz and Wittgenstein in my "Wittgenstein's Anthropology."
43. W. V. O. Quine, *Word and Object*, chapter 2 "Translation and Meaning" (Cambridge, MA: MIT Press, 1960).
44. Barry Hallen and J. Olubi Sodipo, *Knowledge, Belief, and Witchcraft: Analytic Experiments in African Philosophy* (London: Ethnographia Publishers, 1986). This book has been republished with a new Foreword by W. V. O. Quine and a New Afterword by Barry Hallen (Stanford, CA: Stanford University Press, 1997). The Afterword first appeared as "Indeterminacy, Ethnophilosophy, Linguistic Philosophy, African Philosophy," in *Philosophy* 70, 1995, 377–393. These quotes are from the Afterword, p. 130. All references are to the second edition of the book and its Afterword.
45. Geertz, "Found in Translation," p. 810.
46. Hallen and Sodipo, p. 36.
47. Hallen and Sodipo, p. 32.
48. Hallen, in his Afterword, tries to meet Hountondji's criticism, p. 141. We will discuss more of Hountondji's views in chapter 2.
49. Hallen and Sodipo, p. 138.
50. Hallen and Sodipo, p. 136. This, we should add, was true of most sub-Saharan arts and humanities faculties.

51. Hallen and Sodipo, p. 84. These are important findings since most Western analytic philosophers assume that "propositional attitudes" are the same everywhere, that is, they state what is the case (or claimed to be true) of the world they are said to assert in a more or less direct manner.
52. Hallen and Sodipo, p. 139f.
53. Paulin Hountondji, *African Philosophy*, p. 34.
54. Kwasi Wiredu, *Cultural Universals and Particulars: An African Perspective* (Bloomington, IN: Indiana University Press, 1996), p. 4. This book along with Kwame Gyekye's *Tradition and Modernity: Philosophical Reflections on the African Experience* (1997) and Kwame Anthony Appiah's *In My Father's House: Africa in the Philosophy of Culture* (1992) — curiously three Ghanaians — are three of the most striking and philosophically fruitful recent works in setting forward and critically analyzing the larger agenda and providing some methodological reminders for *doing* African philosophy, especially from within the English language tradition.
55. Wiredu, *Cultural Universals*, p. 4f. The project of Ngugi Wa Thiong'o for "decolonising our thinking," see his *Decolonising the Mind: The Politics of Language in African Literature* (1986), is a serious and challenging one. Ngugi's argument is, however, more appropriate to creative "literature" than to philosophy per se. Wiredu does say that "Sooner or later African philosophy will have to be done in an African language or in African languages. The lack of a continental lingua franca is an obvious current disincentive to the use of the vernacular as the medium in academic work," p. 3.
56. Wiredu, *Cultural Universals*, p. 3.

Chapter 2: Foundations of Modern African Philosophy

1. Abiola Irele, "Contemporary Thought in French Speaking Africa," in Albert G. Mosley, *African Philosophy: Selected Readings* (Englewood Cliffs, NJ: Prentice Hall, 1995), p. 264. Originally published in *Africa and the West: The Legacies of Empire*, ed. Isaac James Mowoe and Richard Bjornson (New York: Greenwood Press, 1986). By "younger generation" Irele is referring to those African thinkers educated (mostly in European universities) during or just after the independence movements of the late 1950s and 1960s. Among this generation are Hountondji, Odera Oruka, Franz Fanon, Marcien Towa, Wole Soyinka, and Kwasi Wiredu. Among the "earlier generation" one would include those leaders who charted the independence course, for example, Léopold Senghor, Kwami Nkrumah, Julius Nyerere, and Aime Césaire.
2. As noted earlier, we will refer to the second edition English translation of Hountondji's book with a new and informative introduction by the Author, published in 1996.
3. See "Introduction" to H. Odera Oruka, *Sage Philosophy: Indigenous Thinkers and Modern Debate on African Philosophy* (Leiden, New York: E. J. Brill, 1990), pp. xx–xxii. Specifically, in chapter 6 we will develop this notion introduced in my "Narrative in African Philosophy," *Philosophy* 64, 1989.

4. The best overall summaries of the history and development of modern
   African philosophy are to be found in V.Y. Mudimbe, *The Invention of
   Africa: Gnosis, Philosophy, and the Order of Knowledge* (Blooming-
   ton, IN: Indiana University Press, 1988), chapter 5, "The Patience of
   Philosophy," pp. 135–186, and in Abiola Irele's "Contemporary
   Thought in French Speaking Africa." Both of these focus their analysis
   largely on the Francophone philosophical traditions. Mudimbe extends
   his analysis to some recent theological writings as well. For a general
   survey see D. A. Masolo, *African Philosophy In Search of Identity*
   (Bloomington, IN: Indiana University Press and Edinburgh University
   Press, Ltd, 1994), chapters 6, 7, and 8.
   There are a number of other relevant texts that could be called to
   attention here. One I will note is a very engaging survey of how the
   notion of "African thinking" reflects a history of Africa as the "Other"
   to Western rational imperialism—what the author calls "the dialectics
   of othering in the history of 'African thinking' " (p. 83). This essay, by
   South African philosopher Marlene Van Niekerk, discusses the literature from Western anthropology, colonial history, and philosophy that
   "ghettoized" "African thought" in order to be easily exploited and how
   Africans themselves were complicit in this with such developments as
   "black ethnophilosophy" (following a period of "white ethnophilosophy") and the "negritude" movement. It also discusses what current
   courses of action might result in greater equal respect for "African
   thinking," i.e., "a praxis where classical Western modes of othering as
   distancing of the 'Other' will have to be replaced by taking sides, by
   siding with the 'Other' " (p. 54). This "praxis" would require anyone
   approaching Africa to regard its life and people "as subjects who must
   be listened to instead of being used and treated as objects to be
   observed. A situation of coevalness (Fabian, *Time and the Other: How
   Anthropology Makes its Objects*, 1983; 311) is called for, a sharing of
   the time and the activity of producing knowledge—in other words, a
   situation of dialogue" (p. 53). See Marlene Van Niekerk, "Understanding Trends in 'African Thinking'—a Critical Discussion," antholo-
   gized in, P. H. Coetzee and A. P. J. Roux, ed. *The African Philosophy
   Reader* (London and New York: Routledge, 1998), pp. 52–85. Some of
   the ideas Ms. Van Niekerk surveys will come up in our discussions in
   this chapter as well as in our discussions of "the postcolonial" in
   African thought, and are not unlike—except in their manner of concep-
   tualization and their intellectual origins—our position in chapter 1.
5. Irele, "Contemporary Thought," in Mosley, p. 270.
6. A book following Tempels of importance is Alexis Kagamé, *La Philosophie bantou-rwandaise de l' être* (Brussels, 1956). For an interesting
   discussion of the role that this book along with Tempels' book played
   in the development of African philosophy see Paulin Hountondji,
   African Philosophy: Myth and Reality, pp. 34–44. Also see the introduction to Hountondji by Irele, pp. 15–20.
7. Two paradigmatic ethnographic studies by Western anthropologists
   that underlay the pluralistic view are E. E. Evans-Pritchard's work
   among the Azande and the Nuer, and Marcel Griaule's French team
   working on the Dogon of Mali and Upper Volta (now Burkina Faso).
   There are scores of excellent ethnographic studies of specific African

societies that show their self-consistent and logical forms of life. Cf. also Daryll Forde, ed. *African Worlds: Studies in the Cosmological Ideas and Social Values of African Peoples* (London: Oxford University Press, 1954).

8. Underscoring the distinctive character of particular cultural systems and contributing to both the anthropological and philosophical debate on "relativism" is the well-known book by Melville Herskovits, *Cultural Relativism* (New York: Random House, 1972), p. 33. This quote is part of a discussion of Herskovits in V.Y. Mudimbe, *The Idea of Africa* (Bloomington, IN: Indiana University Press, 1994), pp. 40–50.

9. Hountondji, *African Philosophy*, p. 34 and Notes 3 and 4. Also see Marlene Van Niekerk, "Understanding Trends in 'African Thinking'—a Critical Discussion," cited earlier.

10. See, for example, Soyinka's discussion in *The Burden of Memory, The Muse of Forgiveness* (New York and Oxford: Oxford University Press, 1999), pp. 125–183.

11. This autobiographical note is from his "The Revolution of 1889 and Leo Frobenius" in the collection *Africa and the West: The Legacies of Empire*, ed. Isaac James Mowoe and Richard Bjornson, trans. by Bjornson (New York: Greenwood Press, 1986), p. 77. Senghor's major work on negritude is *Liberté I. Négritude et humanisme* (Paris: Sueil, 1964).

   According to Paulin Hountondji, although the term "negritude" had been used as early as 1932–1934, it was in 1939 that Aimé Césaire, in his poem *Cahier d'un retour au pays natal*, used the term "negritude" with value implications similar to the Paris group. See Hountondji, *African Philosophy*, pp. 158ff. and his Notes 4, 5, and 6 on p. 215.

12. Senghor, "The Revolution of 1889 and Frobenius," p. 78.

13. Senghor, "The Revolution in 1889 and Frobenius," p. 88.

14. Senghor, as found in his essay "Negritude and African Socialism," a lecture given at St. Anthony's College, Oxford, in October 1961. It is collected in P. H. Coetzee and A. P. J. Roux, ed., *The African Philosophy Reader* (New York and London, Routledge, 1998), p. 439.

15. Senghor, "Negritude and African Socialism," p. 440

16. Senghor, "Negritude and African Socialism," p. 447.

17. Senghor, as translated by Wole Soyinka and found in Soyinka, *Myth, Literature and the African World* (Cambridge: Cambridge University Press, 1976), p. 129.

18. Abiola Irele, "Contemporary Thought," in Mosley, p. 270. This essay provides an excellent history of the development of the concept of negritude and the fate it suffered in the postcolonial context by such thinkers as Franz Fanon, Marcien Towa, and Paulin Hountondji—see pp. 266–287.

19. Irele, "Contemporary Thought," p. 267.

20. Irele, "Contemporary Thought," p. 268, my emphasis.

21. Soyinka, *Myth, Literature and the African World*. Soyinka's entire critique of "negritude" is brilliantly analytical. See his pp. 125–136.

22. Hountondji, *African Philosophy*, p. xxiv.

23. Cf. P. O. Bodunrin, "The Question of African Philosophy"; Kwasi Wiredu, *Philosophy and an African Culture* (Cambridge: Cambridge University Press, 1980) and *Cultural Universals and Particulars* (1996); and Odera Oruka, "Mythologies in African Philosophy," *East*

African Journal IX (10), October 1972, and "Four Trends in African Philosophy" collected in his *Sage Philosophy* (Leiden: Brill, 1990)—though this seminal essay was first published in 1981. It is curious, though not wholly surprising, that these Africans are trained in the British analytic philosophical tradition, while the dialectical group reflects its European, French philosophical training.

24. Cf. Hountondji, *African Philosophy* (1976), Eboussi Boulaga, *La Crise de Muntu* (Paris: Présence Africaine, 1977), Marcien Towa, *Essai sur la Problematique Philosophique dans l'Afrique Actuelle*, Point de Vue no. 8, 2nd edition (Yaounde: Editions Clé, 1979), and the excellent critique of the dialectical outlook found in E. Wamba-dia-Wamba, "Philosophy in Africa: Challenges of the African Philosopher," *Mawazo* 5 (2), December 1983, (originally in French, "La philosophie en L'Afrique ou les defis de l'africaine philosophie"), published in *Canadian Journal of African Studies* 13 (1–2), 1979.

25. Bodunrin, "The Question of African Philosophy," p. 173.

26. Wiredu, *Cultural Universals*, p. 153.

27. This view is developed most effectively by Wiredu in his *Philosophy and An African Culture* (1980) and most recently in his *Cultural Universals* (1996).

28. Augustine Shutte, *Philosophy For Africa* (Cape Town: University of Cape Town Press, 1993).

29. Augustine Shutte, *Philosophy For Africa*, p. 5. Shutte confesses to the difficulty of having been trained in the Anglo-American analytical tradition and how this kind of philosophy "seems unwilling or unable to engage with the human issues that arise in our present context in South Africa. Why should this be so?" (p. 7). Wiredu, also, seemed to be aware of this particular difficulty and goes far to overcome any "handicap" that analytic philosophy may give one. See both his *Philosophy and an African Culture* and *Cultural Universals*.

30. As found in Irele, "Contemporary Thought," p. 288.

31. Hountondji, *African Philosophy*, p. 105.

32. Hountondji, *African Philosophy*, p. 33.

33. Hountondji, *African Philosophy*, p. 81.

34. Hountondji, *African Philosophy*, p. 103f.

35. Hountondji, *African Philosophy*, p. 105f.

36. Hountondji, *African Philosophy*, cf. pp. viii–xiv.

37. Irele, "Contemporary Thought," p. 283f. Irele takes these ideas of Towa from Towa's second major book *L'Idée d'une philosophie africaine* (1979).

38. Hountondji, *African Philosophy*, p. 82f.

39. Hountondji, *African Philosophy*, p. 83.

40. Hountondji, *African Philosophy*, p. 83f. Ogotommeli was a sage of the Dogon whose world view was recorded by Marcel Griaule in the classic *Conversations with Ogotemmeli: An Introduction to Dogon Religious Ideas* (London: Oxford University Press, 1965).

41. Hountondji, *African Philosophy*, p. 98ff., also see p. 168.

42. Hountondji, *African Philosophy*, p. 105.

43. Hountondji, *African Philosophy*, p. xxiv.

44. These texts are found in Claude Sumner, ed., *Classical Ethiopian Philosophy* (Los Angeles, CA: Adey, 1994). Mudimbe briefly comments on

some of these texts in his Appendix to his *The Invention of Africa*. See pp. 201–203. See also Teodros Kiros, "Zara Jacob: A Seventeenth-Century Founder of Modernity in Africa," in Kiros, ed., *Exploration in African Political Thought* (New York and London: Routledge, 2001), pp. 69–80.

45. Hountondji, *African Philosophy*, p. 67.
46. Hountondji, *African Philosophy*, p. 67.
47. Hountondji, *African Philosophy*, p. 69.
48. Hountondji, *African Philosophy*, p. 73.
49. Hountondji, *African Philosophy*, p. 106.
50. Hountondji, *African Philosophy*, pp. viii, ix.
51. The defining works of Odera Oruka are his "Four Trends in Current African Philosophy," presented at the William Amo Symposium in Accra, 24–29 July 1978; "Sagacity in African philosophy," *International Philosophical Quarterly*, 23, 1983; and his edited collection, *Sage Philosophy: Indigenous Thinkers and Modern Debate on African Philosophy* (Leiden: E. J. Brill, 1990).
52. H. Odera Oruka, *Sage Philosophy*, p. xv.
53. Odera Oruka, *Sage Philosophy*, p. xxiii. We must remind ourselves that for ancient Greece, "memory" and active dialogue were then "the practice of keeping thought."
54. Odera Oruka, *Sage Philosophy*, p. xx.
55. Odera Oruka, *Sage Philosophy*, p. xxi, and Irele, "Contemporary Thought," in Mosley, p. 284.
56. Odera Oruka, *Sage Philosophy*, p. 44f.
57. Odera Oruka, *Sage Philosophy*, p. 45.
58. Odera Oruka, *Sage Philosophy*, p. 45f. And see transcriptions from Mbuya interviews, pp. 140–141. Gail M. Presbey in "The Wisdom of African Sages," found in *Explorations in African Political Thought*, ed. Kiros, discusses Odera Oruka's project of recording Kenyan sage philosophers and some critics of Odera Oruka.
59. Wiredu, *Cultural Universals*, p. 150.

Chapter 3: Liberation and Postcolonial African Philosophy

1. See especially Nkrumah, *Consciencism: Philosophy and Ideology for Decolonization and Development with Particular Reference to the African Revolution* (London: Heinemann, 1964), 2nd revised edition, *Consciencism: Philosophy and Ideology for Decolonization*, (1970), Nyerere, Ujamaa, *Essays in Socialism* (Oxford: Oxford University Press, 1968), and Senghor, "Negritude and African Socialism," *The African Philosophy Reader*, in Coetzee and Roux. Also see *African Socialism*, ed. William Friedland and Carl Rosberg, Jr. (Stanford, CA: Stanford University Press, 1964), especially Appendices I through VIII, pp. 223–278. These are essays by several of the principal African socialists of the 1950s and 1960s.
2. Nkrumah, *Consciencism*, p. 70.
3. Nyerere, "Ujamaa: The Basis of African Socialism," in *Ujamaa: Essays on Socialism*, p. 12. Also see Nyerere, "Leaders Must Not Be Masters," in E. C. Eze, *African Philosophy: An Anthology*, pp. 77–80.

4. V.Y. Mudimbe, *The Idea of Africa* (Bloomington, IN: Indiana University Press, 1994), p. 42.

5. Mudimbe, *The Idea of Africa*, p. 43.

6. Mudimbe, *The Idea of Africa*, p. 44.

7. Senghor, "Negritude and African Humanism," p. 447.

8. Senghor, "Negritude and African Humanism," p. 444. See also Nyerere's speech "Leaders Must Not be Masters," found in Eze, ed., *African Philosophy: An Anthology*, pp. 77–80.

9. Senghor, "Negritude and African Humanism," p. 442.

10. Senghor, "Negritude and African Humanism," p. 446. This is not far from Tempel's "vital force" in *Bantu Philosophy*. Augustine Shutte brings out the synthesis of Senghor, Tempels' notion of a vital force, and Teilhard de Chardin very explicitly in "African and European Philosophizing: Senghor's 'Civilization of the Universal,' " in ed. *The African Philosophy Reader*, Coetzee and Roux, see especially pp. 432–437.

11. A strong sense of struggle and liberation in this "Marxist syntax" was clearly apparent to me while traveling in Tanzania as late as 1985. Both university students and educated young people working in areas of economic and social development echoed this theme that their reality was one of "struggle" from both external economic and political pressures and with their own will to prevail against great odds. Their philosophy was, simply, that of "liberation." This was not, however, the considered view of many of the "professional" academics—philosophers and social scientists—I met in Dar es Salaam. They were aware of the failed policies of "African socialism" in Tanzania over the past twenty-five years. Within that year Tanzania founding "Father" and President, Julius Nyerere, voluntarily stepped down and the new government moved toward opening its economy toward a more market-oriented structure. Nyerere died in late October 1999, much loved by his fellow Tanzanians and revered throughout Africa.

12. Senghor, "Negritude and African Humanism," p. 444.

13. African political philosophy is still affected by tensions because of the Marxist intellectual training of many of its national leaders—a substantial number of present-day African leaders and technicians were educated in Moscow or in academic centers of Soviet-controlled Eastern Europe from the 1950s well into the 1980s. This tension is reflected in lingering ideological loyalties concerning decisions on economic and social development policy. Political and economic realities at present, even though they are largely driven by capitalistic and democratic thinking, are still shaped from power centers outside of Africa, either "Western" capitalism or under the shadow legacy of "Soviet" or European socialism. Africa is far from controlling its own destiny.

14. Hountondji, *African Philosophy*, p. 171.

15. Nkrumah, *Consciencism*, 2nd edition, p. 78.

16. Gyekye, *Tradition and Modernity*, p. 158f. .

17. Kwame Nkrumah, *Consciencism*, p. 70.

18. Nkrumah, "African Socialism Revisited," *African Forum: A Quarterly Journal of Contemporary Affairs* 1 (3), Winter 1966, 3.

19. Nkrumah, *Consciencism*, p. 99.

20. Nkrumah, *Consciencism,* p. 98
21. Nkrumah's general discussion of "positive and negative action" is on pp. 99–106.
22. Nkrumah, *Consciencism,* p. 79. One must be struck by similarities in Nkrumah's formulation of *consciencism* with Brazilian philosopher and educational theorist Paulo Freire's development of what is translated from the Portuguese as *conscientization.* They were contemporaries and both were fighting against forms of colonial domination. Freire says that "conscientization changes one's perception of the facts based on a critical understanding of them." It was a means of struggle "for social transformation" and liberation.

    Central to Freire's thought is his pedagogical method and its application to literacy education of the urban and rural poor. Here Freire thought that one must expose the imposition of the dominant (colonizing, oppressor) culture on the majority learner's culture. Freire insisted that the learner's culture be respected and that their "popular" experience be the starting point of their education; what they brought to school in their being should be drawn forward from the learners and incorporated in the learning environment itself. Freire believed that it was in the local people's lives, their language, their "festivals, their stories, their mythic figures, and their religiousness," that "the resigned expression of the oppressed" could be transformed into "their possible methods of resistance." He also challenged "first-world" cultures to listen to the voices of the poor. Freire's pedagogical methods are widely used in "third-world" educational systems worldwide and especially in Latin America and Africa. I think it would be fair to say that Freire's literature along with Nkrumah's were major precursors of what is now called "postcolonial studies." See his *Pedagogy of the Oppressed,* trans. Myra Bergman Ramos (New York: The Seabury Press, 1968) and *Letters to Cristina: Reflections on My Life and Work,* trans. Donaldo Macedo with Quilda Macedo and Alexandre Oliveira (New York: Routledge,1996). All the quotes in this note are from this latter work.
23. Nkrumah, "Author's Note" to 2nd edition of *Consciencism.*
24. Hountondji, *African Philosophy,* p. 149. See his larger critique of Nkrumah's revised views in chapter 7, "The idea of philosophy in Nkrumah's *Consciencism.*"
25. Hountondji, *African Philosophy,* p. 149ff.
26. Houndondji, *African Philosophy,* p. 154.
27. Abiola Irele, "In Praise of Alienation," in *The Surreptitious Speech: Présence Africaine and the Politics of Otherness* 1947–1987, ed. V. Y. Mudimbe (Chicago, IL: University of Chicago Press, 1989), p. 202.
28. Emmanuel Chukwudi Eze, *Postcolonial African Philosophy: A Critical Reader* (Oxford: Blackwell Publishers, 1997), p. 5. To underscore and develop this thesis Eze writes:

    > With respect to Africa, then, I use the term "colonialism" as a clustered concept to designate the historical realities of: (1) the European imperial incursions into Africa, which began in the late fifteenth and early sixteenth centuries, and grew into the massive transatlantic slave trade; (2) the violent conquest and occupation of the various parts of the continent by diverse European powers which took place in the late nineteenth and early twentieth centuries; and (3) the forced administration of African lands and peoples which followed this conquest, and which lasted into the years of indepen-

dence in the 1950s and 1960s, and—in the case of Zimbabwe, [Namibia] and
South Africa—into the 1980s and 1990s. Slave trade, conquest, occupation,
and forced administration of peoples, in that order, were all part of an unfolding history of colonialism. (p. 5).

These comprehensive historical realities are widely accepted as part
of what is meant by "colonialism."

29. Prakash's articles are widely cited in postcolonial studies. This quote is
from "Writing Post-Orientalist Histories of the Third World: Perspectives from Indian Historiography," from the anthology: *Postcolonial
Identities in Africa,* ed. Richard Werbner and Terence Ranger (London:
Zed Books LTD., 1996), p. 271. Another widely cited postcolonial theorist is Edward Said, especially his *Orientalism: Western Representation
of the Orient* (London: Routledge and Kegan Paul, 1978), and *The Politics of Dispossession* (London: Vintage, 1995).
30. Trinh T. Minh-ha, *Women, Native, Other: Writing Postcoloniality and
Feminism* (Bloomington: Indiana University Press, 1989). For the
larger context of this remark see pp. 97–101.
31. Eze, *Postcolonial African Philosophy,* p. 7. A larger discussion of all
three of these philosophers is found on pp. 6–10. The larger texts for
these "enlightenment" remarks can be found in Eze's edited collection,
Race and the Enlightenment: A Reader (Oxford: Blackwell, 1997).
32. G. W. F. Hegel, *The Philosophy of History* (New York: Dover Publications, 1956), "Introduction," pp. 91–99. This work was from lectures of
Hegel in 1830–1831. China did not fare much better in Hegel's scheme
of "civilizations" of universal and historical significance.
33. Eze, *Postcolonial,* p. 10.
34. Examples of such applications are many, but I list a few related to
examples given: Adrian A. McFarlane, *A Grammar of Fear and Evil: A
Husserlian-Wittgensteinian Hermeneutic* (New York: Peter Lang,
1996); Chris Gudmunsen, *Wittgenstein and Buddhism* (London: The
Macmillan Press LTD, 1977); Hannah Pitkin, *Wittgenstein and Justice:
On the Significance of Ludwig Wittgenstein for Social and Political
Thought* (Berkeley: University of California Press, 1972), or Edward
Said's, *Orientalism,* utilizing Foucaultian analysis (1978), and Tsenay
Serequeberhan, *The Hermeneutics of African Philosophy: Horizon and
Discourse* (New York: Routledge, 1994), and also Theophilus Okere,
*African Philosophy: A Historico-Hermeneutical Investigation of the
Conditions of Its Possibility* (Lanham, MD: University Press of Amer-
ica, 1983). Serequeberhan's study expands many of the issues taken up
in this chapter.
35. Serequeberhan, *The Hermeneutics of African Philosophy,* p. 119.
36. Ato Quayson, *Postcolonialism: Theory, Practice and Process* (Cambridge and Oxford: Polity Press and Blackwell Publishers, 2000), p. 45ff.
37. Homi Bhabha, "Postcolonial Criticism," in *Redrawing the Boundaries:
The Transformation of English and American Literary Studies,* ed.
S. Greenblatt and G. Dunn, (New York: Modern Language Association
of America), p. 437, as found in Ato Quayson, *Postcolonialism,* p. 140.
Quayson himself is a Ghanaian, an African and Western literary theorist, and is able to give voice to an African postcolony writers.
38. Homi Bhabha, from a lecture, "Literature and the Right to Narrate,"
given at The College of Wooster, Wooster, Ohio, 26 September, 2000.

39. Robert Bernasconi, "African Philosophy's Challenge to Continental Philosophy," in Eze, *Postcolonial African Philosophy: A Critical Reader*, p. 183.
40. Bernasconi chronicles this lapse in Heidegger and others, including to some degree Derrida. See "African Philosophy's Challenge," pp. 184–187.
41. Bernasconi, "African Philosophy's Challenge," p. 188. See his larger discussion pp. 187–189. The notion of "the double bind" here is taken from Derrida's understanding of "deconstruction" as Bernasconi discusses that in this context. The Lucius Outlaw article referred to is "African 'Philosophy': Deconstructive and Reconstructive Challenges," found in *Sage Philosophy*, ed. Odera Oruka pp. 223–248. This Outlaw article is an important one in the area of hermenuetics and African philosophy.

   On the point of the phrase "African philosophy" *not registering*, I do not know how many times I said to British colleagues while in the midst of writing this book of my interest in "African philosophy" only to receive the immediate response: "Is there such a thing?"—this usually ended the conversation, or on a rare occasion it was the beginning of a fruitful conversation. This was also true, to my surprise, of some members of white Eurocentric philosophy faculties encountered in South Africa.
42. Bernasconi, "African Philosophy's Challenge," p. 191.
43. Bernasconi, "African Philosophy's Challenge," p. 190f.
44. Bernasconi, "African Philosophy's Challenge," pp. 191 and 192, respectively.
45. James Baldwin, "Fifth Avenue, Uptown," *Esquire*, June 1960. Reprinted in *The Price of the Ticket* (New York: St. Martins, 1985), p. 211.
46. Abraham, *The Mind of Africa*, p. 160.
47. Mamdani, *Citizen and Subject: Contemporary Africa and the Legacy of Late Colonialism* (Princeton, NJ: Princeton University Press, 1996), p. 19.
48. See again Mamdani, *Citizen and Subject*, p. 19f. and chapter 4, "Customary Law: The Theory of Decentralized Despotism," pp. 108–137.
49. The first few pages of this section, tracing Du Bois' "autobiography of a race concept," are a distillation of the seminal essay of Du Bois, "The Conservation of Races," found in Eze, *Postcolonial African Philosophy*, pp. 269–274, as well as the critical essay on Du Bois by K. A. Appiah from his *In My Father's House*, pp. 28–46 (also in Eze, *Postcolonial African Philosophy*, pp. 275–290).
50. Du Bois, "The Conservation of Races," in Eze, p. 269.
51. Du Bois, "The Conservation of Races," in Eze, p. 270.
52. Du Bois, "The Conservation of Races," in Eze, p. 270.
53. Du Bois, "The Conservation of Races," in Eze, p. 270.
54. Du Bois, "The Conservation of Races," in Eze, p. 270f. My emphasis.
55. Du Bois, "The Conservation of Races," in Eze, p. 271.
56. As found in Appiah, *In My Father's House*, p. 40f. My emphasis.
57. West's remarks were made in a Keynote address at the American Academy of Religion Meetings on November 18, 1995.
58. Fanon, from *Toward the African Revolution* (1988), as cited from Eze, *African Philosophy: An Anthology*, p. 306, my emphasis. This is from a speech of Fanon before the First Congress of Negro Writers and

Artists in Paris, September 1956. Published in the Special Issue of
Présence Africaine, June–November, 1956, and collected in Franz
Fanon, *Toward the African Revolution* (Monthly Review Press, 1988).

Fanon has a larger literature that is widely read and I especially
note, in addition to the above, his *The Wretched of the Earth*, trans.
Constance Farrington (New York: Grove Press, 1963), and *Black Skin,
White Masks*, trans. Charles Lam Markman (New York: Grove
Weidenfeld, 1967). Fanon would also be included in Cornell West's list
of those writers on the question of "race" who had a sense of the tragic and who dealt with great problems of evil.

59. Fanon, *Toward the African Revolution*, in Eze, *African Philosophy*, p. 308.
60. Fanon, *Toward the African Revolution*, in Eze, p. 308.
61. Fanon, *Toward the African Revolution*, in Eze, p. 309.
62. Fanon, *Toward the African Revolution*, in Eze, p. 310.
63. Irele, "Contemporary Thought in French Speaking Africa," p. 277.
64. Irele, "Contemporary Thought in French Speaking Africa," p. 278.
65. Fanon, *Toward the African Revolution*, in Eze, p. 310.
66. See Irele's account of Fanon's visit to Kwame Nkrumah's newly independent Ghana, "Contemporary Thought in French Speaking Africa,"
p. 279f. Fanon remains indispensable for his writings on race and colonialism. For a recent valuable study of Fanon see *Franz Fanon: A Biog-
raphy* by David Macey (New York: Picador USA, 2001).
67. We will not open out this "third-stage" debate, but point the reader to
sources for further reading. See K. Anthony Appiah and Amy Gutmann, ed., *Color Conscious: The Political Morality of Race* (Princeton,
NJ: Princeton University Press, 1997); Mabogo P. More, "Outlawing
Racism in Philosophy: On Race and Philosophy," in *The African Philosophy Reader*, ed. Coetzee and Roux, pp. 364–373; Amy Gutmann,
ed., *Multiculturalism*, with essays by Charles Taylor, Appiah, Jürgen
Habermas, Michael Walzer, and Susan Wolf (Princeton, NJ: Princeton
University Press, 1994); Martha Nussbaum, *For Love of Country:
Debating the Limits of Patriotism*, with responses from Appiah,
Charles Taylor, and others (Boston: Beacon Press, 1996), and P. H.
Coetzee, "Kwame Anthony Appiah: The Triumph of Liberalism" in a
special issue of the journal *Philosophical Papers*, December 2001, ed.
Richard H. Bell. The special issue is on the general topic "African
Philosophy and the Analytic Tradition" and illustrates part of the cur-
rent dialogue that *is* African philosophy.
68. Du Bois, "The Conservation of Races," in Eze, *African Philosophy*,
p. 272.
69. Fanon, *Toward the African Revolution*, in Eze, p. 310.

Chapter 4: African Moral Philosophy I

1. Hountondji, *African Philosophy*, p. xviii.
2. Placide Tempels, *Bantu Philosophy*, English translation (Paris: Présence
Africaine, 1959), p. 58. The reference to "Bantu speaking Africans" in
Tempels is in no way intended as pejorative; it refers to his identification of the major language group in central Africa, which is also linked
to language speakers extending to West and East Africa and well into
Southern Africa.

3. Tempels, *Bantu Philosophy*, p. 35. Abiola Irele in his Introduction to Hountondji's book, *African Philosophy*, says the following of Tempels' book:

> The importance of Tempels' work in the intellectual history of Africa is difficult to overestimate. It is true that his *Bantu Philosophy* remains within the stream of European discourse upon the non-western world and, in the particular instance, upon Africa. Moreover, it was conceived as part of a strategy for the spiritual conquest of Africa. But the concessions which Tempels had to make were on such a scale as to imply the total recognition of the African mind in its own individuality. Hence Tempels' work registers, despite the paternalistic tone of its expression, a decisive break with the ethnocentric emphasis of classical anthropology.
>   But quite apart from this ideological significance which it assumed in the colonial context, *Bantu Philosophy* provided a conceptual framework and reference for all future attempts to formulate the constitutive elements of a distinctive African mode of thought, to construct an original African philosophical system. It is in this respect that Tempels bequeathed to the present generation of African philosophers a problematic question. (p. 17)

4. John Mbiti, *African Religions and Philosophy* (London: Heinemann, 1969), p. 108f, my emphasis.
5. Ifeanyi Menkiti, "Persons and Community in African Traditional Thought," in *African Philosophy: An Introduction*, 3rd edition, ed. Richard A. Wright (Lanham, MD: University Press of America, 1984), p. 176, my emphasis. Also see Gyekye's extended discussion of Menkiti's view and his criticism of it in "Person and Community in African Thought," found in Coetzee and Roux, *The African Philosophy Reader*, p. 318ff.
6. Menkiti, "Persons and Community," in Wright, p. 179.
7. Kwame Gyekye, *Tradition and Modernity: Philosophical Reflections on the African Experience* (Oxford: Oxford University Press, 1997), p. 50.
8. Gyekye, *Tradition and Modernity*, p. 59.
9. Gyekye, *Tradition and Modernity*, p. 54, my emphasis. See also Gyekye in Coetzee and Roux, *An African Philosophy Reader*, p. 327f.
10. Wiredu, *Cultural Universals and Particulars*, p. 71f. Also collected in Mosley, *African Philosophy*, p. 400.
11. W. L. van der Merwe, "African Philosophy and Multiculturalism," p. 76.
12. W. L. van der Merwe, "African Philosophy and Multiculturalism," p. 76.
13. Michael Sandel, "Liberalism and the Limits of Justice," in *What is Justice?*, ed. Robert C. Solomon and Mark C. Murphy (Oxford: Oxford University Press, 1990), p. 354.
14. Alasdair MacIntyre, *After Virtue, A Study in Moral Theory* (Notre Dame, IN: University of Notre Dame Press, 1981), p. 221. As found in Gyekye, p. 59.
15. Gyekye, *Tradition and Modernity*, p. 60, my emphasis.
16. This is a partial listing of communitarian values that Gyekye discusses near the end of chapter 2, *Tradition and Modernity*, see his pp. 62 and 67.
17. Gyekye, *Tradition and Modernity*, p. 67, my emphasis.

18. Appiah, "Ethnic Identity as a Political Source," in *Explorations in African Political Thought*, ed. Kiros, especially pp. 47–53. See also Appiah, "Identity, Authenticity, Survival: Multicultural Societies and Social Reproduction," in *Multiculturalism*, ed. Gutmann, pp. 149–163.

19. Gyekye, *Tradition and Modernity*, p. 70. See also Gyekeye's excellent discussion of the balance of communal well-being and individual rights and duties in his essay "Person and Community in African Thought," in *The African Philosophy Reader*, ed. Coetzee and Roux, pp. 328–334. There the full implication of his notion of "moderate communitarianism" as it may relate to justice is very clear.

20. I have written a book on Simone Weil's view of justice as compassion that details her philosophical ideal of justice and how it contrasts with contemporary Western ideas of justice and individual rights. Among other things, it discusses how her view relates to contemporary communitarian thinking as well as similarities found in her view with recent feminist ethics of care. It also looks at the priority of one's obligation to community and the importance of "self-denial." See Richard H. Bell, *Simone Weil: The Way of Justice As Compassion* (Lanham, MD.: Rowman and Littlefield Publishers, 1998), especially chapters 3 through 7.

21. Simone Weil, *Selected Essays: 1934–1943*, trans. by Richard Rees, (Oxford: Oxford University Press, 1962), p. 21.

22. For a recent general discussion of the concept of "restorative justice" as it may be compared to notions of "retributive justice" and social equality see Jennifer Llewellyn, "Justice for South Africa: Restorative Justice and the South African Truth and Reconciliation Commission," in *Moral Issues in Global Perspective*, ed. Christine M. Koggel (Peterborough, Ontario: Broadview Press, 1999), especially pp. 100–104.

23. Simone Weil, *Selected Essays*, p. 20.

24. See my chapter 4 in *Simone Weil*, especially pp. 61–75.

25. Simone Weil, *Selected Essays*, p. 18.

26. Simone Weil, *Selected Essays*, p. 30. "Harm," in her sense, does not simply mean physical harms or hurts but include denial of human dignity and suffering the loss of self-respect.

27. Simone Weil, *Selected Essays*, p. 30.

28. Simone Weil, *Selected Essays*, p. 28.

29. Simone Weil, *The Need for Roots*, trans. by Arthur Wills with a preface by T. S. Eliot (New York: Harper Colophon Books, 1971), p. 3.

30. See my discussion of this point in *Simone Weil*, p. 129f.

31. Simone Weil, *Selected Essays*, p. 226. For a further discussion of the value of "obligation," "responsibility," and "public interest" over individual needs and rights as Simone Weil develops these see my *Simone Weil*, chapter 7, "Community and Politics: Human Needs and Social Obligations," pp. 123–146.

32. Andrea Nye, *Philosophia: The Thought of Rosa Luxemburg, Simone Weil, and Hannah Arendt* (New York: Routledge, 1994), p. 120. GG is a reference to the collection of notes by Simone Weil edited by Gustav Thibon entitled *Gravity and Grace* (London: Routledge and Kegan Paul, 1972).

33. Simone Weil, "Are We Struggling for Justice?" trans. by Marina Barabas, *Philosophical Investigations* 10:1, January 1987, 5. See also the discussion of consent and refusal in Peter Winch, *Simone Weil:*

"The Just Balance" (Cambridge: Cambridge University Press, 1989, chapter 9, "The Power to Refuse," p. 105ff.

34. Simone Weil, "The Legitimacy of the Provisional Government," trans. by Peter Winch, *Philosophical Investigations* 53, April 1987, 93.

35. Simone Weil, "The Legitimacy of the Provisional Government," p. 94. For further discussion of this notion of justice in relation to community and politics see my chapter 7 "Community and Politics: Human Needs and Social Obligations," in *Simone Weil.*

36. Wole Soyinka, *The Open Sore of the Continent: A Personal Narrative of the Nigerian Crisis* (New York: Oxford University Press, 1996), p. 65.

37. Kwame Anthony Appiah discusses this problem in his *In My Father's House: Africa in the Philosophy of Culture* (Oxford: Oxford University Press, 1992). See his discussion on p. 150. Also, Soyinka, *Open Sore*, p. 65ff. Richard Werbner says in his introduction to *Postcolonial Identities in Africa*, ed. Richard Werbner and Terence Ranger (London: Zed Books Ltd., 1996), "Africa's debts crisis, its increasing economic dependence, its kleptocracies in collusion with transnationals . . . invite the simplistic formulations of neo-colonialism," p. 5.

38. Soyinka, *Open Sore*, p. 109.

39. Simone Weil, *The Need for Roots*, p. 120. This is an apt description of what happened to the South African state under apartheid.

40. Gyekye, *Tradition and Modernity*, p. 72, my emphasis.

41. Gyekye, "Person and Community in African Thought," in *The African Philosophy Reader*, ed. Coetzee and Roux, p. 331.

42. A similar point to this is developed in connection to Simone Weil and the feminist ethics of care in my book, *Simone Weil: The Way of Justice as Compassion*, pp. 86–91.

43. Gyekye, *Tradition and Modernity*, p. 74. Listening carefully to this African philosopher with the attack on the World Trade Center in New York City in mind should heighten awareness of our connectedness and need for greater "moral sensitivities" for "people beyond our immediate communities."

44. Priscilla Hayner comments on the complicated and barbarous nature of the Mozambique civil war. It was a conflict that was said to be embedded in "the spirits of evil." Its enormous atrocities left a *lack of desire* to face its past. See Priscilla B. Hayner, *Unspeakable Truths: Confronting State Terror and Atrocity* (New York and London: Routledge, 2001), pp. 186–195.

45. Wole Soyinka, *The Burden of Memory*, p. 61.

46. Of an estimated two hundred million landmines manufactured and distributed by all producers between 1969 and 1992, there are approximately one hundred million uncleared and unexploded mines that remain planted worldwide. The majority of those are in Southern Africa while the remainder are mostly in Southeast Asia and Afghanistan. Details may be found in *Landmines: A Deadly Legacy* (New York: Human Rights Watch, 1993).

47. The United Nations recently reported that AIDS is the number one killer in sub-Saharan Africa, killing nearly 10 times more Africans than war. In 1998, 200,000 people died as a result of armed conflicts in Africa, compared to about 1.83 million from AIDS. James Wolfensohn, president of the World Bank, remarked: "Just imagine that in

Botswana, Namibia, Zambia and Zimbabwe 25 percent of the people between 15 and 19 years of age are HIV-positive. Just imagine that in Zambia and Zimbabwe there is more chance of a child born today dying of AIDS than of living free of AIDS. A third of teenage girls in many of the countries are subject to the scourge of AIDS. We're losing teachers faster than we can replace them. We're losing judges, lawyers, government officials, persons in the military." And the statistics and laments go on. These facts and comments were found in *The St. Petersburg Times,* Tuesday, January 11, 2000. In a special report, "AIDS at 20," *Newsweek,* June 11, 2001, it was reported that southern African countries have the highest infection rates in the world. It is estimated that between twenty and thirty-six percent of the citizens of South Africa are infected.

48. Soyinka, *The Burden of Memory*, p. 19.
49. Soyinka, *The Burden of Memory*, p. 41f.
50. Simone Weil discusses this concept of suffering as affliction in her essay "Affliction and the Love of God" in *Science, Necessity and the Love of God*, trans. by Richard Rees (London: Oxford University Press, 1968), especially p. 170ff. There are implicit theological implications in her view of affliction, but it is also a very strong moral notion that transcends, or is not limited to, any specific religious doctrine.
51. W. E. Abraham, *The Mind of Africa* (London: Weidenfeld and Nicolson, 1962), p. 32. The general problem of "uprootedness" is discussed in his chapter 1.
52. Appiah, *In My Father's House*, p. 150. "Realist legitimations of nationalism" are not, of course, all that these novels are. We will see more complex and subtle philosophical aspects of some of the novels mentioned here in chapter 6.
53. Appiah, *In My Father's House*, p. 152, my emphasis. Appiah has interesting analyses of several novels of this second stage that show this new narrative concern with suffering and a basic humanism. See his pp. 149–157.
54. Johan Snyman, "To Reinscribe Remorse on a Landscape," *Literature and Theology* 13 (4), December 1999, p. 284.
55. Snyman, "To Reinscribe Remorse," p. 284f.
56. Snyman, "To Reinscribe Remorse," p. 284.
57. Snyman, "To Reinscribe Remorse," p. 289.
58. Antjie Krog, *Country of My Skull* (London: Jonathan Cape, 1999), p. 42f.
59. Antjie Krog, *Country of My Skull*, p. 43.
60. Snyman, "To Reinscribe Remorse," p. 290.
61. Snyman, "To Reinscribe Remorse," p. 291.
62. Fanie Du Toit, "Public Discourse, Theology and the TRC: A Theological Appreciation of the South African Truth and Reconciliation Commission," *Literature and Theology* 13 (4), December 1999, 352.
63. Mahmood Mamdani, "A Diminished Truth," *SIYAYA!*, Issue 3, Spring 1998, Cape Town, p. 40. See also Wilhelm Verwoerd and Mahlubi "Chief" Mabizela, eds., *Truths Drawn in Jest: Commentary on the Truth and Reconciliation Commission Through Cartoons* (Cape Town and Johannesburg: David Philip Publishers, 2000), especially commentary by Wilhelm Verwoerd on cartoons by Zapiro that appeared in *The Sowetan*, p. 142ff.

64. Fanie Du Toit, "Public Discourse," p. 354.
65. Willie Esterhuyse, "Truth as a trigger for transformation: from apartheid injustice to transformational justice," in *Looking Back Reaching Forward: Reflections of the Truth and Reconciliation Commission of South Africa* ed. Charles Villa-Vicencio and Wilhelm Verwoerd (Cape Town: University of Cape Town Press and London: Zed Books Ltd, 2000), p. 145.
66. *Report of the Truth and Reconciliation Commission*, Vol. 1/5, Section 109. The Amnesty hearings continued to the early months of 2001 in order to hear every applicant. See Alex Boraine, *A Country Unmasked: Inside South Africa's Truth and Reconciliation Commission* (Oxford: Oxford University Press, 2000), p. 123.
67. Bessie Head, *Tales of Tenderness and Power* (Johannesburg: A.D. Donker, 1989), p. 41.
68. John Iliffe, *The African Poor: A History* (Cambridge: Cambridge University Press, 1989), p. 3. Iliffe gives numerous similar accounts found throughout the early twentieth century.
69. Iliffe, *The African Poor*, p. 3. He says such a simplistic view of the African past or present "is scarcely worth refuting," though his over 300-page study is a resounding refutation! Written reports of poverty in Ethiopia are as old as any in the ancient Mediterranean world, and the Islamic regions of West Africa have written records of poverty from the late seventeenth and early eighteenth century. In Southern Africa there are Dutch accounts of the poverty among the Khoi people and some Bantu (Xhosa and Herero) from the same period as the Islamic regions.
70. Iliffe, *The African Poor*, p. 7.
71. Iliffe, *The African Poor*, p. 7f, my emphasis. Much has been written in the past decade on the multidimensional aspects of understanding poverty. We take a brief look at some of these new developments as they may apply to Africa below.
72. See comparative figures in Iliffe, p. 231 and throughout his chapter "The Growth of Poverty in Independent Africa," pp. 230—259.
73. Iliffe, *The African Poor*, p. 230.
74. Iliffe, *The African Poor*, p. 1. Desmund Tutu has expressed this same sentiment a number of times, referring to the resilience and dignity of the victims of apartheid evident through the hearings of the TRC.
75. See Nussbaum and Sen, ed., *The Quality of Life* (New York: Oxford University Press, 1993). A summary of their respective views can be found in David A. Crocker, "Functioning and Capability: The Foundations of Sen's and Nussbaum's Development Ethic," *Political Theory* 20(4), November 1992, 584–612. Also Nussbaum discusses numerous examples from women's lives in the African context in her *Sex and Social Justice* (Oxford: Oxford University Press, 1999). See especially chapter 1, "Women and Cultural Universals," pp. 29–54.
76. Amartya Sen, *Inequality Reexamined* (Cambridge, MA: Harvard University Press, 1995), p. 2. See also Sen, "Capability and Well-Being," in *The Quality of Life*, and Crocker, "Functioning and Capability," p. 595f.
77. Sen, *Inequality Reexamined*, p. 107.
78. A recent article in *The New York Times*, "How to Define Poverty? Let us Count the Ways," by Louis Uchitelle, Saturday, May 26, 2001,

shows how the U.S. government has used a fixed income level to measure poverty since the mid-1960s. This is way behind the current discussions and thinking among development ethicists, social
policymakers and even The World Bank.
79. In our next chapter we will explore the meaning and use of the concept
ubuntu (love, forgiveness, generosity) as it is given new life through
the "Truth and Reconciliation Commission" process and used as common coinage by such thinkers as Desmond Tutu.
80. There is a growing "new discipline" called "international development
ethics," which is interdisciplinary rather than the preserve of just
philosophers. Sen's and Martha Nussbaum's works have been vital to
the formation of this new discipline. A wider consensus on development policy as it relates to issues such as hunger and poverty is sought
from both "insiders" and "outsiders" concerned with any new development strategies. Also central to international development ethics are
issues concerning the overall well-being of people in ways that Sen has
suggested. David A. Crocker says, for example, that

> Nutritional well being is only one element in human well-being; the over-
> coming of transitory or chronic hunger also enables people and their gov-
> ernments to protect and promote other ingredients of well-being. Being
> adequately nourished, for instance, contributes to healthy functioning that is
> both good in itself and indispensable to the ability to avoid premature death
> and fight off or recover from disease. Having nutritional well-being and good
> health, in turn, is crucial to acquiring and exercising other valuable capabili-
> ties such as being able to learn, think, deliberate, and choose as well as to be
> a good pupil, friend, householder, parent, worker, or citizen.

Crocker, "Hunger, Capability, and Development," in ed. *World
Hunger and Morality*, ed. Aiken and La Follette (Upper Saddle River,
NJ: Prentice Hall, 1996). For a foundational essay in development
ethics see David A. Crocker, "Toward Development Ethics," *World
Development*, 19: 5, 1991, 457–483.
81. As found in Uchitelle, *The New York Times*, May 26, 2001.
82. David A. Crocker, "Functioning and Capability: The Foundations of
Sen's and Nussbaum's Development Ethic, Part 2," in *Women,
Culture, and Development: A Study of Human Capabilities*, ed.
Martha Nussbaum and Jonathan Glover (Oxford: Clarendon Press,
1995), p. 159.
83. Sen, *Inequality Reexamined*, p. 112f, my emphasis. See also Crocker,
"Hunger," p. 611. For other relevant philosophical literature on international development ethics related to justice and building "civic
society," see David A. Crocker and Toby Linden, ed., *Ethics of Consumption: The Good Life, Justice and Global Stewardship* (Lanham,
MD: Rowman and Littlefield, 1998), and essays in *The Quality of Life*.

Chapter 5: African Moral Philosophy II

1. I have been helped immensely by Wilhelm Verwoerd, formerly of the
Stellenbosch University philosophy faculty and researcher for the TRC
from April 1996 to June 1998. The critical and evaluative literature in
response to the TRC process is diverse and growing. New plays, books,
documentary films, and articles are proliferating. In this section I have

tried to give a limited survey and some critical coherence to the best of this literature and show the problems and promise of the continuing TRC process.

2. Desmond Tutu, *Hope and Suffering* (London: Collins Fount Paperback, 1984), p. 29.
3. Tutu, *Hope and Suffering*, p. 29.
4. Tutu, *Hope and Suffering*, p. 31.
5. Desmond Tutu, *No Future Without Forgiveness* (London and Johannesburg: Rider and Random House), 1999, p. 9.
6. Nelson Mandela, *Long Walk to Freedom, The Autobiography of Nelson Mandela* (Boston: Little, Brown & Company, 1994), p. 322.
7. Nelson Mandela, *Long Walk to Freedom*, p. 544.
8. See Alastair Sparks, *Tomorrow Is Another Country* (Johannesburg: Struik, 1994); the BBC television documentary "The Death of Apartheid" screened in 1995 is based largely on Sparks' book. Waldmeir, *Anatomy of a Miracle*, Mandela, *Long Walk to Freedom*, and F. W. de Klerk, *The Last Trek, A New Beginning* (London: Macmillan, 1999).
9. Soyinka, *The Burden of Memory*, especially chapter II, "L. S. Senghor and Negritude."
10. Soyinka, "The Past Must Address its Present," in *Wole Soyinka: An Appraisal*, ed. Adewale Maja-Pearce, (Oxford: Heinemann Educational Publishers, 1994), p. 19.
11. See, Alex Boraine, *A Country Unmasked: Inside South Africa's Truth and Reconciliation Commission* (Oxford: Oxford University Press, 2000), p. 425.
12. Gyekye, *Tradition and Modernity*, p. 71.
13. Gyekye, *Tradition and Modernity*, p. 73.
14. Gyekye, *Tradition and Modernity*, p. 73.
15. Joe Slovo is associated with introducing the "sunset clause" that would enable the National Party government to share in power during the first few years of majority rule. Cf. Waldmeir, *Anatomy*, pp. 213–215 and 222. Kadar Asmal perhaps deserves most credit for shaping the idea of a Truth and Reconciliation Commission that originated out of the ANC. See Boraine, *A Country Unmasked*, pp. 12–14 and 260. There were many South African citizens and leaders of different ethnic origins (whites, mixed race, and South Africans of Indian and Malay descent) who actively fought against apartheid and whose supererogatory acts helped in the freedom struggle and social transition process.
16. Boraine, *A Country Unmasked*, pp. 261 and 362. There are recent studies of the South African concept of *ubuntu* that link it both to Mandela's Xhosa upbringing and to Tutu's Christian theology. See William I . Zartman, *Traditional Cures for Modern Conflicts* (London: Lynne Rienner Publishers, 2000). Zartman says, for example, that in Xhosa society, "*ubuntu* is an expression of our collective personhood and invokes images of group support, acceptance, co-operation, care and solidarity" (p. 170). *Ubuntu* is linked to Tutu's Christian theology in Michael Battle, *The Ubuntu Theology of Desmond Tutu* (Cleveland, OH: The Pilgrim Press, 1997).
17. Boraine, *A Country Unmasked*, p. 423.
18. Boraine, *A Country Unmasked*, p. 425.

19. Waldmeir, *Anatomy*, p. 268. Tutu says the same of *ubuntu* in his book *No Future Without Forgiveness*, pp. 34–36.

20. Desmond Tutu, *No Future Without Forgiveness*, p. 36.

21. For broad and insightful discussions of the relationship of vengeance and forgiveness and of the relationship of truth commissions to justice in the wake of the "mass atrocities" of this century, see Martha Minow, *Between Vengeance and Forgiveness: Facing History after Genocide and Mass Violence*, foreword by Judge Richard J. Goldstone (Boston: Beacon Press, 1998), and Priscilla B. Hayner, *Unspeakable Truths*.

    For a severely realistic, if not overly grim, look at the extent of division between black and white and among rival Black groups in South Africa, read the brutally honest account of apartheid evils and the possibility or impossibility of reconciliation in Rian Malan's *My Traitor's Heart* (London: Vintage, 1991). This gives one a clear view of just how intractable the South African transition would seem and gives one an appreciation for the sense of balance struck between the political realities and a desire for unity and reconciliation.

22. Minow, *Between*, p. 174.

23. As found in Minow, *Between*, p. 81.

24. *Report of the Truth and Reconciliation Commission*, Vol. 1/5, Section 103, my emphasis.

25. The concept of "restorative justice" is inscribed in the *TRC Report*. See Volume I, chapter 5.

26. Tutu, *No Future Without Forgiveness*, p. 51f.

27. Trudy Govier and Wilhelm Verwoerd draw attention to "trust" in discussing various meanings of reconciliation. Reconciliation can be seen as an instrument that supports movement toward a just society — an instrument for the building or rebuilding of trust, especially between large social groups "in the aftermath of alienation or tension." Govier and Verwoerd, "Trust and the Problem of National Reconciliation," unpublished essay, p. 5.

28. As found in Boraine, *A Country Unmasked*, p. 426.

29. Johnny de Lange, "The Historical Context, Legal Origins and Philosophical Foundation of The South African Truth and Reconciliation Commission," in *Looking Back Reaching Forward, Reflections of the Truth and Reconciliation Commission of South Africa*, ed. Charles Villa-Vicencio and Wilhelm Verwoerd (Cape Town: University of Cape Town Press; London: Zed Books Ltd., 2000), p. 24.

30. The commission was legislated into being by the National Unity and Reconciliation Act (No. 34 of 1995). For a brief overview of the Commission's mandate, structure, and process see Patricia B. Hayner, *Unspeakable Truths*, pp. 40–45.

31. Boraine, *A Country Unmasked*, p. 291.

32. Jane Taylor, *Ubu and the Truth Commission* (from the production by William Kentridge and The Handspring Puppet Company) (Cape Town: University of Cape Town Press, 1998), p. X.

33. *Ubu and the Truth Commission*, p. iv. This confirms part of Franz Fanon's account discussed in chapter 3 of the psychological response of the colonial oppressor when confronted by the oppressed.

34. This is found in Jacques Derrida's *The Truth in Painting*, collected in *Art and Its Significance: An Anthology of Aesthetic Theory*, ed.

Stephen David Ross (Albany: State University of New York Press, 1994), p. 402.

35. Taylor, *Ubu and the Truth Commission*, pp. viii–ix.
36. Minow, *Between*, p. 78. See also de Lange in *Looking Back Reaching Forward*, ed. Villa-Vicencio and Verwoerd, especially pp. 22–26.
37. Bessie Head who has a great gift for the expression of rage among those who are powerless, writes of how overwhelmed the ordinary black person felt in South Africa—this was from an essay of hers in the mid–1960s: "There are huge armies prepared for war against unarmed people and we are all overwhelmed with fear and agony, not knowing where it will end" (from *A Woman Alone*, p. 31). To be so overwhelmed with fear and agony easily renders one silent.
38. Simone Weil, *The Iliad or The Poem of Force*, trans. by Mary McCarthy (Wallingford, PA: Pendle Hill Pamphlet, no. 91, 1981), p. 14. This is a line from her analysis of Homer's *Iliad* where she is referring to the grieving wives and widows of those dying in war "far from hot baths." The grieving gives all pause for reflection about what has gone wrong.
39. Elizabeth Wolgast, *The Grammar of Justice* (Ithaca: Cornell University Press, 1987), p. 203.
40. Wolgast, *The Grammar of Justice*, p. 128. Again she says: "Outrage is required of any person of moral dimension, anyone expecting respect as a member of the moral community, or silence and complacency in the face of wrongdoing are themselves a kind of moral offense" (p. 139). A similar theme is struck in Judith N. Shklar's *The Faces of Injustice* (New Haven: Yale University Press, 1990), where she provides a more historical look at how "the sense of injustice as a fundamental experience plays a relatively small part in classical ethics," and argues for greater attention to "the voice of the victims" in its many forms (p. 85ff.). An argument similar to Wolgast and Shklar can be found in Jonathan Allen's "Balancing Justice and Social Unity: Political Theory and the Idea of a Truth and Reconciliation Commission," *University of Toronto Law Journal* 49, 1999, 315–353.
41. This would have to be further argued, but Minow in *Between Violence and Forgiveness* and Hayner in *Unspeakable Truths* suggest some of the important differences.
42. Andrew Brien, "Mercy Within Legal Justice," *Social Theory and Practice* 24 (1), Spring 1998, 103.
43. *Ubu and the Truth Commission*, p. viii.
44. See Vol. 1/5, Sections 10–28 of the *Report*, "Promoting National Unity and Reconciliation."
45. Within the "merciless" framework of apartheid, there were, of course individual acts of mercy shown to victims by persons who were members of the power structure. Some of these came out in the public hearings and show the meaning and value of reconciliation. See the case of "the angel of mercy," Ilene Crouse in her acts of kindness to the tortured Ivy Gcina. *Report*, Vol. 5/9, Sections 66–69.
46. Andrew Brien, "Mercy Within Legal Justice," p. 104.
47. Andrew Brien, "Mercy Within Legal Justice," p. 83f. This is the definition given by Seneca in the *De Clementia*, and Brien goes on to discuss the dynamics of "power and vulnerability . . . in which an act of mercy

occurs" (p. 84). Another essay that argues for the inclusion of mercy within a legal justice system, and that I find remarkably compatible to both the TRC's conception of restorative justice and Simone Weil's notion of justice as compassion, is Martha Nussbaum's "Equity and Mercy" in her *Sex and Social Justice* (Oxford: Oxford University Press, 1999), pp. 154–183. Nussbaum also discusses Seneca's ideas of mercy within the framework of what she calls the "equity tradition."

48. *Report*, Vol. 1/5, Section 109.
49. Brien, "Mercy Within Legal Justice," p. 106.
50. Nussbaum, *Sex and Social Justice*, p. 159.
51. Nussbaum, *Sex and Social Justice*, p. 170.
52. Jonathan Allen, "Balancing Justice and Social Unity," p. 332f.
53. One of the most useful critical surveys made of the TRC hearings and its overall process is found in the political cartoons (from conservative to liberal) that appeared in South Africa's leading newspapers throughout the commission's process. A selection, with commentary on those cartoons by South African journalists, academics, and researchers associated with the TRC, was made by Wilhelm Verwoerd and Mahlubi "Chief" Mabizela, published as *Truths Drawn in Jest: Commentary on the Truth and Reconciliation Commission Through Cartoons* (Cape Town: David Philip Publications, 2000). This collection also serves as a summary of the mandate of the TRC and of its overall effectiveness.
54. Mahmood Mamdani, "A Diminished Truth," *SIYAYA!* Issue 3, spring 1998, Cape Town, p. 40.
55. This is a view expressed by Rick de Satgé in "Reconstruct," *Quarterly Supplement to the Mail & Guardian*, 15–21 March, 1996, p. viii. See Wilhelm Verwoerd's discussion of this in "Individual and/or Social Justice After Apartheid?" The South African Truth and Reconciliation Commission, *The European Journal of Development Research* 11(2), December 1999, 131f.
56. Mamdani, "A Diminished Truth," p. 40. See also a discussion of broader criticisms of the TRC by Mamdani in Antjie Krog, *Country of My Skull*, p. 112f.
57. Sampie Terreblanche, "Dealing with Systemic Economic Injustice," in *Looking Back*, ed. Villa-Vicencio and Verwoerd, pp. 265–276. I believe this essay to be a very important one in the overall discussion of the TRC process.
58. Terreblanche, p. 272. Mamdani's position is most clearly articulated in his essay "Reconciliation Without Justice," *Southern African Review of Books*, November/December 1996.
59. Terreblanche believes that the TRC was "restrained by the recalcitrant attitude the majority of businesses took toward anyone who dared to blame them for being an integral part of racial capitalism, or who suggested that they benefited." He goes on to note that "it is presently politically very incorrect to acknowledge any association, whatsoever, with the now discredited apartheid system. It is also politically incorrect to be too harsh on business" (p. 273). See also Antjie Krog's account of Terreblanche's testimony during the business community's submission before the TRC, *Country of My Skull*, pp. 239–241.
60. Terreblanche, p. 271.

61. This is from Goldstone's Foreword to Minow, *Between,* p. xii. Goldstone is a Judge on the Constitutional Court, South Africa, and former Chief Prosecutor, International Criminal Tribunals for the former Yugoslavia and Rwanda. He played an active part in exposing the injustices and human rights crimes of apartheid throughout his career as a lawyer and judge in South Africa.

    Another important "community" that made submissions to the Commission were "religious communities." Iain S. Maclean notes: "The existence of the TRC and the submissions made before it by all churches as well as by other religions suggest that the TRC served as a vehicle for public confession that these religious and confessional traditions were perhaps unable to accomplish among themselves. The TRC process could be a microcosm of a larger movement to build a common future from the divided memories of the past." Maclean, "Truth and Reconciliation: Irreconcilable Differences? An Ethical Evaluation of the South African TRC," *Religion and Theology* 6–3, 1999, 287.

62. For a further discussion of Weil's view on punishment and justice see Ronald K. L. Collins and Finn E. Nielsen, "The Spirit of Simone Weil's Law," found in the Appendix to my *Simone Weil: The Way of Justice as Compassion,* especially pp. 227–232, and in my chapter 6, "Civil Society and the Law," p. 116f.

63. Boraine, *A Country Unmasked,* p. 120. See a larger discussion of this challenge, pp. 117–121. For a fuller description of these court challenges to the TRC see TRC *Report,* Vol. I, chapter 7, "Legal Challenges."

64. Boraine, *A Country Unmasked,* p. 431.

65. Wiredu, *Cultural Universals and Particulars,* p. 182f. Also in Coetzee and Roux, *The African Philosophy Reader,* p. 374.

66. Soyinka, *The Burden,* p. 81.

67. Soyinka, *The Burden,* p. 92. It should be noted that reparations were part of the South African TRC recommendations in their final report of October 1998. They suggested that individual monetary grants be given to some 20,000 people found to be victims by the TRC. The Government has to date budgeted about 600 million Rand or about 100 million dollars, about one-fifth of the estimated need. The recommended maximum grant is $3,830 dollars a year, payable for six years. See Tutu, *No Future,* p. 58. The reparations, however, are slow in coming from the government and there is a growing suspicion even among former commission staff that "justice delayed is justice denied." See the story on the front page of the *Cape Times,* Friday February 25, 2000. The headline reads: "Budget has 'failed' apartheid victims." See also the essay by former TRC Commissioner Wendy Orr, "Reparations Delayed is Healing Retarded," in *Looking Back,* ed. Villa-Vicencio and Verwoerd, pp. 239–249.

    Other recommendations of the TRC report were: "Businesses should assist the reconstruction of . . . oppressed communities, through, amongst others, a wealth tax, a one-off corporate and private income and a retrospective surcharge on corporate profits. It also suggested a 'business reconciliation fund' to be administered by the business sector itself, to help entrepreneurs from marginalised communities." These were noted by Fanie Du Toit, in his "Public Discourse," p. 355.

68. Soyinka, *The Burden*, p. 91.
69. Soyinka, *The Burden*, p. 86. In the single case of Nigeria's former ruler, Sani Abacha, it was reported in the *Cape Times*, Wednesday, February 9, 2000: "Nigeria's late military ruler, General Sani Abacha, and his family stole $4.3 billion from public funds during his four and one-half years in power.... The figure is the first given by the current government of the sum illegally transferred from public accounts by Abacha, his relatives and associates during his 1993–1998 regime" (p. 2). See also *Newsweek*, "Where Did the Money Go?" March 13, 2000.
70. Soyinka, *The Burden*, p. 86f.
71. Soyinka, *The Burden*, p. 86.
72. Soyinka, *The Burden*, p. 89.
73. Soyinka, *The Burden*, pp. 179 and 181.
74. Verwoerd, "Individual and/or Social Justice After Apartheid?," *The European Journal of Development Research* 11 (2), December 1999, 136.
75. Verwoerd, "Individual," p. 124.
76. Nussbaum, *Sex and Social Justice*, p. 166f.
77. The *Report* reflects this effort as one of "bridge building." See Vol. 1/5, Sections 101–111, "Responsibility and Reconciliation."
78. Verwoerd, "Towards a Recognition of our Past Injustices," in Villa-Vicencio and Verwoerd, p. 163f.
79. See Fanie Du Toit, "Public Discourse," p. 350, and our discussion in chapter 4. *Ubu and the Truth Commission* is also an excellent example of showing the tensions and disruptions that exist in such a dialogue between strangers.
80. Villa-Vicencio, "Getting on With Life," in *Looking Back*, ed. Villa-Vicencio and Verwoerd, p. 199, my emphasis.
81. As found in Antjie Krog, *Country of My Skull*, p. 111.
82. See again Villa-Vicencio, "Getting on With Life," in *Looking Back*, pp. 205–207. Charles Villa-Vicencio has become the Executive Director of the new "Institute for Justice and Reconciliation" opened in May 2000. The aim of this Institute is to try and further the work begun by the TRC through coordination of various NGO's efforts toward peace, justice, and reconciliation in South African civil society. The Institute will be undertaking an extensive program of publishing and broadcasting as well as promoting conferences on ways to realize justice, and reconciliation.
    Priscilla Hayner reminds us through several examples of truth commissions that "reconciliation" means different things in different contexts. See Hayner, *Unspeakable Truths*, pp. 192 and 195.
83. "Reading through the wound" is a notion I first heard from Old Testament theologian Walter Brueggemann, who said that all human situations in the twentieth century must be so read. All social texts, he believed, must be read through the wound. For him this is no less than what one well versed in biblical texts must do — a reading through the suffering servant and the crucified Christ. (From a talk given at Cambridge University on September 12, 1999.)

Chapter 6: Narrative in African Philosophy

1. Edward Said, *Culture and Imperialism* (1994), p. xiii.
2. Annie Gagiano, *Achebe, Head, Marechera*, p. 37.
3. This last point is made very nicely by Jane Heal in her essay "Wittgenstein and Dialogue," *Proceedings of the British Academy*, 85, 63–83, in *Philosophical Dialogues: Plato, Hume, Wittgenstein*, ed. Timothy Smiley (Oxford: Oxford University Press, 1995). Ms. Heal sees the central place of dialogue in Wittgenstein's thought that places it in its proper Socratic tradition and understands the importance of a two-way conversation for philosophy itself. See especially her pp. 76, 77.
4. I mentioned earlier that Odera Oruka had characterized my use of "narrative" as another "trend" in African philosophy subsequent to his original "four trends." This he drew from my article "Narrative in African Philosophy," *Philosophy*, 64, 1989. What follows in the first two sections of this chapter is an expansion and philosophical refinement of what was written there, especially in pp. 372–375. The third section of this chapter is further development of the idea of "narrative in African philosophy"; it includes some material from my essay "Understanding African Philosophy from a Non-African Point of View," in Eze, *Postcolonial Philosophy: A Critical Reader*, and the fourth section of this chapter pushes the boundaries of the concept of narrative and the aesthetic consciousness even further in the arts.
5. Gyekye, *Tradition and Modernity*, pp. 116–119. I once sat with twenty Samburu village elders under a large thorn tree in northern Kenya for over three hours as they discussed the relative merits of building and supporting a local elementary school in their village versus "busing" their children to a distant District school. They could come to a decision only after each elder had put forward his argument.
6. Kwasi Wiredu, *Cultural Universals and Particulars*, see his discussion on p. 188f.
7. Wiredu, *Cultural Universals*, p. 185f.
8. Wiredu, *Cultural Universals*, p. 186.
9. Wiredu, *Cultural Universals*, p. 187.
10. Mamdani, *Citizen and Subject*, p. 45. The reordering of communities by chiefs' rivalries and subjects' consensual loyalties is also discussed by Bessie Head in her study/novel of nineteenth-century Botswanan communal structures, *A Bewitched Crossroad: An African Saga* (1984).
11. See Mamdani, *Citizen and Subject*, pp. 43–48.
12. Mamdani, *Citizen and Subject*, p. 46.
13. Mamdani, *Citizen and Subject*, p. 48.
14. E. Wamba-dia-Wamba, "Experience of Democracy in Africa: Reflections on Practices of Communalistic Palaver as a Social Method of Resolving Contradictions among the People." A paper discussed in a Seminar in the Department of Theory and History of State Law, Faculty of Law, University of Dar es Salaam, 17 May 1985, p. 5. Unpublished. Wamba-dia-Wamba is a Congolese historian and philosopher who has taught at the University of Dar es Salaam for the past decade

or so. In 1999 he returned to the Congo to head up a faction of "rebels" against the Laurent Kabila government.

15. Wamba-dia-Wamba, "Experience of Democracy," p. 24f.
16. Wamba-dia-Wamba, "Experience of Democracy," p. 30.
17. Wamba-dia-Wamba, "Experience of Democracy," p. 31, my emphasis.
18. Wamba-dia-Wamba, "Experience of Democracy," p. 32f.
19. Wamba-dia-Wamba has some very telling comparisons between Socrates and the palavering community in his concluding pages, 45–49.
20. This, of course, is an autobiographical remark. In comparing a view of language represented in his earlier work, the *Tractatus*, with his later views, he now calls our attention to the fact that both views show us something of our world even though they may do this in different ways. The whole of the *Philosophical Investigations* illustrates how language in all its ordinary formulations *show (zeigen)* rather than propositionally *say (sagen)* what is characteristically understood about our world in its many "forms of life."
21. The idea of an "iconic tradition" within African culture was developed by Soyinka in a lecture "Icons for Self Retrieval: The African Experience," given at Oberlin College, Oberlin, Ohio, 14 November 1985.
22. Soyinka, "Icons for Self Retrieval," Oberlin lecture, 1985.
23. Soyinka, *Myth, Literature and the African World*, p. 98, my emphasis.
24. For discussions of Kuria examples see Malcolm Ruel, *Belief, Ritual and the Securing of Life*, pp. 12–16.
25. See Ato Quayson's *Strategic Transformations in Nigerian Writings* (Bloomington, IN; Indiana University Press, 1997), in which he discusses such transformations from orality to literary text in four Nigerian writers from the late nineteenth century to the present.
26. Chinua Achebe writes: "If an author is anything he is a human being with heightened sensitivities; he must be aware of the faintest nuances of injustice in human relations." [Achebe, *Morning Yet on Creation Day: Essays*. (London: Heinemann, 1975), p. 79.] And Bessie Head said that she viewed her "own activity as a writer as a kind of participation in the *thought* of the whole culture." (Head, *A Woman Alone*, p. 101.)
27. Edward Said, *Culture and Imperialism* (1994), p. xiii.
28. Soyinka, *Myth, Literature and the African World*, p. 125f.
29. Soyinka, *Myth, Literature and the African World*, p. 123.
30. Soyinka, *Myth, Literature and the African World*, p. 117.
31. Soyinka, *Myth, Literature and the African World*, p. 118.
32. Soyinka, *Myth, Literature and the African World*, p. 119, my emphasis.
33. Soyinka, *Myth, Literature and the African World*, p. 117.
34. Soyinka, *Myth, Literature and the African World*, p. 105.
35. Soyinka, *Myth, Literature and the African World*, p. viii.
36. See Ifi Amadiume, "Gender, Political Systems and Social Movements: A West African experience," in *African Studies in Social Movements*, ed. Mahmood Mamdani and E. Wamba-dia-Wamba (Dakar, Senegal: CODESRIA, 1995), and Mahmood Mamdani, *Citizen and Subject*, p. 40f. I think this is apparent in Bessie Head's work as well. This is clearly implied in the analysis of her work in Gagiano, *Achebe, Head, Marechera*, see chapter 3, "Bessie Head."

37. Achebe, *Things Fall Apart*, pp. 120–122.
38. Ato Quayson, *Postcolonialism*, p. 95.
39. Quayson, *Postcolonialism*, p. 93, my emphasis.
40. Quayson draws this point in part from Homi Bhabha's critical meth-
    ods, see *Postcolonialism*, p. 94f. Quayson applies this to the reading of
    the novels *Sozaboy* by Ken Saro-Wiwa (1985) and Ben Okri's *The
    Famished Road* (1992) and *Songs of Enchantment* (1993). See his
    pp. 95–102.
41. As found in Quayson, *Postcolonialism*, p. 101.
42. Quayson, *Postcolonialism*, p. 101.
43. Kane, *Ambiguous Adventure* (Portsmouth, NH: Heinemann Educa-
    tional, 1989), p. 34.
44. Kane, *Ambiguous Adventure*, p. 84. My parenthetical interpolation.
45. Kane, *Ambiguous Adventure*, p. 149f.
46. Sources in Heidegger that would bear out this comparison could be
    found in his "The Origin of a Work of Art," and in the essays, "On the
    Question of Being" and "On the Essence of Truth." In the latter he
    says that truth as "unconcealment" is "a disclosive letting beings be."
    In Martin Heidegger, *Pathmarks*, ed. William McNeill (Cambridge:
    Cambridge University Press, 1998), p. 147f.
47. Kane, *Ambiguous Adventure*, p. 151.
48. Kane, *Ambiguous Adventure*, p. 152.
49. Bessie Head, *Tales of Tenderness and Power*, p. 141.
50. These stories and more are collected in *Tales of Tenderness and Power*.
51. Bessie Head, *A Woman Alone*, p. 66.
52. Annie Gagiano, *Achebe, Head, Marechera*, p. 160.
53. Gagiano, *Achebe, Head, Marechera*, p. 160. Gagiano writes at length
    about the importance of the example of Khama III in *Serowe*, leader of
    the Sotho people who knew how to exercise a form of "powerless
    power." Head's understanding of power was that it was potentially
    embodied in powerlessness that is accompanied by such virtues as a
    willingness to accommodate and adapt, to shelter and preserve, accom-
    panied by a compassionate dignity. This she believed characterizes
    Southern Africa's most impressive leaders (see Gagiano, pp. 164–168).
54. Bessie Head, *A Woman Alone*, p. 79.
55. Bessie Head, *Tales of Tenderness and Power*, p. 72.
56. As found in George Pattison, *Kierkegaard: The Aesthetic and the Reli-
    gious* (London: Macmillan, 1992), p. 167.
57. Annie Gagiano, *Achebe, Head, Marechera*, p. 276.
58. Gagiano, *Achebe, Head, Marechera*, p. 276 and Note 2, p. 278.
59. John M. Chernoff, *African Rhythm and African Sensibility* (Chicago
    and London: The University of Chicago Press, 1979), p. 21.
60. Chernoff, *African Rhythm*, p. 33.
61. Andrew Tracey, "African Values in Music," in *Festschrift for Gerhard
    Kubik's 60th Birthday* (Frankfurt: Peter Lang, 1994), p. 271. Tracey is
    Director of the International Library of African Music at Rhodes Uni-
    versity, Grahamstown, South Africa.
62. Chernoff, *African Rhythm*, pp. 149 and 151, also see pp. 114, 126f., and
    138–140.

63. Chernoff, *African Rhythm*, p. 36f.
64. Soyinka, "Death and the King's Horseman," p. 309.
65. Chinua Achebe says of such events, "The masquerade (which is really an elaborated dance) not only moves spectacularly but those who want to enjoy its motion fully must follow its progress up and down the arena." It is "the art form par excellence for it subsumes not only the dance but all other [iconic] forms — sculpture, music, painting, drama, costumery, even architecture." Achebe, "The Igbo world and its art," *Hopes and Impediments: Selected Essays* 1965–87, p. 44. Also in Eze, *African Philosophy*, p. 436.

   The notion that African music includes dance and other movement forms is widely accepted. Tracey notes the importance of body extension in performing music (p. 277), and Gerhard Kubik in his *Theory of African Music*, (Wilhelmshaven: Florian Noetzel Verlag, 1994) says that " 'African music' in an extended sense also includes 'dance'," and "Movement style is what sets African and Afro-American [music] apart from the rest of the world" (pp. 9 and 37, respectively).
66. Chernoff, *African Rhythm*, p. 3.
67. Chernoff, *African Rhythm*, p. 114.
68. Tracey, "African Values in Music," p. 282f. What Chernoff and Tracey say above could apply as well to the performance of jazz. American jazz audiences, however, are generally more contemplative, evoking more individual responses than communal participation with the music.
69. *Indaba* is a Zulu word meaning a coming together or symposium in which participants contribute equally toward the solution of a problem. "It suggests combined efforts at working towards consensus through discussion of matters concerning the group as a whole." See Ingrid Bianca Byerly, "Mirror, Mediator, and Prophet: The Music *Indaba* of Late-Apartheid South Africa," *Ethnomusicology* 42 (1), Winter 1998, 1.
70. Byerly, "Music *Indaba*," p. 37. In this long essay, Byerly surveys a multiplicity of *Indaba* forms that developed in South Africa, especially in the period from 1960 to the first democratic election in 1994—all of which served some social and political end in subverting or critiquing apartheid and lifting up various values of peace, equality, cooperation, and reconciliation.
71. Chernoff, *African Rhythm*, p. 65. Another example of this fusion and balance in contemporary African music can be seen in the example of a pop concert given by Malian singer Salif Keita I experienced in Windhoek, Namibia, on October 15, 1994. An account of this concert may be found in my "Understanding African Philosophy from a Non-African Point of View," in Eze, *Postcolonial African Philosophy*, p. 215f.
72. K. A. Appiah, *In My Father's House*. Appiah's point is here compressed from his chapter "The Postcolonial and the Postmodern," pp. 137–139.
73. William James, *Varieties of Religious Experience*, p. 409.
74. Appiah, *In My Father's House*, p. 139.
75. Appiah, *In My Father's House*, p. 139.
76. Appiah, *In My Father's House*, p. 157.

Chapter 7: Some Concluding Remarks

1. I borrow this phrase from Willian Stringfellow's title: *An Ethic for Christians and Other Aliens in a Strange Land* (Waco, TX: Word, Inc., 1973).
2. Karen Auble from her Senior Independent Study Thesis at The College of Wooster, *What is Becoming of Me: Personal Agency As National Possibility in the Post-Apartheid Narrative*, March 2001, p. 24.
3. Heidegger, "The Origin of the Work of Art," in *Art and its Significance: An Anthology of Aesthetic Theory*, ed. Steven David Ross (Albany: State University of New York Press, 1994), pp. 261 and 265.

bibliography

Abraham, W. E. *The Mind of Africa*. London: Weidenfeld and Nicolson, 1962.

Achebe, Chinua. *Morning Yet on Creation Day: Essays*. London: Heinemann, 1975.

———. *Hopes and Impediments: Selected Essays* 1965–1987. New York: Doubleday, 1988.

———. *Things Fall Apart*. New York: Anchor Books, 1994.

Adorno, Theodor W. *Negative Dialectics*. London: Routledge, 1973.

Aiken, William and Hugh La Follette, ed. *World Hunger and Morality*, 2nd edition. Upper Saddle River, NJ: Prentice Hall, 1996.

Allen, Jonathan. "Balancing Justice and Social Unity: Political Theory and the Idea of a Truth and Reconciliation Commission." *University of Toronto Law Journal* 49, 1999, 315–353.

Amadiume, Ifi. "Gender, Political Systems and Social Movements: A West African Experience." In *African Studies in Social Movements*, ed. Mahmood Mamdani and E. Wamba-dia-Wamba. Dakar, Senegal: CODESRIA, 1995.

Appiah, Kwame Anthony. *In My Father's House: Africa in the Philosophy of Culture*. New York: Oxford University Press, 1992.

Baldwin, James. "Fifth Avenue, Uptown." *Esquire*, June 1960. Reprinted in *The Price of the Ticket*. New York: St. Martins Press, 1985.

Bates, H., V. Y. Mudimbe, and Jean O'Barr, eds. *Africa and the Disciplines: The Contribution of Research in Africa to the Social Sciences*. Chicago: University of Chicago Press, 1993.

Bell, Richard H. "Understanding the Fire-Festivals: Wittgenstein and Theories in Religion." *Religious Studies* 14, 1978, 113–124.

———. "Wittgenstein's Anthropology: Self-understanding and Understanding Other Cultures." *Philosophical Investigations* 7(4), October 1984, 295–312.

———. "Narrative in African Philosophy." *Philosophy* 64, 1989, 363–379.

———, ed. *Simone Weil's Philosophy of Culture*. Cambridge: Cambridge University Press, 1993.

———. "Religion and Wittgenstein's Legacy: Beyond Fideism and Language Games." In ed. *Philosophy and the Grammar of Religious Belief*, Timothy Tessin and Mario von der Ruhr. London: St. Martins Press, 1995.

———. "Understanding African Philosophy from a Non-African Point

View: An Exercise in Cross-Cultural Philosophy." In *Postcolonial African Philosophy: A Critical Reader*, ed. E. C. Eze. Oxford: Blackwell Publishers, 1997.

———. *Simone Weil: The Way of Justice As Compassion*. Lanham, MD: Rowman and Littlefield Publishers, 1998.

———, ed. "African Philosophy and the Analytic Tradition." Special issue of *Philosophical Papers*, October 2001.

Bell, Richard H., and Ronald E. Hustwit, eds. *Essays on Wittgenstein and Kierkegaard*. Wooster, OH: The College of Wooster, 1979.

Bernasconi, Robert. "African Philosophy's Challenge to Continental Philosophy." In *Postcolonial African Philosophy: A Critical Reader*, ed. E. C. Eze. Oxford: Blackwell Publishers, 1997.

Bhabha, Homi. "Postcolonial Criticism." In *Redrawing the Boundaries: The Transformation of English and American Literary Studies*, ed. S. Greenblatt and G. Dunn. New York: Modern Language Association of America, 1992.

Bodunrin, P. O. "The Question of African Philosophy." *Philosophy* 56, 1981, 161–179.

Boraine, Alex. *A Country Unmasked: Inside South Africa's Truth and Reconciliation Commission*. Oxford: Oxford University Press, 2000.

Boulaga, Eboussi. *La Crise de Muntu*. Paris: Présence Africaine, 1977.

Brien, Andrew. "Mercy Within Legal Justice." *Social Theory and Practice* 24(1), Spring 1998, 83–110.

Byerly, Ingrid Bianca. "Mirror, Mediator, and Prophet: The Music *Indaba* of Late-Apartheid South Africa." *Ethnomusicology* 42(1), Winter 1998, 1–44.

Cavell, Stanley. *The Claim of Reason*. Oxford: Oxford University Press, 1979.

———. *This New Yet Unapproachable America: Lectures on Emerson after Wittgenstein*. Albuquerque, NM: The Living Batch Press, 1989.

Chernoff, John M. *African Rhythm and African Sensibility*. Chicago and London: The University of Chicago Press, 1979.

Cioffi, Frank. *Wittgenstein on Freud and Frazer*. Cambridge: Cambridge University Press, 1998.

Coetzee, P. H., and A. P. J. Roux, ed. *The African Philosophy Reader*. London and New York: Routledge, 1998.

Collins, Ronald K. L., and Finn E. Nielsen. "The Spirit of Simone Weil's Law." In Appendix to R. H. Bell, *Simone Weil: The Way of Justice as Compassion*. Lanham, MD: Rowman and Littlefield Publishers, 1998.

Crocker, David A. "Functioning and Capability: The Foundations of Sen's and Nussbaum's Development Ethic." *Political Theory* 20(4), November 1992, 584–612.

———. "Functioning and Capability: The Foundations of Sen's and Nussbaum's Development Ethic, Part 2." In *Women, Culture, and*

Development: A Study of Human Capabilities, ed. Martha Nussbaum and Jonathan Glover. Oxford: Clarendon Press, 1995.

———. "Hunger, Capability, and Development." In *World Hunger and Morality,* ed. William Aiken and Hugh La Follette. Upper Saddle River, NJ: Prentice Hall, 1996.

Crocker, David A., and Toby Linden, ed. *Ethics of Consumption: The Good Life, Justice and Global Stewardship.* Lanham, MD: Rowman and Littlefield Publishers, 1998.

de Klerk, F. W. *The Last Trek, A New Beginning.* London: Macmillan, 1999.

de Satgé, Rick. "Reconstruct." *Quarterly Supplement to the Mail & Guardian,* 15–21 March, 1996.

Derrida, Jacques. *The Truth in Painting.* Collected in *Art and Its Significance: An Anthology of Aesthetic Theory,* ed. Stephen David Ross. Albany: State University of New York Press, 1994.

Diop, Cheikh Anta. *The African Origin of Civilization: Myth or Reality,* trans. Mercer Cook. Westport, CT: Lawrence Hill and Company, 1974.

———. *Precolonial Black Africa: A Comparative Study of the Political and Social Systems of Europe and Black Africa from Antiquity to the Formation of Modern States,* trans. Harold Salemson. Trenton, NJ: African World Press Edition, 1987.

Douglas, Mary. *Implicit Meanings: Essays in Anthropology.* London and Boston: Routledge & Kegan Paul, 1975.

Du Bois, W. E. B. *Dusk of Dawn: An Essay Toward an Autobiography of a Race Concept.* New York: Harcourt, Brace and Company, 1940.

———. "The Conservation of Races." In *Postcolonial African Philosophy: A Critical Reader,* ed. E. C. Eze. Oxford: Blackwell Publishers, 1997.

Du Toit, Fanie. "Public Discourse, Theology and the TRC: A Theological Appreciation of the South African Truth and Reconciliation Commission." *Literature and Theology* 13(4), December 1999, 340–357.

Evans-Pritchard, E. E. *Nuer Religion.* Oxford: Clarendon Press, 1956.

———. *Witchcraft, Oracles and Magic among the Azande.* Abridged with an introduction by Eva Gillies. Oxford: Clarendon Press, 1976.

Eze, Emmanuel Chukwudi, ed. *Postcolonial African Philosophy: A Critical Reader.* Oxford: Blackwell Publishers, 1997.

———, ed. *Race and the Enlightenment: A Reader.* Oxford: Blackwell Publishers, 1997.

———, ed. *African Philosophy, An Anthology,* Oxford: Blackwell Publishers, 1998.

Fanon, Franz. *The Wretched of the Earth,* trans. Constance Farrington, New York: Grove Press, 1963.

————. *Black Skin, White Masks,* trans. Charles Lam Markman, New York: Grove Weidenfeld, 1967.

————. *Toward the African Revolution.* Monthly Review Press, 1988. In *African Philosophy: An Anthology,* ed. E. C. Eze. Oxford: Blackwell Publishers, 1998.

Forde, Daryll, ed. *African Worlds: Studies in the Cosmological Ideas and Social Values of African Peoples.* London: Oxford University Press, 1954.

Freire, Paolo. *Pedagogy of the Oppressed,* trans. Myra Bergman Ramos. New York: The Seabury Press, 1968.

————. *Letters to Cristina: Reflections on My Life and Work,* trans. Donaldo Macedo with Quilda Macedo and Alexandre Oliveira. New York: Routledge, 1996.

Friedland, William H. and Carl G. Rosberg, Jr., ed. *African Socialism.* Stanford, CA: Stanford University Press.

Gagiano, Annie. *Achebe, Head, Marechera: On Power and Change in Africa.* Boulder, CO: Lynne Rienner Publishers, 2000.

Geertz, Clifford. *The Interpretation of Cultures.* New York: Basic Books, 1973.

————. "Found in Translation: On the Social History of the Moral Imagination." *The Georgia Review* 31, Winter 1977, 788–810.

Giddens, Anthony. *Sociology: A Brief but Critical Introduction.* New York: Macmillan Education, 1982.

Griaule, Marcel. *Conversations with Ogotemmeli: An Introduction to Dogon Religious Ideas.* London: Oxford University Press, 1965.

Gudmunsen, Chris. *Wittgenstein and Buddhism.* London: The Macmillan Press LTD, 1977.

Gutmann, Amy. ed. and intro. *Multiculturalism: Examining the Politics of Recognition.* Princeton, NJ: Princeton University Press, 1994.

Gyekye, Kwame. *Tradition and Modernity: Philosophical Reflections on the African Experience.* Oxford: Oxford University Press, 1997.

Hallen, Barry. "A Philosopher's Approach to Traditional Culture." *Theoria to Theory* 9, 1975.

————. "Robin Horton on Critical Philosophy and Traditional Thought." *Second Order,* 1, 1977.

————. "Indeterminacy, Ethnophilosophy, Linguistic Philosophy, African Philosophy." *Philosophy* 70, 1995, 377–393.

Hallen, Barry, and J. Olubi Sodipo. *Knowledge, Belief, and Witchcraft: Analytic Experiments in African Philosophy.* London: Ethnographia Publishers, 1986. Second edition with new Afterword by Barry Hallen. Stanford, CA: Stanford University Press, 1997.

Hayner, Priscilla B. *Unspeakable Truths: Confronting State Terror and Atrocity.* New York and London: Routledge, 2001.

Head, Bessie. *A Bewitched Crossroad: An African Saga*. Johannesburg: A.D. Donker, 1984.

———. *Tales of Tenderness and Power*. Johannesburg: A.D. Donker, 1989.

———. *A Woman Alone: Autobiographical Writings*. London: Heinemann, 1990.

Heal, Jane. "Wittgenstein and Dialogue." In *Philosophical Dialogues: Plato, Hume, Wittgenstein*, ed. Timothy Smiley. Proceedings of the British Academy, 85, 63–83. Oxford: Oxford University Press, 1995.

Heidegger, Martin. "The Origin of the Work of Art." In *Art and its Significance: An Anthology of Aesthetic Theory*, ed. Steven David Ross. Albany: State University of New York Press, 1994.

———. *Pathmarks*. ed. William McNeill. Cambridge: Cambridge University Press, 1998.

Herskovits, Melville. *Cultural Relativism*. New York: Random House, 1972.

Hollis, Martin, and Steven Lukes, ed. *Rationality and Relativism*. Oxford: Basil Blackwell, 1982.

Horton, Robin. *Patterns of Thought in Africa and the West*. Cambridge: Cambridge University Press, 1994.

Horton, Robin, and Ruth Finnegan, ed. *Modes of Thought: Essays on Thinking in Western and Non-Western Societies*. London: Faber and Faber, 1973.

Hountondji, Paulin J. *Sur la philosophie Africaine*. Paris: Maspero, 1976.

———. *African Philosophy: Myth and Reality*, 2nd edition. Bloomington and Indianapolis: Indiana University Press, 1996.

Iliffe, John. *The African Poor: A History*. Cambridge: Cambridge University Press, 1989.

Irele, Abiola. "Contemporary Thought in French Speaking Africa." In *Africa and the West: The Legacies of Empire*, ed. Isaac James Mowoe and Richard Bjornson, trans. by Bjornson. New York: Greenwood Press, 1986.

James, William. *Varieties of Religious Experience* (The Gifford Lectures, Edinburgh, 1901–1902). New York: Macmillan, 1961.

Kagamé, Alexis. *La Philosophie bantou-rwandaise de l' être*. Brussels, 1956.

Kane, Chiekh Hamidou. *Ambiguous Adventure*. Portsmouth, NH: Heinemann Educational, 1989.

Kerr, Fergus. "Metaphysics and Magic: Wittgenstein's Kink." In *Post-secular Philosophy*, ed. Phillip Blond. London and New York: Routledge, 1998.

Kierkegaard, Søren. *On Authority and Revelation*, trans. Walter Lowrie. New York: Harper & Row, 1966.

Kiros, Teodros, ed. with a preface by K. Anthony Appiah. *Explorations in*

African Political Thought: Identity, Community, Ethics. New York and London: Routledge, 2001.

Krog, Antjie. *Country of My Skull.* London: Jonathan Cape, 1998.

Kubik, Gerhard. *Theory of African Music.* Wilhelmshaven: Florian Noetzel Verlag, 1994.

Landmines: A Deadly Legacy. New York: Human Rights Watch, 1993.

Llewellyn, Jennifer. "Justice for South Africa: Restorative Justice and the South African Truth and Reconciliation Commission." In *Moral Issues in Global Perspective,* ed. Christine M. Koggel. Peterborough, Ontario: Broadview Press, 1999.

Maclean, Iain S. "Truth and Reconciliation: Irreconcilable Differences? An Ethical Evaluation of the South African TRC." *Religion and Theology,* 6–3, 1999.

MacIntyre, Alasdair. "Is Understanding Religion Compatible with Believing?" In *Rationality,* ed. Brian Wilson. New York: Harper Torchbooks, 1970.

———. *After Virtue, A Study in Moral Theory.* Notre Dame, IN: University of Notre Dame Press, 1981.

Maja-Pearce, Adewale. *Wole Soyinka: An Appraisal.* Oxford: Heinemann Educational Publishers, 1994.

Malan, Rian. *My Traitor's Heart.* London: Vintage, 1991.

Mamdani, Mahmood. *Citizen and Subject: Contemporary Africa and the Legacy of Late Colonialism.* Princeton, NJ: Princeton University Press, 1996.

———. "Reconciliation Without Justice," *Southern African Review of Books,* November/December 1996.

———. "A Diminished Truth," *SIYAYA!* Issue 3, Spring 1998, Cape Town, 38–40.

Mandela, Nelson. *Long Walk to Freedom: The Autobiography of Nelson Mandela.* Johannesburg: Macdonald Purnell, 1994.

Masolo, D. A. *African Philosophy In Search of Identity.* Bloomington, IN: Indiana University Press, 1994.

Mbiti, John. *African Religions and Philosophy.* London: Heinemann, 1969.

McFarlane, Adrian A. *A Grammar of Fear and Evil: A Husserlian-Wittgensteinian Hermeneutic.* New York: Peter Lang, 1996.

Menkiti, Ifeanyi. "Persons and Community in African Traditional Thought." In *African Philosophy: An Introduction,* ed. Richard A. Wright, 3rd edition, Lanham, MD: University Press of America, 1984.

Minh-ha, Trinh T. *Women, Native, Other: Writing Postcoloniality and Feminism.* Bloomington, IN: Indiana University Press, 1989.

Minow, Martha. *Between Vengeance and Forgiveness: Facing History after Genocide and Mass Violence.* Foreword by Judge Richard J. Goldstone. Boston: Beacon Press, 1998.

Mosley, Albert G., ed. *African Philosophy, Selected Readings.* Upper Saddle River, NJ: Prentice Hall, 1995.

Mowoe, Isaac James, and Richard Bjornson, ed. *Africa and the West: The Legacies of Empire,* trans. by Bjornson. New York: Greenwood Press, 1986.

Mudimbe, V. Y. *The Invention of Africa: Gnosis, Philosophy, and the Order of Knowledge.* Bloomington, IN: Indiana University Press, 1988.

———, ed. *The Surreptitious Speech: Présence Africaine and the Politics of Otherness* 1947–1987. Chicago, IL: University of Chicago Press, 1989.

———. *The Idea of Africa.* Bloomington, IN: Indiana University Press, 1994.

Mulhall, Stephen. *On Being in the World: Wittgenstein and Heidegger On Seeing Aspects.* London: Routledge, 1990.

Nkrumah, Kwame. *Consciencism: Philosophy and Ideology for Decolonization and Development with Particular Reference to the African Revolution.* London: Heinemann, 1964.

———. "African Socialism Revisited." *African Forum: A Quarterly Journal of Contemporary Affairs* 1(3), Winter 1966.

———. *Consciencism: Philosophy and Ideology for Decolonization,* 2nd revised edition. London: Heinemann, 1970.

Nussbaum, Martha. *Sex and Social Justice.* Oxford: Oxford University Press, 1999.

Nussbaum, Martha, and Jonathan Glover, ed. *Women, Culture, and Development: A Study of Human Capabilities.* Oxford: Clarendon Press, 1995.

Nussbaum, Martha with Respondents. *For Love of Country: Debating the Limits of Patriotism,* ed. Joshua Cohen. Boston: Beacon Press, 1996.

Nussbaum, Martha, and Amartya Sen, ed. *The Quality of Life.* New York: Oxford University Press, 1993.

Nye, Andrea. *Philosophia: The Thought of Rosa Luxemburg, Simone Weil, and Hannah Arendt.* New York: Routledge, 1994.

Nyerere, Julius K. *Ujamaa: Essays on Socialism.* London: Oxford University Press, 1968.

Okere, Theophilus. *African Philosophy: A Historico-Hermeneutical Investigation of the Conditions of Its Possibility.* Lanham, MD: University Press of America, 1983.

Oruka, H. Odera. "Mythologies in African Philosophy." *East African Journal* IX(10), October 1972.

———. "Four Trends in African Philosophy." In *Philosophy in the*

Present Situation of Africa, ed. Diemer Alwin. Weisbaden, Germany: Franz Steiner Erlagh GmBH, 1981.

———. "Sagacity in African Philosophy." *International Philosophical Quarterly*, 23, 1983, 383-393.

———. *Sage Philosophy: Indigenous Thinkers and Modern Debate on African Philosophy*. Leiden, New York: E. J. Brill, 1990.

Pattison, George. *Kierkegaard: The Aesthetic and the Religious*. London: Macmillan, 1992.

Pitkin, Hannah. *Wittgenstein and Justice: On the Significance of Ludwig Wittgenstein for Social and Political Thought*. Berkeley: University of California Press, 1972.

Pittman, John P., ed. *African-American Perspectives and Philosophical Traditions*. New York: Routledge, 1997.

Quayson, Ato. *Strategic Transformations in Nigerian Writings*. Bloomington, IN: Indiana University Press, 1997.

———. *Postcolonialism: Theory, Practice and Process*. Cambridge and Oxford: Polity Press and Blackwell Publishers, 2000.

Quine, W. V. O. *Word and Object*. Cambridge, MA: MIT Press, 1960.

Ruel, Malcolm. "Icons, Indexical Symbols and Metaphorical Action: An Analysis of Two East African Rites." *The Journal of Religion in Africa*, June 1987, 98–112.

———. *Belief, Ritual and the Securing of Life: Reflexive Essays on a Bantu Religion*. Leiden: E. J. Brill, 1997.

Said, Edward. *Orientalism: Western Representation of the Orient*. London: Routledge and Kegan Paul, 1978.

———. *The Politics of Dispossession*. London: Vintage, 1995.

Sandel, Michael. "Liberalism and the Limits of Justice." In *What is Justice?*, ed. Robert C. Solomon and Mark C. Murphy. Oxford: Oxford University Press, 1990.

Sen, Amartya. *Inequality Reexamined*. Cambridge, MA: Harvard University Press, 1995.

Senghor, Leopold. *Liberté I. Négritude et humanisme*. Paris: Sueil, 1964.

———. "The Revolution of 1889 and Leo Frobenius." In *Africa and the West: The Legacies of Empire*, ed. Isaac James Mowoe and Richard Bjornson. New York: Greenwood Press, 1986.

———. "Negritude and African Socialism." A lecture given at St. Anthony's College, Oxford, in October 1961. Collected in *The African Philosophy Reader*, ed. P. H. Coetzee and A. P. J. Roux. London and New York: Routledge, 1998.

Serequeberhan, Tsenay, ed. *African Philosophy: The Essential Readings*. New York: Paragon House, 1991.

———. *The Hermeneutics of African Philosophy: Horizon and Discourse*. New York: Routledge, 1994.

Shklar, Judith N. *The Faces of Injustice*. New Haven: Yale University Press, 1990.

Shutte, Augustine. *Philosophy For Africa*. Cape Town: University of Cape Town Press, 1993.

Smith, Jonathan Z. "When the Bough Break." *History of Religions* XII, May 1973, 342–371.

Snyman, Johan. "To Reinscribe Remorse on a Landscape." *Literature and Theology* 13(4), December 1999, 284–298.

Soyinka, Wole. *Myth, Literature and the African World*. Cambridge: Cambridge University Press, 1976.

———. "Icons for Self Retrieval: The African Experience." A lecture given at Oberlin College, Oberlin, Ohio, 14 November 1985.

———. *Art, Dialogue and Outrage: Essays on Literature and Culture*. New York: Pantheon Books, 1993.

———. *The Open Sore of the Continent: A Personal Narrative of the Nigerian Crisis*. New York: Oxford University Press, 1996.

———. *The Burden of Memory, The Muse of Forgiveness*. New York, Oxford: Oxford University Press, 1999.

———. Death and the King's Horseman. In *Contemporary African Plays*, ed. Martin Banham and Jane Plastow. London: Metheun Publishing Limited, 1999.

Sparks, Alastair. *Tomorrow Is Another Country*. Johannesburg: Struik, 1994.

Sumner, Claude, ed. *Classical Ethiopian Philosophy*. Los Angeles, CA: Adey, 1994.

Suzman, Helen. *In No Uncertain Terms: A South African Memoir*. New York: Alfred A. Knopf, 1993.

Tambiah, Stanley. *Magic, Science, Religion, and the Scope of Rationality*. Cambridge: Cambridge University Press, 1990.

Taylor, Jane. *Ubu and the Truth Commission*. From the production by William Kentridge and The Handspring Puppet Company. Cape Town: University of Cape Town Press, 1998.

Tempels, Placide. *Bantu Philosophy*. English translation. Paris: Présence Africaine 1959.

Thiong'o, Ngugi Wa. *Decolonising the Mind: The Politics of Language in African Literature*. Portsmouth, NH: Heinemann, 1986.

Towa, Marcien. *Essai sur la Problematique Philosophique dans l'Afrique Actuelle*. Point de Vue no. 8, 2nd edition. Yaounde: Editions Clé, 1979.

Tracey, Andrew. "African Values in Music." In *Festschrift for Gerhard Kubik's 60th Birthday*. Frankfurt: Peter Lang, 1994.

Truth and Reconciliation Commission of South Africa Report, 5 vols. Cape Town: Truth and Reconciliation Commission, 1998. Distributed by Cape Town: Juta & Company, and New York: Grove Dictionaries, 1999. The full report can be found on line at www.truth.org.za.

Tutu, Desmond. *Hope and Suffering*. London: Collins Fount Paperback, 1984.

———. *No Future Without Forgiveness*. London and Johannesburg: Rider & Random House, 1999.

van der Merwe, W. L. "African Philosophy and Multiculturalism." *South African Journal of Philosophy*, 16(3), 1997.

Verwoerd, Wilhelm. "Individual and/or Social Justice After Apartheid?" The South African Truth and Reconciliation Commission." *The European Journal of Development Research* 11(2), December 1999.

Verwoerd, Wilhelm, and Mahlubi "Chief" Mabizela, ed. *Truths Drawn in Jest: Commentary on the Truth and Reconciliation Commission Through Cartoons*. Cape Town: David Philip Publications, 2000.

Villa-Vicencio, Charles, and Wilhelm Verwoerd, ed. *Looking Back Reaching Forward: Reflections of the Truth and Reconciliation Commission of South Africa*. Cape Town: University of Cape Town Press and London: Zed Books Ltd., 2000.

Waldmeir, Patti. *Anatomy of a Miracle*. London: Penguin Books, 1997.

Wamba-dia-Wamba, Ernest. "Philosophy in Africa: Challenges of the African Philosopher." *Mawazo* 5(2), December 1983, 76–93. Originally in French, "La philosophie en L'Afrique ou les defis de l'africaine philosophie." *Canadian Journal of African Studies* 13(1–2), 1979, 223–239.

———. "Experience of Democracy in Africa: Reflections on Practices of Communalistic Palaver as a Social Method of Resolving Contradictions among the People." A paper presented in the Department of Theory and History of State Law, Faculty of Law, University of Dar es Salaam, 17 May 1985. Unpublished.

Weil, Simone. *Selected Essays: 1934–1943*, trans. by Richard Rees. Oxford: Oxford University Press, 1962.

———. "Affliction and the Love of God." In *Science, Necessity and the Love of God*, trans. by Richard Rees. London: Oxford University Press, 1968.

———. *The Need for Roots*, trans. by Arthur Wills with a preface by T. S. Eliot. New York: Harper Colophon Books, 1971.

———. *Gravity and Grace*, ed. Gustav Thibon. London: Routledge and Kegan Paul, 1972.

———. *The Iliad or The Poem of Force*, trans. by Mary McCarthy. Wallingford, PA: Pendle Hill Pamphlet, no. 91, 1981.

———. "Are We Struggling for Justice?," trans. by Marina Barabas. *Philosophical Investigations* 10(1), January 1987, 1–10.

———. "The Legitimacy of the Provisional Government," trans. Peter Winch. *Philosophical Investigations* 53, April 1987, 87–98.

Werbner, Richard, and Terence Ranger, ed. *Postcolonial Identities in Africa*. London: Zed Books Ltd., 1996.

Wilson, Brian, ed. *Rationality*. New York: Harper Torchbooks, 1970.

Winch, Peter. *The Idea of the Social Sciences and its Relation to Philosophy*. London: Routledge & Kegan Paul, 1958.

———. "Understanding a Primitive Society." *American Philosophical Quarterly* I, 1964, 307–324.

———. *Simone Weil: "The Just Balance"*. Cambridge: Cambridge University Press, 1989.

———. "Can We Understand Ourselves." *Philosophical Investigations* July 1997, 193–204.

———. "Critical Notice" on Norman Malcolm, *Wittgensteinian Themes, Essays 1978–1989*. *Philosophical Investigations* 20(1) January 1997, 51–64.

Wiredu, Kwasi. *Philosophy and an African Culture*. Cambridge: Cambridge University Press, 1980.

———. *Cultural Universals and Particulars: An African Perspective*. Bloomington IN: Indiana University Press, 1996.

Wittgenstein, Ludwig. *Philosophical Investigations*, ed. G. E. M. Anscombe and R. Rhees, trans. G. E M. Anscombe. Oxford: Basil Blackwell, 1953.

———. "Remarks on Frazer's *Golden Bough*," trans. A. C. Miles and Rush Rhees, with an "Introductory Note" by Rush Rhees. *The Human World* 3, May 1971, 18–41.

———. *Philosophical Grammar*, ed. Rush Rhees, trans. A. J. P. Kenny. Oxford: Blackwell, 1974.

———. *Remarks on the Philosophy of Psychology*, vol. I, trans. G. E. M. Anscombe. Oxford: Basil Blackwell, 1980.

———. *Culture and Value*, ed. and trans. Peter Winch. Chicago: University of Chicago Press, 1980.

———. *Philosophical Occasions* (1912–1951), ed. James Klagge and Alfred Nordmann. Indianapolis, IN: Hackett Publishing Co., 1993.

Wolgast, Elizabeth. *The Grammar of Justice*. Ithaca: Cornell University Press, 1987.

Wright, Richard, ed. *African Philosophy: An Introduction*. 3rd edition. Lanham, MD: University Press of America, 1984.

index

M17
22г